Introduction to Counselling Skills

Text and Activities

Richard Nelson-Jones

SAGE Publications

London • Thousand Oaks • New Delhi

KU-755-752

© Richard Nelson-Jones 2000

First published 2000

All rights reserved. No part of this publication may be reproduced, stored in a retrieval system, transmitted or utilized in any form or by any means, electronic, mechanical, photocopying, recording or otherwise, without permission in writing from the Publishers.

SAGE Publications Ltd
6 Bonhill Street
London EC2A 4PU

SAGE Publications Inc.
2455 Teller Road
Thousand Oaks, California 91320

SAGE Publications India Pvt Ltd
32, M-Block Market
Greater Kailash – I
New Delhi 110 048

British Library Cataloguing in Publication data

A catalogue record for this book is available
from the British Library

ISBN 0 7619 6185 2
ISBN 0 7619 6186 0 (pbk)

Library of Congress catalog card number 99–72928

Typeset by Mayhew Typesetting, Rhayader, Powys
Printed in Great Britain by Biddles Ltd, Guildford, Surrey

Contents

List of Activities

Preface

Welcome to *Introduction to Counselling Skills: Text and Activities*. In this introductory but challenging counselling skills text, I aim to provide a basic, straightforward and practical presentation of some central skills of being in a helping role with another person. One way of looking at these skills is that they are generic and relevant to all situations where one person attempts to draw out another's resources and develop their potential.

Once familiar with these basic skills, you may wish to learn more advanced skills that reflect one or more differing theoretical approaches to counselling and helping. My other skills book, *Practical Counselling and Helping Skills: Text and Exercises for the Lifeskills Counselling Model*, reviews advanced as well as introductory counselling skills, but here I address only the fundamentals of effective counselling and helping. Nevertheless, learning and applying such fundamentals is an ongoing process that will extend far beyond any introductory counselling skills course.

In today's highly mechanised and fast-moving society there is a great need for people with the inner strength and ability to access their humanity in the service of others. To be skilled you also need to be humane. Do not be afraid to share your humanity. Your ability to release your compassion and caring in a disciplined way is essential to truly skilled counselling and helping. It is in the context of humane person-to-person relationships that you can best comfort other human beings and assist them to make better choices which create more happiness in their own and others' lives.

For whom is this book intended? I assume that most people using this book will be enrolled in introductory counselling skills courses. Such courses may be starting points for those studying to become professional counsellors and counselling psychologists. However, numerous people use counselling skills as part of other roles, for instance: teachers, social workers, probation workers, health professionals, managers, supervisors, personnel officers, welfare officers and pastoral care workers. In addition, much training in counselling skills takes place in voluntary agencies: for example, agencies dealing with distressed relationships, suicidal people, women's concerns, men's concerns, migrant and racial concerns, gay and lesbian concerns, substance abuse, dying and bereavement, and spiritual development.

A number of issues either were present at the start of or emerged during the writing of this text. First, the purposes of introductory counselling skills courses differ. For example, the British Association for Counselling has separate codes of ethics and practice for counsellors and for those using counselling skills to enhance their performance in other roles. I have tried to write an introductory counselling skills text relevant to both those studying to become counsellors and those learning counselling skills to incorporate into other roles.

Another issue concerns how to define an introductory counselling skills course. I selected two criteria: first, not more than 100 contact hours; and second, for those training to become counsellors, preparatory courses that precede supervised placements. Nevertheless, introductory counselling skills courses of up to 100 contact hours vary in length: for example, short courses of up to 30 contact hours, medium-length courses of say 30 to 60 hours, and longer courses of 60 to 100 hours. Thus, already we have six types of introductory counselling skills courses depending on purpose (counsellor training or counselling skills training) and length (short, medium, longer). In addition, there are different settings for introductory counselling skills courses: for example, colleges and universities, organisations, voluntary agencies and private training institutes.

There are also many training issues connected with introductory counselling skills courses: for example, whether and how to integrate personal development with skills development, how to give students confidence in their skills without turning them into instant experts, how to phase in the development of skills, and how to give students an idea of how introductory counselling skills can be broadened and deepened when used by experienced counsellors.

I have grappled with issues of purpose, length and how best to train students in counselling skills when writing this book. Many of these problems are inherent in a book of this nature. I hope, as is the case with many counselling clients, awareness of the issues has helped me to address them better than if I had remained unaware. However, because of the undesirability and impossibility of being all things to all people, trainers and students will have to draw from the book those aspects that best suit their particular purposes.

What, then, are the book's contents? In Part 1, 'Introduction', the first chapter surveys introductory counselling skills training, explores your motivation, and defines counselling skills. Helpers and clients are seen as both thinkers and doers. Accordingly Chapters 2 and 3 assist you to become more aware of how you use your mind and how you communicate. Chapter 4 presents a simple three-stage relating-understanding-changing model of the helping process for assisting clients to manage problem situations better. Chapter 5 looks at some learning skills you can use to get the most out of your counselling skills training group.

Parts 2 to 4 of the book examine each stage of the relating-understanding-changing helping process model. In Part 2, 'The relating stage', Chapter 6 explores elements of the helping relationship, Chapter 7 focuses on how you can listen better, and Chapter 8 on some skills for starting the helping process.

In Part 3, 'The understanding stage', Chapter 9 primarily reviews how to use questioning skills to clarify understanding, whereas Chapter 10 focuses on a variety of skills helpers can use to broaden and deepen understanding: for instance, challenging and providing feedback.

In Part 4, 'The changing stage', Chapter 11 presents both a problem solving and a changing communications and thoughts approach to this stage. Chapters 12 and 13 review a range of basic helping strategies for assisting clients to communicate, act and think more effectively.

In Part 5 of the book, 'Practical considerations', Chapter 15 reviews some ethical issues connected with how helpers use counselling skills and shows how some of these same issues are relevant to introductory counselling skills training. Lastly, Chapter 16 presents ways in which you can maintain and develop both your counselling skills and your humanity.

What are some of the main features of *Introduction to Counselling Skills*? This book focuses both on observable counselling skills and also on the mental processes that can enhance or interfere with your communicating these skills effectively. Throughout, I emphasise that to be a genuinely skilled helper you need to offer humane and compassionate relationships to clients. I provide a simple three-stage relating-understanding-changing helping process model to guide your use of counselling skills.

I highlight the applied nature of learning counselling skills in numerous ways: by interview excerpts, case examples and by activities at the end of each chapter. Furthermore, I provide some suggestions on how to use your training group to best effect.

I have tried to write this book guided by the KISA or 'Keep It Simple, Author!' principle. Furthermore, to help the book's flow, I have limited the use of citations.

I thank the following people who contributed to the development and publication of this book. Susan Worsey, Ziyad Marar and Melissa Dunlop at Sage Publications participated in the decision to commission the book. Melissa Dunlop also provided unobtrusive but highly welcome support throughout the book's development.

From the beginning I thought that this was an easy book to write, but a difficult book to write well. Because I was afraid that I might make a mess of it, I requested Sage to ask Brian Thorne to act as consultant to the book and provide feedback on drafts of chapters as I went along. Fortunately Brian accepted and I think the book is much stronger and more sympathetic as a result of his participation. I also thank Dave Mearns who was kind enough to provide feedback on some of the early chapters. In addition, I appreciate Mary Williams and Jim McLennan who responded to queries about ethical codes in the Australian Guidance and Counselling Association and Australian Psychological Society, respectively.

Learning counselling skills and using them well is an exciting challenge. We are all students as we try to become and remain more competent and less artificial persons and helpers. This is a lifelong learning process. As student to student, I hope this book gives you pleasure, knowledge and skills in the crucial endeavour of helping others, and ourselves too, to live more kindly, happily and fully.

Richard Nelson-Jones

PART 1

INTRODUCTION

1 What are Counselling Skills?

*If you contribute to other people's happiness, you will find
the true good, the true meaning of life.*
                                                The Dalai Lama

Chapter outcomes

By studying and doing the activity in this chapter you should be able to:

- *understand the growth and range of introductory counselling skills training courses;*
- *list some good, pragmatic and potentially harmful motives for why you want to learn counselling skills;*
- *categorise the kinds of people who use counselling skills;*
- *understand the definition of key terms relevant to this book;*
- *understand some purposes of using counselling skills; and*
- *understand that counselling skills involve mental processes as well as external communication.*

So you want to learn more about counselling skills? If so, you are far from alone. Over 30 years ago, when I first learned counselling skills, there were few opportunities to do so. Since then the situation has changed dramatically. There has been increasing recognition of the importance of counselling skills and a corresponding growth in introductory counselling skills courses.

Introductory counselling skills courses may be part of specialised courses leading to diplomas or certificates in counselling. Sometimes they form part of undergraduate psychology and behavioural science courses and they often form part of the training for a broad range of helping service professions – for example, social work, nursing, careers work and human resource management. Furthermore, there is a growing recognition that counselling skills are useful in business and industry: for instance, in dealings with clients and in the management and supervision of staff. Organisations with a commitment to staff development may run their own counselling skills courses or assist their staff to gain counselling skills on outside courses. In addition, there are a growing number of private training institutes running counselling skills courses. Furthermore, numerous voluntary agencies offer introductory skills courses.

There are a number of reasons for the burgeoning demand for counselling skills training. There has been an increasing recognition that helping other people to use more of their potential and make better choices is an activity that requires skills rather than one that can be left to chance. Many of the traditional approaches to helping others can be damaging: for instance, 'I know better than you' advice or 'You will be all right' reassurance. Furthermore, there is a growing research literature whose findings indicate the need for training in specific helping skills.

Modern society is full of highly visible problems that require addressing to protect those both directly and indirectly involved: for example, relationship breakdown, juvenile delinquency and substance abuse. In addition, many people require assistance with everyday transitions and choices: for example, choosing a career, studying effectively, selecting a mate wisely, handling work challenges and stress, retiring and dying with dignity.

Another reason for the increasing demand for counselling courses is that people are becoming increasingly articulate about their rights and want to move beyond constricting ways of living: for instance, the women's and men's movements, racial and cultural minorities and the gay and lesbian movement. In addition, many people now regard themselves as consumers of professional services and are more assertive about being treated like persons. Abrupt insensitivity on the part of doctors, nurses, lawyers, bank managers, teachers and university lecturers is less likely to be tolerated now than previously, though sometimes this can lead to vexatious litigation. Furthermore, attitudes to management, supervision, and dealing with the public are changing with a move to more cooperative and less authoritarian ways of dealing with staff and clients.

There has been a lessening of respect for traditional sources of authority – for example the church and the older generation – and increasingly people are seeking assistance in finding their own solutions to life's problems. In addition, the public at large is becoming more psychologically minded and sophisticated. There is a growing willingness to seek help with problems and psychological pain rather than hide them behind stiff upper lips and lace curtains.

Last, but far from least, the increasing demand for counselling skills training comes from those who want to become more skilled. Box 1.1 provides brief illustrations of some students attending introductory counselling skills training courses. As mentioned in the preface these introductory courses can vary in length (short, medium and longer) and purpose (counsellor training and counselling skills training). In addition, counselling skills can be taught as part of broader undergraduate courses. In the box some different formats for counselling skills training are also illustrated, for instance, full time, evening, one half-day a week and a two-day workshop. Notice that the box contains more illustrations of women than men – women still tend to outnumber men in counselling skills training. Also, with one exception, all the students are mature.

Box 1.1   Some illustrative counselling skills students and introductory courses

Short introductory courses

Sophie, 36, is a secondary school English teacher who attends an introductory counselling skills evening course lasting 25 contact hours – 10 weekly two-and-a-half-hour sessions – run by a private counselling skills training organisation. Sophie wanted to attend the course because she saw an increasing need to use counselling skills in the racially mixed and multicultural environment of her school. Sophie is thinking of training to become a full-time school or college counsellor.

Lauren, a 19-year-old psychology student, is taking a one-semester, 26-contact-hour Introduction to Counselling subject involving two hours a week for 13 weeks. This is taught by a lecturer in a university psychology department. The department sees counselling skills as useful for all applied areas of psychology, including applied research. One of the reasons Lauren is taking the course is to discover in which branch of psychology she wants to specialise. Lauren's options include counselling, clinical and organisational psychology.

Zohra, 39, is a middle manager in a telecommunications firm who attends a 15-contact-hour, two-day counselling skills short course, run in the office of an external training organisation, as part of her firm's staff development programme. Zohra decided to take the course because she conducts frequent performance appraisals and wants to improve her skills at developing the human resources that she manages. Zohra also thinks that attending the course might improve her promotion prospects.

Medium-length introductory course
Tim, a 46-year-old engineer, is attending a 40-contact-hour introductory counselling skills class run by a gay voluntary agency that runs a telephone counselling and a befriending service for those with HIV and Aids, their carers and for the worried well. The course consists of a 16-contact-hour, two-day introductory block and then eight weekly three-hour sessions. Having been through the anguish of losing Adrian, his partner, to Aids two years ago, Tim is strongly motivated to comfort and strengthen others in their suffering.

Longer length introductory courses
Becky, 42, is attending a 120-contact-hour Certificate in Counselling Skills course that meets half a day a week throughout the academic year. The course, which is run by the counselling staff in the college adult education department, consists of two 60-contact-hour modules: introductory counselling skills and intermediate counselling skills. After bringing up her family, Becky has decided to move back into the workforce. One of the reasons Becky was selected for the course was that she had done volunteer telephone counselling. Becky's main interest is in personal, relationship, sexual and family counselling.

Roger, 27, trained in nursing and is now attending the 75-contact-hour introductory counselling skills module on a 450-hour Diploma in Counselling course run by the Centre for Counselling Studies at his university. Roger's major interest is in working as a qualified counsellor in a health care team. Also, Roger is considering becoming a nurse educator later in his career.

Motives for learning counselling skills: the good, the pragmatic and the potentially harmful

Why do you want to learn counselling skills? Often students applying to counselling courses will reply: 'I'm good at listening to other people', 'I'm the sort of person my friends bring their problems to' and 'I like helping others'. Another viewpoint was offered me by Andy West, former head of Dillons London University Bookshop's counselling and psychology section, who observed: 'Most people who go on counselling courses need counselling themselves.'

People's motives for being counsellors and helpers can be complex and vary over time. I encourage you to recognise some of your motives for learning counselling skills and to gain insight into how these may influence your contact with clients. I divide the following discussion of motives into the good, the pragmatic and the potentially harmful. However, the categories overlap and intertwine.

The good

Many people wishing to learn counselling skills do so with some degree of altruistic motivation. In its pure form, altruism is unselfish concern for the welfare of others. Characteristics of an altruistic mind include sensitively perceiving others' thoughts, feelings and life experiences and a desire to help others. Characteristics of altruistic communication include engaging in kind, affectionate, considerate and benevolent actions. Helper altruism represents the concept of *agape* or unselfish love. Clients are prized for themselves and helped to unfold their unique potentials.

Many explanations exist for altruism. One is that humans are altruistic by nature, that ignorance and anxiety interferes with showing this innate altruistic nature and that people repress and deny the angelic parts of their genetic endowment. Another explanation is that humans are altruistic by nurture – that you can be brought up to be unselfishly concerned with others. Still another explanation is that humans match one another's altruistic behaviours, though this explanation is more relevant for everyday relationships than for helping relationships where the balance of power and obligation is uneven.

A further explanation is that altruism results from individuals successfully taking responsibility for their mental and spiritual development. Such individuals may be humanists endeavouring to implement their humanistic values or they may be motivated by religious faiths. Here altruism cannot be assumed; rather good thoughts and actions result from the disciplined and ongoing purification of your mind.

Most truly altruistic individuals combine the contributions of nature, nurture and self-development. For instance, the late Carl Rogers, the founder of person-centred counselling, was altruistic by nature, by his Christian upbringing and through continued striving to become a more genuinely loving person. However, Rogers was also a human being, subject to worldly motivations and frailties (Cohen, 1997).

Possibly, far more counselling skills students are at the relatively shallow 'feel good' end of altruism than at the tough mentally developed 'deep commitment' end of altruism. Of course, there are many of you in the middle, striving to become more loving people in your helping and private lives. Also, a number of counselling students either have or will attain a higher level of altruism through working through the torment of personal pain and unhappiness. David Grayson's observation 'Back of tranquillity lies always conquered unhappiness' is relevant to the deepening maturity and altruism of many people in the helping professions. Psychological pain, if correctly handled, can liberate altruistic tendencies to comfort and assist others who suffer.

The pragmatic

You may be motivated to become a counselling skills student because you correctly consider you possess the right stuff to help others. You may be emotionally intelligent with a capacity to recognise and skilfully manage emotions in yourself and others (Goleman, 1995). In addition, you may be naturally curious about 'what makes people tick'. You enjoy the challenge of understanding yourself and your clients so that you can become a more effective helper.

Most counselling skills students need to earn a living and all aspire to gain fulfilment and satisfaction from helping others. There may be a good fit between your personality and the role demands of helping service careers. Noted American psychologist John Holland proposed a theory of personality types asserting that special heredity and experiences led to the characteristics of six main personality types: realistic, investigative, artistic, social, enterprising and conventional (Holland, 1973). Though Holland viewed individuals more in terms of personality type profiles than single personality types, he considered the social personality type likely to predominate in profiles of helping profession workers. Illustrative characteristics of the social personality type are: responsible, helpful, friendly, idealistic, feminine, insightful and kind. If a good match exists between your personality and career, you are more likely to enjoy its challenges and to work hard at becoming more competent than if doing uncongenial work.

Many other practical reasons exist for learning counselling skills. Those of you using counselling skills as part of other roles may become more proficient at your jobs if you can incorporate counselling skills into them. By learning counselling skills you may also add another string to your range-of-career-skills bow. In addition, status, recognition and promotion may stem from possessing counselling skills. Furthermore, if either employed by others or self-employed, you may make more money if you learn counselling skills. There is an important role in private practice for qualified counsellors and counselling psychologists. Counselling skills practitioners have as much right to be paid for their services as lawyers or car mechanics. However, if you wish to become fabulously wealthy it is generally better to seek a career outside the helping professions.

The potentially harmful

Potentially harmful motives for learning counselling skills contain hidden agendas that serve helpers' rather than clients' needs. All helpers honest about themselves realise that they experience some difficulty perceiving clients independent of their own prior conditioning and current wants and wishes. Dangerous helpers are seriously deficient in their capacity to perceive and prize the separateness and difference of clients. A reasonable degree of self-awareness and commitment to developing your own mind and communication skills is essential to becoming an effective helper.

Helping others has its potential dark or shadow side. The following are five danger signals you can look out for in yourself and others.

Unresolved emotional pain
Earlier I mentioned that some people come through tough breaks in their lives stronger and more altruistic persons. On the other hand, some students enter counselling skills training as a way of working on their own concerns at one remove. A paradox can exist in that sometimes those students most in need of counselling help are so heavily defended that they are unable to acknowledge how disturbed they are. Counselling course tutors try to screen out such students during their selection procedures. However, most counselling courses at one time or another contain a few unsuitable students, some of whom still pass their courses by completing formal assessment requirements.

Wanting to dominate and control
Some individuals have a strong need to advise, dominate and control others. Their 'I know what is best for you' attitude undermines their clients' needs to develop as strong and independent persons. Helpers can possess strongly held values without imposing them on their clients.

Excessive need for approval
Probably all helpers like being liked by most clients most of the time. However, this differs from a compulsive wish to be liked by all clients all

the time. Skilled helpers require sufficient sense of their own worth to withstand and constructively use their clients' expressions of negative feelings. Furthermore, they require sufficient detachment to understand that clients' positive feedback may sometimes represent underlying agendas about dependency and approval. Some counselling skills students confuse friendship, focused on meeting mutual needs, with the disciplined use of counselling skills focused on meeting clients' needs. Do-gooding, where the hidden agenda is what a great person you are, is another variation of excessive approval seeking.

Seeking intimacy and sex

Some students are attracted to helping because it provides opportunities for psychological closeness they find difficult to obtain otherwise. Afraid to take the risks of authentic living, they are attracted by the limited nature of the helping role. In addition, some students can see helping as a way of spending time with sexually attractive people, even though most stop short of sexual relationships.

Possessing a victim mentality

In their pasts, many helping profession students have been subject to psychological abuse and sometimes to sexual abuse and physical violence as well. In addition, these students may have been adversely affected by broader social, economic and cultural factors. However, be careful not to stay stuck in perpetually seeing yourself as the victim of negative personal and external circumstances and, then, encouraging your clients to do likewise. In a widely publicised speech at a European Trauma Conference, Yvonne McEwan highlighted this concern when she claimed that the counselling profession was contributing to Britain becoming a nation of victims (*Daily Telegraph*, 27 September 1997). Students can collectively act out victim mentalities on their counselling skills courses as well as individually in their later helping roles. A difference exists between assertively confronting personal and social injustices and wallowing in unproductive and often aggressive self-pity.

Box 1.2, describing my entry into counselling, provides a case example illustrating good, pragmatic and potentially harmful motives for learning counselling skills. My good motive was that I was genuinely interested in wanting to improve the lot of others as well as of myself. My pragmatic motives were that counselling suited my interests and aptitudes and was likely to provide me with a fulfilling career. My potentially harmful motives were that I was far too anxious to function effectively as a counsellor and that, without fully acknowledging it, I was seeking to deal with my own problems through studying counselling. I needed to develop my own skills, inner strength and capacity to create happiness before I could be of real help to others.

Box 1.2 My entry into counselling

Though born and largely educated in Britain, in the early 1960s while in my mid-20s I enrolled in the Stanford University School of Business in California for a Masters in Business Administration, having previously laboured through an undergraduate degree in economics at Cambridge University. As part of my Stanford course, I studied an organisational psychology subject in which I was one of the top students. I also studied an economics course in which I was one of the bottom students.

To help pay for my education, I had obtained a position as a postgraduate student resident assistant (RA) in an on-campus undergraduate residence hall. One of the RA's functions was to act as 'dormitory counsellor' and, in this capacity, my group of eight RAs met regularly with the university counselling centre staff. Gradually, over my first term at Stanford, I became aware that my interest in becoming a counsellor and in helping people was winning out over my waning interest in a business career.

Also, I was developing an emerging awareness that I was a pretty 'screwed up' young man who was not nearly as happy as I would like to have been. The origins of my unhappiness, high anxiety and low self-esteem lay in a family life distorted by the emotionally and practically controlling behaviour of my basically very kind-hearted but deeply maritally distressed parents. My father, who had very fixed ideas of right and wrong, had broken off with his own family of origin who were never mentioned at home. When feeling down, my mother ruthlessly burdened her three sons with her marital pain and demanded sympathy. From adolescence on, I never felt emotionally safe with either parent.

During the vacation at the end of my first term, I went along as a client to what was then called the Stanford University Counselling and Testing Center for some career counselling. There I received both individual counselling and vocational testing. After some three counselling sessions, which incorporated considering my test battery results, both I and my counsellor thought there was sufficient evidence that I might succeed in a counselling career.

At registration day for the second term, I went to the professor in the Stanford School of Education responsible for enrolling students in the Masters in Counselling and Guidance and was admitted virtually on the spot. My admission was helped by my already being a 'dormitory counsellor', my very good organisational psychology grade, my high score on a business school intellectual aptitude test and my showing evidence of a rational decision making process to become a counsellor (in the early 1990s I gave a seminar at Stanford and discovered how much more difficult it had become to get into what is now the Counseling Psychology program). Later I proceeded to complete a PhD at Stanford with a double major in counselling and guidance and in the study of higher education.

Along with my new studies I started a series of 50 or so individual counselling sessions with the then counselling centre director Dr John Black, a skilled client-centred counsellor. Also, I attended a series of three different psychotherapy groups at the Stanford Medical Center. In particular, the work I did with John Black provided a very solid foundation for turning my life around. However, sometimes nowadays I still regard myself a little like Humpty Dumpty – not quite all put back together again, though still able to manage life quite adequately.

Helpers and counselling skills

Who uses counselling skills?

Five main categories of people use counselling skills:

- *Professional counsellors* Counselling specialists, suitably trained and accredited, and paid for their services. Such people include: counsellors, psychologists and psychiatrists.
- *Voluntary counsellors* People trained in counselling skills who work on a voluntary basis in settings such as Relate or Relationships Australia, youth counselling services, church-related agencies and numerous other voluntary agencies.
- *Those helpers using counselling skills as part of their jobs* Here the main focus of the job may be: nursing, teaching, preaching, supervising or managing; providing services such as finance, law, recreation or funerals; trade union work and so on. These jobs require people to use counselling skills some of the time if they are to be maximally effective.
- *Informal helpers* All of us have the opportunity to assist others, be it in the role of partner, parent, relative, friend or work colleague.
- *Counselling and helping students* Students on supervised placements as part of counselling and the helping service courses.

Throughout this book, I mainly use the term 'helper' to refer to both counsellors and helpers. Both counsellors and helpers use counselling skills. The most significant reason for preferring the term 'helper' is that many of the readers of this introductory counselling skills book are unlikely to regard themselves as either counselling students, prospective counsellors or actual counsellors. The term 'helper' is more inclusive and less formal than the term 'counsellor'. Throughout the book I use the term 'client' for persons who are recipients of helpers' counselling skills. Already the term 'client' encompasses those receiving counselling services provided by professional and voluntary counsellors. The term 'client' is inclusive in that it can incorporate many other categories of people, for instance patients and employees, who might benefit from helpers using counselling skills. Box 1.3 provides brief definitions of some key terms used in this book.

Box 1.3   Defining key terms used in this book

Regarding counselling skills

Counselling skills are helper-offered communication skills, accompanied by appropriate mental processes, for developing relationships with clients, clarifying and expanding their understanding, and, where appropriate, assisting them to develop and implement strategies for changing how they think, act and feel so that they can attain life affirming goals.

Helper is an inclusive term to describe people who use counselling skills whether as professional or voluntary counsellors, as part of other roles or informally.

Helping describes the use of counselling skills by helpers.

Client is an inclusive term to describe all those people with and for whom helpers use counselling skills.

Regarding learning introductory counselling skills

Skills training group refers to a time-limited structure for a set of applied activities, that include instruction, demonstration, practice and group interaction, for imparting and learning counselling skills mainly focused on helping individual clients.

Trainer refers to all those suitably qualified and experienced persons who perform the trainer role in counselling skills training groups.

Student refers to all persons who participate in counselling skills training groups with the purpose of learning counselling skills.

Why use counselling skills?

The following discussion concerning counselling skills goals assumes that clients are the vast majority of ordinary people with problems of living, transition and decision making. Many such people function reasonably well and some are functioning well above average. Rather than considering severely disturbed clients, this discussion is mainly limited to the level of disturbance indicated by Albert Ellis' term 'nicely neurotic' (Ellis, 1996).

In a nutshell, I see the main purpose or goal of using counselling skills as assisting clients to develop personal skills and inner strength so that they can create happiness in their own and others' lives. Helpers help clients to help themselves. As such, helpers use counselling skills to develop clients' capacity to use their human potential both now and in future.

Helpers' use of counselling skills can be broken down into five different goals. Some of these goals may seem more modest than my 'nutshell' suggestion, but nevertheless may be the appropriate goal in the circumstances.

The first or *supportive listening goal* is to provide clients with a sense of being understood and affirmed. Attaining this goal requires helpers to be skilled at listening to clients, taking their perspectives and sensitively showing them that they have been heard accurately. The primary purpose of introductory counselling skills training is to help students become better at listening and showing understanding to clients. Everything else is secondary and dependent upon making some progress towards this primary goal. Helpers with good listening skills can comfort, ease suffering, heal psychological wounds and act as sounding boards for moving forward. An employee just made redundant, a patient recently given a diagnosis of a life-threatening illness, or a schoolchild who has been bullied, for instance, may above all need helpers able to listen deeply. Be careful never to underestimate the power of effective listening both for comforting and for empowering clients.

Second, there is the *managing a problem situation goal*. Clients may want help dealing with specific situations that are problematic for them. In addition, helping may best proceed if a specific situation within a larger problem is addressed rather than trying to deal with the whole problem. With a shy college student client, rather than focus on the broader problem of shyness, helper and client might focus on a particular shyness situation of importance to the client, such as starting a conversation with a classmate. Supportive listening and managing a problem situation goal are perhaps the easiest skills for beginning students and informal helpers.

Third there is the *problem management goal*. Though some problems are limited, many other problems can be larger and more complex than specific situations within them. For example, George's problem was that he felt depressed. Together, the helper and George identified the following dimensions to his problem: obtaining or creating employment for himself; being more assertive with his wife; participating in recreational outlets; reactivating his friendship network; and learning to sleep better. Another example is that of a client with children going through a divorce. Here dimensions of the problem might include: obtaining a just divorce settlement; maintaining self-esteem; relationships with children; a possible move of home; and learning to live as a single adult again. Egan's book *The Skilled Helper* (1998) is a prime example of a book that has its major focus on problem management.

Fourth, there is the *altering poor skills that create problems goal*. Other terms for poor skills include 'problematic', 'deficient' or 'insufficiently effective' skills. Here the assumption is that problems tend to repeat themselves. In the past clients may have been repeating underlying mind skills and communication or action skills deficiencies and are at risk of continuing to do so again. For instance, workers who keep moving jobs may again and again set themselves up to become unhappy or to get fired. Another example is that of clients poor at public speaking who require skills both for now and in future. Thus the problem is not just the presenting problem, but the poor skills that create, sustain or worsen the problem.

Fifth, there is the *bringing about a changed philosophy of life goal*. Here, clients can competently manage problem situations, manage problems and alter problematic skills as a way of life. Such people might be termed self-actualising, fully functioning or even enlightened. However, this fifth or elegant goal is beyond the scope of this beginning counselling skills book.

What are counselling skills?

What is a skill?
One meaning of the word 'skills' pertains to *areas* of skill, for instance listening skills or disclosing skills. Another meaning refers to *level of competence*, for instance skilled or unskilled in an area of skill. However competence in a skill is best viewed not as an either/or matter in which helpers either possess or do not possess a skill. Rather, within a skills area, it is preferable to think of helpers as possessing *good skills* or *poor skills* or a mixture of the two. In all skills areas helpers are likely to possess mixtures of strengths and deficiencies. For instance, in the skills area of listening, you may be good at understanding clients, but poor

at showing your understanding. Similarly, in just about all areas of their functioning, clients will possess a mixture of poor and good skills.

A third meaning of skill relates to the *knowledge and sequence of choices* entailed in implementing the skill. The essential element of any skill is the ability to make and implement sequences of choices to achieve objectives. For instance, if as a helper you are to be good at listening deeply and accurately to your clients, you have to make and implement effective choices in this counselling skills area. The object of counselling skills training is to help students, in the skills areas targeted by their training groups, move more in the direction of making good rather than poor choices: for example, in the skills area of active listening making good choices for not only understanding but also showing your understanding to clients.

Counselling skills originate in the mind

When thinking of any area of counsellor or client communication, there are two main considerations: first, what are the components of skilled external behaviour and, second, what interferes with or enhances enacting that behaviour. Thus a helper skill like active listening consists both of skilled interpersonal communication and skilled intrapersonal mental processing. The term 'cognitive behaviour' can obscure the point that outer behaviour originates in the mind. Partly because I now live in a Buddhist culture (Thailand), where the religion lays great stress on mental development, more and more I emphasise the primacy of mind and that both thinking and behaviour are fundamentally mental processes. Although I distinguish between helpers' communication skills and mind skills in the context of this introductory skills textbook, the distinction is somewhat artificial since external communication as well as inner thoughts are created in the mind.

Counselling skills as mind and communication skills

Counselling skills involve mental processing both to guide external behaviour and to ensure thinking that supports rather than undermines skilled external communication. Let us take the skill of active listening. To some extent it is easy to describe the central elements of the external communication involved, as I do in Chapter 7. On paper, these external communication skills may appear straightforward. However, most counselling skills students and many experienced helpers struggle to listen well. The question then arises: 'If the external communication skills of listening well are so relatively easy to outline, why don't counselling skills students and helpers just do them?' The simple answer is that your mind can both enhance and get in the way of your external communication. Thus counselling skills are both mind and communication skills. As the book progresses I elaborate the theme that how well your mind processes both past and present information influences how well you communicate counselling skills to clients both now and in future.

Summary

Based on an increasing recognition of the need for effective counselling and helping, there is a burgeoning demand for introductory counselling skills training courses. Settings for such courses include colleges and universities, voluntary agencies, organisations and private training facilities.

Students are encouraged to explore their good, pragmatic and potentially harmful motives for wanting to learn counselling skills. Worked-through emotional pain provides one explanation for altruism. Pragmatic motives include considerations such as: good personality and career fit; interest in 'what makes people tick'; increasing your range of skills and becoming more competent; and status, recognition, promotion prospects and money. Potentially harmful motives include unresolved emotional pain, wanting to dominate and control, excessive need for approval, seeking intimacy and sex, and possessing a victim mentality. Most students' and helpers' motives are mixed.

Five main categories of people use counselling skills: professional counsellors, voluntary counsellors, those using counselling skills as part of their jobs, informal helpers and counselling and helping students on supervised placements. The terms 'helper' and 'client' are inclusive terms for those using and receiving counselling skills, respectively. Goals for using counselling skills include: supportive listening, managing a problem situation, problem management, altering poor skills that create problems, and changing clients' philosophies of life.

Counselling skills are sequences of choices originating in the mind in specific skills areas. They are helper-offered communication skills, accompanied by appropriate mental processes, for developing relationships with clients, clarifying and expanding their understanding and, where appropriate, assisting them to develop and implement strategies for changing how they think, act and feel so that they can attain life affirming goals.

Introduction to activities

Each chapter in this book ends with some activities to help you develop your knowledge and skills. Though my assumption is that readers are learning introductory counselling skills in training groups, this may not always be the case. Nevertheless, you may still want to perform the activities either with a partner or, where possible, on your own. You will enhance the value of this book if you undertake the activities diligently. While practice may not make perfect, it certainly can increase your competence.

Trainers and students can decide how to proceed with each activity: for instance, whether the activity should be done as a whole group exercise, in threes, pairs, individually or using any combination of these approaches. When doing the activities, all concerned should ensure that no one feels under pressure to reveal any personal information that she or he does not want to. To save repetition, I only mention these instructions once here and not at the start of each activity.

Activity

Activity 1.1   My motives for learning counselling skills

Answer the following questions concerning your motives for learning counselling skills.

The good

1   To what extent are you motivated by altruism?
2   To what extent does worked through emotional pain contribute to your altruistic motives?
3   How strong are your altruistic motives?

The pragmatic

4   Which of the following pragmatic motives for learning counselling skills apply to you? How important is each motive?

   • good personality and career fit
   • interest in 'what makes people tick'
   • increasing my range of skills
   • increasing my competence at my job
   • increased status
   • greater recognition
   • improved promotion prospects
   • financial considerations
   • others not mentioned above

The potentially harmful

5   Which of the following potentially harmful motives for learning
counselling skills apply to you? How important is each motive?

- unresolved emotional pain
- wanting to dominate and control
- excessive need for approval
- seeking intimacy and sex
- possessing a victim mentality
- others not mentioned above

Putting it all together

6   Summarise and prioritise the strands in your current motivation
for wanting to learn counselling skills.

7   How do you think that your potentially harmful motives might
influence your work with clients and what do you intend to do
about them?

8   How and why did you choose your current introductory counselling skills training course?

9   How well motivated are you to work hard as an introductory
counselling skills training group student?

2 Creating Your Mind

Something we were withholding made us weak
until we found it was ourselves.

Robert Frost

Chapter outcomes

By studying and doing the activities in this chapter you should be able to:

- *gain information relevant to your personal development and self-awareness as a helper;*
- *possess insight into what the term 'mind' means;*
- *understand some contexts for creating your mind;*
- *understand some of the mental processes by which counselling skills students, trainers, helpers and clients create their minds; and*
- *learn counselling skills more efficiently and enjoyably.*

All contact between helpers and clients consists of both external and internal communication. Internal communication within the mind is important both in its own right and also because it drives external communication. In this chapter I provide a framework for understanding how your mind influences how you help. Much of the following discussion also provides a framework for understanding clients' minds.

An important issue in counselling skills training is the influence of your level of self-awareness and personal development on how you help clients. Self-awareness and personal development are concepts that require greater clarity if you are to know how to improve yourself. Here I substitute the ideas of mind-awareness, mind skills and mental development for self-awareness and personal development. This will give you some tools to move beyond self-awareness to genuine personal development. You can become more skilled at super-thinking or thinking about and influencing how you think. By strengthening your mind you increase your ability to offer genuine helping relationships focused on meeting clients' goals and needs.

Understanding your mind

What is mind?

Let us start our task of helping you become mentally tougher and more able to relate to clients as they really are by exploring how you create your mind. The word mind has many meanings. Though the relationship between mind and brain is a hotly debated minefield, one way to view your mind is that it is the psychological manifestation of your brain. An important meaning of mind is that of intellectual capacities or powers, so-called grey matter. The noun 'intellect' refers to the faculty of reasoning, knowing and understanding. An intelligent person is quick of mind. However, people with high IQs do not always fare well in dealing with the practicalities of life. As anyone who has spent time in universities knows, high intellectual intelligence is no guarantee of communicating well to others. Also, high IQ people can use their quickness of mind against themselves: for instance, avoiding personal responsibility by being facile at making excuses.

A debate exists as to whether there are other types of intelligence than quickness of mind. For example, Gardner has proposed six types of intelligence: linguistic, musical, logical-mathematical, spatial, bodily-kinaesthetic and personal. The personal 'intelligences' consist of two aspects: first, access to your own feeling life and, second, '*the ability to notice and make distinctions among other individuals* and, in particular, among their moods, temperaments, motivations, and intentions' (Gardner, 1993: 240).

Similarly a concept termed emotional intelligence has been proposed (Goleman, 1995). Goleman proposes that in a sense people have two minds and two different, yet overlapping, kinds of intelligence: rational and emotional. Emotional intelligence can be broken down into five domains: knowing one's emotions; managing emotions; motivating oneself; recognising emotions in others; and handling relationships.

Emotions can intertwine with how intelligently you think and act. Carl Rogers often emphasised the role of emotions in being rational. The more you are open to your significant feelings and experiences, the more likely you are to be rational. Rogers' ideal was that of wholeness rather than living in a compartmentalised world of body and mind.

Your mind consists of visual images as well as verbal symbols. You thought in visual images before you thought in words. Verbal thinking requires the acquisition of learned symbols or a language in which to talk to yourself. As such, unlike visual imagery, the verbal part of thinking represents a secondary or learned rather than a primary or genetic process.

Levels of mind

Freud's view of mind was in terms of three main levels of consciousness: conscious, preconscious and unconscious (Freud, 1976). Here, I add super-conscious as a fourth level of consciousness. The boundaries between these levels may be imprecise.

- *Conscious thinking* is a state of possessing a present awareness in your mind of some material. Unlike the preconscious and the unconscious, consciousness has no memory and is usually very transitory.
- *Super-conscious thinking* is a state of thinking about how you think. When you are in a super-conscious state, you are not only aware of mental content, but think about the processes of your mind. Super-cognition involves the capacity to distance yourself from your thought processes so that you can monitor, evaluate and, if necessary, change them.
- *Preconscious thinking* consists of thoughts that can be brought into awareness relatively easily. Much preconscious material finds its way into consciousness without any need for professional counselling assistance. Automatic thoughts are a kind of preconscious thinking that may require professional assistance to bring the thoughts into awareness. Such thoughts emerge automatically and can be extremely rapid. Beck provides the example of a patient describing to him sensitive sexual conflicts. The following 'secondary' stream of preconscious automatic thoughts accompanies the patient's description: 'I am not expressing myself clearly . . . He is bored with me . . . He probably can't follow what I'm saying . . . This

probably sounds foolish to him . . . He will probably try to get rid of me' (Beck 1976: 32).

- *Unconscious thinking* is frequently inadmissible to consciousness because of the anxiety it generates. In other words, with the unconscious the censorship on material coming into awareness can be very strong indeed. Such material is subject to repression. Repression has been jokingly described as 'forgetting and then forgetting that you have forgotten.' Often the word depth is used to describe the unconscious. Psychological theorists differ regarding the content of the unconscious. For example, Freud viewed humans as repressing anxieties associated with conflicts over infantile sexuality. Other theorists view avoiding anxieties about death as the main agenda for repression. Another viewpoint is that altruism as well as aggression may be subject to repression.

Contexts for creating your mind

You create your mind and thoughts within three important contexts: biological, social and cultural, and from the learning influences of your past. Biological influences include: evolutionary traces and instincts; your sex; and the genetic components of intellectual and emotional intelligence and of sexual and affectionate orientation.

Throughout history, people's minds have been influenced by social and cultural considerations: for instance the time in which you live; technological change; culture; social class; and attitudes towards gender. For example, the following characteristics may be more representative of Asian than western cultures: filial piety; emphasis on harmonious group relationships; saving face rather than confrontation; fatalism or accepting events as predetermined; and appearing modest (Ho, 1992). The prevailing economic system is another social and cultural context that influences the content of your mind. Prominent among capitalist values are those of competition, consumerism, accumulation of wealth and individualism.

Influences from your past can be viewed on at least four levels: acquisition, maintenance, activation and change. First, the way in which you initially *acquired* or learned what and how to think: when you were young, in particular, this was mainly a matter of what others, for instance your parents, did to you. Second, how you have *maintained* and continue to maintain both helpful and unhelpful thoughts and thought processes: as you grow to be an adult, this represents more what you have done and keep doing to yourself rather than what others have done or keep doing to you. Responsibility for creating your mind becomes more personal than external. Third, how you *activate* your learned and maintained mental strengths or vulnerabilities in face of different life events: for instance, stressful experiences such as taking examinations, redundancy or a relationship break-up. Fourth, how you can *change* and lay to rest the ghosts of your past so that you become happier, stronger and more fulfilled both now and in future. Recognising the need for and possibility of change is the point at which many people enter counselling. Some people, however, enrol on counselling skills courses instead and hope to help themselves by helping others.

Empowering your mind

You can both learn counselling skills and help others much more effectively if you harness your mind's potential. How can you control your thoughts so that you can beneficially influence how you communicate? First, you can understand that you have a mind with a capacity for super-conscious thinking – or thinking about thinking – that you can develop. Second, you can become much more efficient in thinking about your thinking if you view your mental processes in terms of skills that you can train yourself to control. Third, in daily life as well as in your counselling skills training, you can assiduously practise using your mind skills to influence your communication (Nelson-Jones, 1999a).

There follow descriptions of six central mental processes or mind skills. These skills are derived from the work of leading cognitive therapists, such as Aaron Beck and Albert Ellis. Though I illustrate the skills more from the perspective of counselling skills students than of clients, these mind skills are just as relevant to clients. Conversely, Chapter 13 of this book, which focuses on strategies for changing clients' thinking, is also relevant to counselling students.

Creating self-talk

There is a joke about a psychoanalyst who remained silent for three sessions. At the end of each the client was charged one hundred pounds. Half-way through the fourth session the client requested permission to ask a question and said: 'Do you by any chance need a partner?' In other words, the client's self-talk was: 'This analyst is in on a good racket. Let's see if I can get in on it too!'

Try a simple mind experiment. For the next 30 seconds, close your eyes and try and think of nothing. Some readers trained in meditation techniques may be successful in stilling the mind. Most readers will become conscious that thinking of nothing is very difficult and that one has a constant stream of intrusive verbalisation – including telling oneself to think of nothing!

Self-talk goes by numerous other names including: inner mono-logue, inner dialogue, inner speech, self-verbalising, self-instructing and talking to yourself. You talk to yourself even when you remain silent. In any helping relationship, there are at least three conversations going on: your public conversation and helper and client private self-talk.

All verbal thinking can be regarded as self-talk. However, here I focus on a specific area of self-talk, namely instructing yourself so that you may cope with specific learning counselling skills and helping situations better. You may be aware of much of your self-talk, yet awareness is no guarantee of skilful self-talk. In addition, some of your self-talk is preconscious or automatic. This is not necessarily bad. For instance, if you have learned to drive a car, you first received instruc-tions which you then consciously told yourself to the point where these self-instructions became automatic. In some instances, your automatic self-talk may be unhelpful. Without knowing it, you are creating inept or unskilful thoughts that depower rather than empower you.

Negative self-talk can be contrasted with coping self-talk. You can distinguish between coping ('doing as well as I can') and mastery ('I have to be perfect'). Coping emphasises competence rather than perfection. In reality, most people use a mixture of negative and coping self-talk.

Negative self-talk refers to anything that you say or fail to say to yourself before, during or after specific situations that contributes to potentially avoidable negative feelings, physical reactions and com-munications. When American psychologists Philip Kendall and Steven Hollon researched their *Anxious Self-Statements Questionnaire*, they dis-covered three main types of anxious statements: those reflecting inability to maintain a coping view of the future, for instance 'I can't cope' and 'I can't stand it anymore'; those reflecting self-doubt, for instance 'Will I make it?'; and those suggesting confusion and worry regarding future plans, for instance 'I feel totally confused' (Kendall and Hollon, 1989).

If you create negative self-statements, such as the above, you weaken yourself internally through unskilful thinking. You are less in control of your feelings and thoughts. You also put yourself at risk of communicating externally in inappropriate ways: for example, by excessive approval seeking.

Box 2.1 illustrates the self-talk of two students before attending the first session of their counselling skills training group, where neither knows anyone else. Usually people mix negative with coping self-talk, but here I highlight the differences.

Box 2.1   Creating negative and coping self-talk

Situation
Thinking of attending the first session of a counselling skills training group.

Negative self-talk: Self-doubting Donna/Don
'I don't know anyone. I am sure that all the other students will be much more experienced than me and know much more about counselling skills than I do. I'm worried what they and the trainer are going to think of me. Will I make a complete fool of myself? Will I get so far behind that I will never catch up? I sometimes do not come over as well as I would like and then start getting nervous which makes matters even worse. I'm worried that this will happen in this first skills group session. I may start blushing and stammering. I can feel my heart pounding just at the thought of it. I so want to be liked and to get an excellent grade.'

Coping self-talk: Confident Christine/Chris
'I'm looking forward to going to the first session. I am going to enjoy the group and get a lot out of it. I've been wanting to learn more about counselling skills for some time and it's just great to be getting started. I'm also looking forward to meeting the other group members and seeing if I can make some new friends. I know I may be a little nervous at the first session, but that's life. I'll just tell myself to calm down and take it easy. If I start talking too quickly, I can slow my speech. In the past I've always been a good student and I am optimistic about doing well again this time.'

With coping self-talk you calm yourself down, become clear as to your goals, and coach yourself in appropriate communications to attain them. Also, you increase your confidence by acknowledging strengths, support factors and previous success experiences. Altering your goal from mastery to coping is likely to increase your self-support and to decrease your self-oppression. You now possess an attainable standard toward which to strive. Remember, you can use your self-talk skills before, during and after specific counselling skills training and helping situations.

The fact that you choose to use coping self-talk to manage a situation or problem does not preclude your using other mind skills as well. For instance, self-doubting Donna/Don also needs to alter her/his rule about demanding acceptance from everyone. In addition, Donna/Don may require better communication skills, for instance those of striking up conversations with fellow students. If anything, regard coping self-talk as a necessary part of, rather than as a sufficient whole for dealing with, specific situations in your skills training and helping work.

Creating visual images

Do not underestimate the importance of your visual images. Noted psychotherapist Arnold Lazarus writes: 'Through the proper use of mental imagery, one can achieve an immediate sense of self-confidence, develop more energy and stamina, and tap into one's own mind for numerous productive purposes' (1984: 3). Also, the proper use of mental imagery can help you improve your counselling skills.

Try a simple mind experiment. Think of someone you love or like. Put down the book and hold the thought for about 15 seconds. Then think of someone you dislike. Again, put down the book and hold the thought for about 15 seconds. Almost certainly, in both instances you saw visual images of these people. To use a computer analogy, you called up visual images onto your screen.

When experiencing any significant feeling or sensation, you are likely to think in pictures as well as words. Probably, then, your relationships with your fellow counselling skills students and helping clients take place on a pictorial level. Not only do you see them face-to-face, but you store pictures about them in your mind and, even when absent, you may relate to these mental pictures.

Counselling skills students can differ not only in how much they visualise but also in how vividly. Possessing full awareness of a visual image means that the image is very vivid. Vividness incorporates the degree to which all relevant senses – sight, smell, sound, taste and touch – are conjured up by the visual image. Another possible aspect of vividness is the extent to which visual images elicit or are accompanied by feelings, for instance hope and sadness.

Some of you either possess well-developed powers of imagery or can develop the skills of visualising vividly. Others of you may experience much difficulty in visualising vividly and need to emphasise other ways of controlling your thinking. In general, the more you can experience the senses and feelings attached to your images, the better you can use visualising as a self-helping skill.

As with self-talk, the visual images you create can be negative, coping or a mixture of both. For instance, confident Christine/Chris accompanied her/his coping self-talk with visual images of performing competently at her/his first counselling skills training group session. On the other hand, self-doubting Donna/Don created visual images of performing incompetently, of others' negative evaluations and of reacting by blushing and stammering.

Box 2.2 provides another example of how you can create either helpful or harmful visual images to accompany your self-talk. The example here is of that of a mature student holding down a job who is on the way to a counselling skills evening class after a stormy work-place staff meeting lasting all afternoon. Though life is not always this simple, frequently by using good visualising skills you can make it much less difficult.

Box 2.2   Creating harmful and helpful visual images

Situation
On the way to a counselling skills evening class after a stormy workplace staff meeting that lasted all afternoon.

Negative self-talk and visual images: Angry Andrea/Andy
'I'm absolutely furious that my so-called colleagues did not support me. I can just see them sitting there smugly looking after their own interests. They don't really seem to care for the clients. I'm picturing myself at the meeting getting attacked and outvoted. In particular, I can see Dave and Sharon coming on strong and ganging up on me. They look so aggressive and as if they are enjoying putting me down. I just can't get their faces out of my mind.'

Coping self-talk and visual images: Focused Fran/Frank
'Let's leave office politics at the office. You can't win them all. I'm on my own time now. Calm down and breathe slowly and regularly. Imagine that peaceful place on the beach I like to mentally visit when I'm feeling stressed . . . (conjures up the sights, sounds, smell, taste and touch sensations of the scene). Enjoy the calm peaceful sensations attached to lying there and relaxing without a care in the world . . . (stays in the scene). Now I'm on my way to my counselling skills class that I enjoy. I can see the friendly faces of my trainer and fellow students and the fun we have together learning counselling skills with all its ups and downs. I'm starting to feel better already.'

Creating rules

Rules are the 'dos' and 'don'ts' by which you lead your life. All counselling skills students have inner rule-books that guide how you live and help. You may be aware of some of your personal and helping rules, but there are others of which you are unaware. Some of these latter rules are preconscious and moderately accessible to awareness. However, others may be more threatening and anxiety evoking. Consequently, you may have even more difficulty acknowledging them.

Who sets your rules? The answer is that you probably think you do, but frequently this is not the case. Influences from your past and present have helped create and sustain your rules: for example, your family, religion, gender, culture, race, peer group, age, exposure to the media and so on.

You may have rational and altruistic reasons for creating and sustaining your rules. In addition, you may sustain some rules through less rational factors. Habit, or persisting communicating in the same old unexamined way, is one such factor. Fear is another important factor. You may be afraid that you will lose out in some significant way if you examine and change your rules.

Wanting immediate gratification is a third factor keeping you stuck in unproductive rules. Like a child you may demand that you must have what you want NOW, NOW, NOW, rather than balance longer term with shorter term considerations. Ellis, the founder of rational-emotive behaviour therapy, considers that people create and maintain much of their distress and unhappiness through demanding and absolutistic thinking, making demands, rather than through preferential thinking, having preferences (Ellis, 1995; 1996).

Box 2.3 focuses on the counselling skills trainer rather than the counselling skills student. Perhaps it is easier to start by seeing irrationality in others before exploring it in yourself. This box emphasises the distinction between demanding and preferring. Notice that each of the demanding trainer's unrealistic rules has been reworded to become the preferential trainer's realistic rules. No prizes for guessing in whose skills group you would rather be. In reality, both trainers and students are likely to possess various combinations of realistic and unrealistic rules. For me, becoming more comfortable in the trainer role over time was both cause and result of a shift to possessing more preferential rules. I felt much less need to prove myself and hence I could relax more.

Box 2.3   Creating unrealistic and realistic rules

Situation

The conscious and preconscious rules of trainers thinking about leading a counselling skills group.

Unrealistic rules: Demanding Dannie/Dan

- 'I must be the perfect trainer'
- 'I must be liked by all the students'
- 'I must always be in control of the training group'
- 'Students should find learning counselling skills easy'
- 'I must appear as an expert counsellor to students'

Realistic rules: Preferential Paula/Paul

- 'I'd prefer to be a highly competent trainer and I'll do my best for the students'
- 'I'd prefer to be liked, but it is also important to stay focused on the task and to be true to myself'
- 'I'd prefer to influence the training group to attain its goals, but total control is both undesirable and unrealistic'
- 'Students are likely to vary in how easy they find learning counselling skills and it is preferable that students learn skills thoroughly rather than quickly'
- 'It is preferable for skills trainers to be highly competent counsellors. However, I can still be honest about my strengths and my limitations'

Creating perceptions

One of the most influential approaches to cognitive psychotherapy is that of American psychiatrist Aaron Beck (Beck, 1976; Beck and Weishaar, 1995). Whereas Ellis emphasises preferential thinking, based on realistic rules, Beck emphasises propositional thinking, based on testing the reality of your perceptions about yourself, others and your environment. Both preferential and propositional thinking are useful mind skills. In this section, I focus more on how accurately you perceive yourself rather than on how accurately you perceive others.

Your self-concept

Your self-concept is your picture of yourself, what you think of as 'I' or 'Me'. It consists of a series of different perceptions about yourself of varying degrees of accuracy. Areas of your self-concept concern perceptions regarding your: family of origin, current relationships, body image, age, gender, sexual orientation, culture, race, social class, religious beliefs, health, work, study activities, leisure pursuits and tastes and preferences, among others.

Centrality is one dimension of your self-concept: 'What is really important to me?' For instance, if a committed Christian, your faith is fundamental to your self-concept. Another dimension of self-concept is that of your positive and negative evaluations of personal charac-teristics: 'What do I like and dislike about myself?' A further important dimension of self-concept is that of how confident a person you are. You may accurately perceive your level of confidence or over- or under-estimate it.

The self-concepts of all counselling skills students contain percep-tions of varying degrees of accuracy about your skills: for example, perceptions of your listening skills and questioning skills. You may accurately perceive your skill level in a particular area or perceive youself as either more or less skilled than you really are.

The process of perceiving

Some counselling students possess a tendency to underestimate skill levels. Psychologists McKay and Fanning (1992) use the term patho-logical critic to describe the pathological inner voice that attacks and judges you. While all students have areas on which they need to work, when in pathological critic mode they perceive their skills far too negatively. For example, negative perceptions that you may hold about your listening skills include that they are hopeless, unchangeable and worse than those of your fellow students.

Conversely, counselling students can perceive their skill levels too positively, even to the extent of becoming instant experts. Sometimes you may use self-protective habits that defend your current estimation of your ability. You may deny certain aspects of the feedback that you receive from your trainer and fellow students: for instance, that you are too inclined to give advice rather than listen. Alternatively you may distort and selectively filter out incoming information: for example, only partly acknowledging the full extent of a piece of positive or negative feedback.

One of the principal skills of learning to perceive more accurately is that of being able to distinguish fact from inference. Take the statement 'All Aborigines walk in single file, at least the one I saw did'. That you saw one Aborigine is fact, that all Aborigines walk in single file is inference or factually unsupported supposition. Whether as a counsel-ling skills student, helper or private individual, guard against tendencies to jump to unwarranted conclusions. Also, be prepared to change or modify your conclusions in light of emerging information.

Box 2.4 depicts a counselling skills student, who initially jumps to an unduly negative conclusion about her/his level of performance, and then reality-tests the perception to see how accurately it fits the available facts.

Box 2.4   Creating and reality-testing perceptions

Situation
A student assessing her/his performance just after the half way stage of a 60-hour introductory counselling skills course.

Reality-testing Raelene/Ray's initial perception
'I'm doing poorly on my counselling skills course.'

Reality-testing Raelene/Ray challenging the initial perception
'I know that I have a tendency to put myself down. Where is the evidence that I'm doing poorly? I started off the course listening poorly. I'd never had any training in listening skills and thought the best way to help people was to give good advice. Also, I felt intimidated because the other students are older and more experienced than me. However, the feedback I've received both from the trainer and from my fellow students is that they think I'm improving. In fact, on my middle of course assessment cassette, I received an above average grade. The trainer gave me some feedback about how I might improve, but that does not mean that I am doing poorly. What is a realistic skills level for this stage of the course? I think I expect too much of myself too soon. So far I have had limited opportunity to practise my skills and they still do not feel natural to me. I'm very aware of thinking about what I do all the time. Also, along with learning new skills I'm having to unlearn some bad old habits.'

Reality-testing Raelene/Ray's revised perception
'While I wish I were doing better, my progress is satisfactory for this stage of the course.'

Creating explanations

There is a joke about a psychological researcher who had trained a frog to jump when he said 'jump'. One day he decided to extend his research by cutting off one of the frog's rear legs and then saying 'jump'. The frog jumped sideways. Then he cut off the second rear leg and said 'jump'. The frog did not move. The psychologist's explanation for this was that the frog had suddenly gone deaf!

Explanations of cause are the reasons you give yourself for what happens. These explanations can influence how you think about your past, present and future. Also, explanations of cause influence how you feel, physically react and act. Frequently, people make explanatory errors that interfere with their motivation and effectiveness. Let's take the example of the women's movement. When women explained their lack of status as due to male dominance, they were relatively powerless. However, when women also attributed their lack of status to their own insufficient assertion, they empowered themselves.

Counselling students can stay stuck in personal problems through wholly or partially explaining their causes inaccurately. Your unresolved personal problems may negatively intrude into your counselling skills training and helping work. Possible faulty explanations for the causes of problems include: 'It's my genes', 'It's my unfortunate past', 'It's my bad luck', 'It's my poor environment', 'It's all their fault', or 'It's all my fault'. Sometimes counselling students succumb to the temptation of externalising problems: they are the victims of others' inconsiderate and aggressive behaviours. Such students explain cause from outside to inside. However change usually requires explaining cause from inside to outside.

As a counselling skills student you can strengthen or weaken your motivation to attain higher skills levels by how you explain the causes of your successes and failures. For instance, you may rightly or wrongly assign the causes for your good or poor counselling skills performance to such factors as: prior experience, ability, effort, anxiety, task difficulty, trainer competence, adequacy of training environment, opportunities to practise your skills, competing demands from other subjects on your course, financial worries, external work pressures, external relationship pressures, supportive home environment, supportive work environment or luck, to mention but some.

Excuses, excuses, excuses. Unfortunately some students are adept at making excuses that mask an inability to assume genuine personal responsibility for becoming more skilled. Assuming personal responsibility for your counselling skills involves the ability to explain cause accurately and, where possible, to address relevant considerations constructively.

Box 2.5 examines how students can create either harmful or helpful explanations for what happens both inside and outside their counselling skills classes. The differences are exaggerated to make the point about the importance of creating accurate explanations.

Box 2.5   Creating harmful and helpful explanations

Harmful explanations: Victim Vicky/Vic

Vicky/Vic is a person for whom anger is never far below the surface. Vicky/Vic constantly externalises the cause of not only past but present problems and difficulties on to other people. S/he feels keenly that s/he was not given sufficient love by her/his parents and, consequently, will always be disadvantaged in life because of them. Currently Vicky/Vic is in an unhappy relationship where s/he blames her/his partner for creating all their mutual misery.

In regard to counselling skills training, Vicky/Vic considers that it is up to the trainer and the other group members to make sure s/he does well. Vicky/Vic is quick to complain when difficulties occur in the training group – for instance, a handout is not forthcoming or the video malfunctions – whether or not these are beyond the control of the trainer. Bringing to skills training an underlying 'Ain't it awful' attitude to life, Vicky/Vic looks for allies to turn the training group into a students versus trainer 'us-them' combative environment.

Helpful explanations: Personally responsible Rhonda/Ron

Rhonda/Ron grew up in an unhappy home where s/he feels s/he was not given sufficient love by her/his parents. However, Rhonda/Ron worked through the pain and anger to understand that neither parent received a good emotional start in life and that it was unproductive to keep blaming them. Rather than focusing on the past, Rhonda/Ron has assumed personal responsibility for her/his own happiness and fulfilment in her/his present and future. Rhonda/Ron is in a stable relationship in which both partners treat one another with respect. When problems occur, they both accept responsibility for adopting a cooperative approach to solving them.

In regard to counselling skills training, Rhonda/Ron accepts responsibility for making the most of the opportunities that are either provided or that s/he can create. S/he works hard to keep her/his side of the skills training contract. If difficulties occur in the training group, Rhonda/Ron is no doormat. S/he accepts what cannot be immediately changed, for example the photocopy machine breaking down, and assertively collaborates with the trainer and fellow students to improve matters that can be changed.

Creating expectations

Humans seek to predict their futures so that they can influence and control them. Consequential thinking entails creating expectations about the consequences of your communication and actions. For good or ill, you create and influence your own consequences, including your own and others' feelings, physical reactions, thoughts and communications.

Consequential thinking can be overdone. Harmful anxiety is a feeling generated by excessive preoccupation with dangerous consequences. Also, you can freeze yourself with indecision if you spend too much time trying to predict consequences. Furthermore, in both your helping contacts and in daily life, you can lose all spontaneity if continually preoccupied with the consequences of your communication. You create expectations about the positive and negative consequences of your own and others' communication. Sometimes you make accurate inferences concerning consequences. On other occasions you may overestimate or underestimate the probability of loss or gain.

In counselling skills training and in helping, you create expectations of varying degrees of accuracy about your competence and coping ability. Such expectations influence how confident you feel and how you communicate. Communicating counselling skills competently is not simply a matter of knowing what to do. You need the confidence to use your skills. Expectations about competence differ from expectations about outcomes. Expectations about competence involve your predictions about your ability to accomplish a certain level of performance, for instance listening. Outcome expectations involve your predictions about the likely consequences of your performance; for instance if you listen skilfully to clients then they will experience and explore their feelings more fully.

Expectations about your level of competence also influence how much effort to expend and how long to persist in the face of setbacks and difficulties. Unlike self-doubt, strong expectations of competence strengthen your resilience when engaging in difficult tasks. In addition, expectations about your level of competence influence how you think and feel. If you judge yourself insufficiently competent in dealing with the demands of your skills training group, you tend to exaggerate your personal deficiencies, become disheartened more easily and give up in face of difficulties. If you possess a strong sense of personal competence, though you may be temporarily demoralised by setbacks, you are more likely to stay task-oriented and to intensify your efforts when your performance in skills training falls short of your goals.

Related to your expectations about your level of competence are your expectations about your ability to cope with difficult situations and people. In your counselling skills training and helping work, lack of confidence about your ability to cope with difficulties, crises and critical incidents can worsen how you handle them, if and when they occur. Ironically, at the times when you need to be at your most realistic and rational, your emotional brain can take over and strong feelings can overcome reason.

Box 2.6 illustrates how one student started out on an introductory skills training course by having unrealistic expectations about her counselling skills that interfered with and undermined how she interviewed. Then, as the course progressed, she learned more realistic expectations that supported her interviewing.

Box 2.6   Creating harmful and helpful expectations

Situation
A counselling skills student being required to hand in an end-of-course assessment videotape of a full single helping interview and then being asked to resubmit it.

Harmful expectations: Desperately striving Susan
Susan was a married student with three children and a successful husband who fully supported her in taking a Diploma in Counselling course. Some 20 years previously, Susan had completed an undergraduate psychology major and now, with her parenting duties lightening, Susan wanted to train for a counselling career. At the end of her first semester counselling skills class, Susan handed in a very poor final assessment videotape in which she was far too controlling and did not listen properly to her client.

Rajiv, Susan's skills trainer, was aware that she was strong in the academic components of the course and related well to her fellow students. However, he considered Susan's anxiety level was too high in her practical skills work. Consequently, rather than fail her videotape, Rajiv had a chat with Susan to explore what was going on. Susan admitted to being highly anxious over making the assessment videotape.

As the conversation continued, it transpired that Susan had tremendously high expectations for herself. Susan related how, when growing up, she felt she always had to strive to prove herself to her mother who had continuously favoured her older sister and who regarded her as 'Susan also ran'. Now Susan was making herself anxious again trying to meet inner expectations that had outlived any purposes they may have served in her past and were positively counter-productive now. Susan thought her new insight very useful to understanding and moving beyond her present impasse.

Helpful expectations: Reasonably striving Susan
Rajiv and Susan agreed that she could resubmit her final assessment videotape in three weeks' time. During the intervening period Rajiv gave Susan three extra individual supervisions focused on helping her become

more relaxed both mentally and in her external communication. Susan , increasingly learned a more realistic set of expectations about interviewing competently for this stage of the course and not having to prove her worth as a person to an external authority figure. She gained a level of anxiety which was sufficient to help her strive for interviewing competence, but not so high that her mind created incompetence. Susan passed her resubmitted videotape assessment with no trouble at all.

The same human clay

Counselling skills students, trainers, helpers and clients share a common humanity. Though this chapter mainly focuses on the mental processes or mind skills of counselling skills students, much of its contents apply to everyone. All of us are made of the same human clay and, thus, possess good and poor mind skills. In successful counselling skills training you can build on your mental strengths and move your weaknesses more in the direction of strengths. Furthermore, counselling skills training can fruitfully go beyond focusing on helping you understand your mental processes in helper–client contacts to incorporate helping you understand your mental processes as a student. This additional focus should accelerate your learning about how to create your mind more skilfully, thus contributing to the effectiveness and fun of your training experience.

Summary

Your mind can be viewed as the psychological manifestation of your brain. You can use your mind to further heightened self-awareness and personal development. Levels of thinking include: conscious, super-conscious, preconscious and unconscious. Contexts for creating your mind include: biological, social and cultural; and the learning influences of your past. Influences from your past can be viewed on four levels: acquisition, maintenance, activation and change.

You can harness your mind's potential both to learn counselling skills and to help clients more effectively. You can view your mental processes as skills that you can train yourself to control. When faced with specific situations you can substitute coping self-talk and visual images with an emphasis on calming and coaching yourself, for negative ones. In addition, you can substitute realistic rules based on preferential thinking, for unrealistic rules based on demanding thinking.

Your perceptions include your self-concept or how you picture yourself. You can have perceptions of varying degrees of accuracy about your counselling skills. You can perceive more accurately if you become skilled at distinguishing fact from inference and reality-testing the accuracy of your perceptions. You can create explanations that can allow you to stay stuck in unproductive patterns of behaviour, for instance blaming others. Alternatively, you can create explanations that acknowledge your personal responsibility for developing yourself as a student, helper and person. You can also create expectations that enhance rather than interfere with your learning counselling skills and helping clients. Students, trainers, helpers and clients are made of the same human clay and possess the same mental processes.

Activities

Activity 2.1   Creating self-talk and visual images

Part A   Creating self-talk

1   To what extent are you aware of your tendency to use self-talk before, during and after specific situations that may be stressful? To what extent is your self-talk either negative or coping or a mixture of both?

2   Think of a particular situation in relation to introductory counselling skills training or helping that you might experience as stressful.

Negative self-talk

3.1   Using Self-doubting Donna/Don as an example, develop negative self-talk in regard to the situation.

3.2   What would be the consequences of your negative self-talk on how you feel and communicate?

Coping self-talk

4.1   Using Confident Christine/Chris as an example, develop coping self-talk, focused on calming and coaching yourself, in regard to the situation.

4.2   What would be the consequences of your coping self-talk on how you feel and communicate?

Part B *Creating visual images*

1   To what extent are you aware of your tendency to use visual imagery before, during and after specific situations that may be stressful? To what extent are your visual images either negative or coping or a mixture of both?

2   Think of a particular situation in relation to introductory counselling skills training or helping that you might experience as stressful (it may be the same situation as in Part A above).

Negative self-talk and visual images

3.1   Using Angry Andrea/Andy as an example, develop negative self-talk and visual images in regard to the situation.

3.2   What would be the consequences of your negative self-talk and visual images on how you feel, physically react and communicate?

Coping self-talk and visual images

4.1   Using Focused Fran/Frank as an example, develop coping self-talk and visual images, focused on calming and coaching yourself, in regard to the situation.

4.2   What would be the consequences of your coping self-talk and visual images on how you feel, physically react and communicate?

5   As appropriate, in all learning counselling skills and helping situations, practise substituting coping self-talk and visual images for negative self-talk and visual images.

Activity 2.2   Creating rules

Demanding rules about yourself as a learner

1   Using Demanding Dannie/Dan as an example, list at least three unrealistic and demanding rules you either do or might possess concerning how you should learn introductory counselling skills.

2   What are likely to be the consequences of possessing the above demanding rules on your feelings, physical reactions and communication?

Preferential rules about yourself as a learner

3   Using Preferential Paula/Paul as an example, restate the demanding rules you listed above into more preferential rules about learning introductory counselling skills.
4   What are likely to be the consequences of possessing the above preferential rules on your feelings, physical reactions and communication?
5   As appropriate, in all learning counselling skills and helping situations, practise substituting preferential rules for demanding ones.

Demanding and preferential rules concerning your trainer(s)

Repeat the above activity, but this time list demanding rules that you might have about your counselling skills group trainer(s) and restate them into more preferential rules.

Activity 2.3   Creating perceptions

Part A   My self-concept

Either verbally or in writing describe how you see yourself in such a way that another person might really get to know you. In your description, indicate

- what is central to you;
- some aspects of yourself you regard positively and some aspects you regard negatively;
- how confident you see yourself as a person; and
- how you view your counselling skills.

Part B   Perceiving accurately

Think of a situation in regard to either learning introductory counselling skills or in your workplace where you may be jumping to a conclusion based on inference rather than on fact. Taking Reality-testing Raelene/Ray as an example, articulate a process of questioning the adequacy of your initial perception and replacing it with a more realistic perception.

Activity 2.4   Creating explanations

Part A   Assessing my level of personal responsibility

1   To what extent do you consider you are realistic in assuming personal responsibility for what happens in your life?
2   Do you have any tendencies to play the victim and unreasonably blame others for what happens to you? If so, what do you intend doing about it?

Part B   Explanations for how successful I will be in learning counselling skills

1   Using the rating scale below, rate the importance you attach to each of the listed factors to explaining how successful you will be in learning introductory counselling skills:
   4   Extremely important
   3   Very important
   2   Moderately important
   1   Slightly important
   0   Of no importance

Your rating	*Factors*
_____	my prior experience at helping
_____	how able I am
_____	the amount of effort I will make
_____	how anxious I will get
_____	the difficulty of the learning tasks
_____	how competent the trainer(s) is
_____	how good the training facilities are
_____	the opportunities I will get to practise my skills
_____	competing demands from other elements of the course, if relevant
_____	financial worries
_____	the degree of support from my work environment
_____	the degree of support from my home environment
_____	my physical health
_____	luck
_____	other factors not mentioned above (please specify and rate each)

2   Summarise your main explanations for how successful you will be in learning introductory counselling skills.

3   Can you alter any of your explanations to increase your chances of success? If so, what revised explanations might you have?

Activity 2.5   Creating expectations

Part A   *Expectations of skills training*

Expectations about training group outcomes

1   What are your expectations about the goals and outcomes of your introductory skills training group?

2   What are your fellow students' expectations about the goals and outcomes of your introductory skills training group?

3   What are your trainer's expectations about the goals and outcomes of your introductory skills training group and do they diverge from students' expectations?

Expectations about training group processes

1   What are your expectations about the processes of your introductory skills training group?

2   What are your fellow students' expectations about the processes of your introductory skills training group?

3   What are your trainer's expectations about the processes of your introductory skills training group and do they diverge from students' expectations?

Part B   *Expectations about myself*

1   What are your expectations about how you will perform during the training group and how realistic are they?

2   What are your expectations about the outcomes you will personally obtain from your training group and how realistic are they?

3 Creating Your Communication and Feelings

Don't walk ahead of me,
I may not follow.
Don't walk behind me,
I may not lead.
Just walk beside me,
And be my friend.
                    Anon

Chapter outcomes

By studying and doing the activities in this chapter you should be able to:

- *understand how helpers and clients can create verbal communication;*
- *understand how helpers and clients can create vocal communication;*
- *understand how helpers and clients can create bodily communication;*
- *appreciate the importance of understanding communication in its cultural context;*
- *as appropriate, change some of your verbal, vocal and bodily communication;*
- *understand what is meant by the term 'feelings';*
- *acknowledge some important physical reactions associated with feelings; and*
- *establish some connections between mind, communication, feelings and physical reactions.*

Counselling skills students, helpers and clients use mental processes to create external communication. You always have choices in how you communicate. However, you may have limited awareness about the fact that you are always choosing, what some of your choices are, and how sometimes you can make different and better choices.

Often, in the first session of my workshops, I use a simple demonstration to make the point that people may be insufficiently aware that they can choose how to communicate. I ask for a volunteer to sit opposite me and go through three steps concerning bodily communication. First, I ask the volunteer to describe what the concept of bodily communication means to her or him. Here people tend to answer very much from their heads. Second, I use a Gestalt counselling awareness exercise in which I instruct the volunteer to say 'I am aware . . .' as they become aware of any aspect of their bodily communication: for example, 'I am aware that I have my legs crossed above my ankles'. The volunteer may do this awareness exercise for a minute or two. Then I tell the volunteer to say 'I choose to . . .' before any aspect of their bodily communication: for instance, 'I choose to cross my legs above my ankles'. After a minute or two I hold a feedback session in which I ask how the volunteer experienced each of the different steps. More often than not, volunteers acknowledge feeling more empowered when saying 'I choose to . . .' than in the other two steps. Also, frequently volunteers get themselves into more comfortable sitting positions during the 'I choose to . . .' step.

Creating your communication

When creating their roles, actors like Emma Thompson and Mel Gibson are continually choosing their verbal and non-verbal communication. Similarly, a major function of movie directors like Stephen Spielberg is to help actors make skilled choices in how they come across on the screen. In your helping relationships, you too can take care to choose how best to communicate. Also, you can assist clients to make better communication choices.

All communication messages are encoded by senders and then decoded by receivers (Duck, 1998). You may possess either poor encoding skills or poor decoding skills or various mixtures of both. Another way of putting this is to use the terms 'communication skills' for encoding skills and 'discrimination skills' for decoding skills. Discrimination skills are highly relevant to communication skills because if you do not discriminate another's communications accurately, you will probably respond inappropriately.

In helping conversations, mistakes can be made by both parties. Senders may not send the messages they wish to send. Much human communication is either poor or unintentional. Also, senders sometimes intentionally seek to deceive. At the receiving end helpers and clients with poor listening skills may decode even the clearest of messages wrongly. However, you are much more likely to be misunderstood if you have poor communication skills.

There are five main ways helpers and clients can create communication or send messages. *Verbal* communication consists of messages that you send with words: for example, saying 'I understand what you are saying' or 'I don't understand'. *Vocal* communication consists of messages that you send through your voice: for instance, through your volume, articulation, pitch, emphasis and speech rate. *Bodily* communication consists of messages that you send with your body: for instance, through your gaze, eye contact, facial expression, posture, gestures, physical proximity and clothes and grooming. *Touch* communication is a special category of bodily communication. Messages that you send with your touch include: what part of the body you use, what part of another's body you touch, and how gentle or firm you are. *Taking action* communication consists of messages that you send when you are not face to face with others: for example, sending a follow up note to a client who has missed an appointment.

In particular, when reading the following sections on verbal, vocal and bodily communication, consider whether clients will experience your communication as comfortable.

Verbal communication

Let's look at some dimensions of verbal communication or talk. *Language* is an obvious dimension. Language consists of many elements other than whether people are English speaking or not. For instance, there may be a formal language, words either BBC or ABC news readers might use, as well as an informal or colloquial language, words you might use with mates in the pub. Another dimension of language is use of visual imagery: for example, 'I feel like a bird in a cage', and metaphors, for instance 'It's a glaring error'. Also, your language is very much governed by the social rules attached to the context in which conversations take place: for instance, you may use different language in the home, the pub and the helping interview.

Another dimension of talk is *content*. Content may refer to topic area, problem area or the task being undertaken, such as learning counselling skills. In addition, content refers to the focus of talk, whether it be about yourself, others or the environment. Furthermore, content can refer to the evaluative dimension of talk: for example, depressed clients may say many negative things about themselves such as 'I'm worthless' and 'I just don't seem to care any more'.

A further dimension of talk is the *amount* of speech. 'Shyness' is a term commonly attached to people who experience difficulty when it comes to their turn to talk. In some but not all counselling approaches clients talk more than helpers. However, some clients may be talkative from the start, others warm up as helping progresses, and yet others talk haltingly throughout even though the helping may be successful. Counselling skills students and helpers can also talk too much or too little.

Honesty is an important dimension of talk. Counselling students, helpers and clients can use words to share personal information honestly. You can also use words so as not to communicate genuinely. In helping relationships, trust may need to be established before clients reveal more threatening information. Thus initial talk may mask more important agendas. Indeed, clients may need to get in touch with and acknowledge some information within themselves prior to sharing it with you.

Both helpers and clients may use words for self-protective purposes and to manage the impressions another has of them. Much of this concealment is motivated by anxiety and may be below your awareness. Sometimes the concealment represents consciously economising on the truth. On other occasions it may entail outright lying.

Yet another dimension of talk is that of *ownership* of speech. Thomas Gordon (1970), in his book *Parent Effectiveness Training*, makes a useful distinction between 'You' messages and 'I' messages. 'You' messages focus on the other person and can be judgemental: for example, 'You don't appreciate what I'm doing for you' or 'You're not listening to me properly'. 'I' messages use the word 'I' and are centred in you as the sender: for instance, 'I feel unappreciated' or 'I'm experiencing not being heard correctly'.

How skilled are you at creating verbal communication? In your counselling skills training group, are you able to say what you mean and mean what you say? When you help others, are you able to find the right words for the right occasion or are you at a loss for words? In your private life, do you speak to much or too little or roughly the right amount?

Vocal communication

As the old saying goes: 'It ain't what you say, but how you say it'. When talking, your overall communication consists of voice and body *framing* communications which may or may not match your verbal communication, the *literal* content of what you say. These framing communications are extremely important. Your vocal and bodily communications can either correspond to, heighten, lessen or contradict the intention of your verbal communication. For instance, a helper says to a client Dave 'I'm really concerned about you', in a monotonous voice at the same as time as looking down and away. Here, it does not take an expert decoder to surmise that this helper is not particularly concerned with Dave.

If you can create appropriate vocal communications, you have acquired a very useful skill in dealing with fellow students, clients and colleagues. Your vocal messages can speak volumes about what you truly feel and how emotionally responsive you are to others' feelings. Following are five dimensions of vocal messages. They form the acronym VAPER – volume, articulation, pitch, emphasis and rate.

Volume refers to loudness or softness. You need to disclose at a level of audibility that is comfortable and easy for clients to hear. Some counselling students let their voices trail away at the end of sentences. Some unnecessarily soften their voices to match their clients' voices. Though a booming voice overwhelms, speaking too quietly may communicate that you are a 'wimp'. A firm and confident voice is a good starting point from which you can make variations as appropriate, for instance by speaking more gently or more loudly.

Articulation refers to the clarity of your speech. You are easier to understand if you enunciate words well. *Pitch* refers to the height or depth of your voice. An optimum pitch range includes all the levels at which a pleasing voice can be produced without strain. Errors of pitch include either being too high pitched or too low pitched.

It is important that your voice uses *emphasis* when responding to clients' feelings and nuances and when sharing your feelings. You may use too much emphasis and seem melodramatic or too little emphasis and come across as wooden. In addition, you may use emphasis in the wrong places.

Often speech *rate* is measured by words per minute. Your speech rate depends not only on how quickly you speak words, but on the frequency and duration of pauses between them. If you speak very quickly, you may appear anxious and clients may have difficulty understanding you.

On the other hand, a speech rate which is too ponderous can be boring. However, pausing and being silent at the right times is another important aspect of speech rate.

Bodily communication

If you want to do a brief activity that highlights the importance of bodily communication, sit back to back with another counselling skills student and try to hold a conversation. You are now having to communicate as if blind. How did you experience not being able to see one another? Not surprisingly, back to back conversations are sometimes used when training telephone helpers.

Both when speaking and listening you disclose yourself through how you create your bodily communication. For instance, whether speaking or listening, if you continue looking out of the window without a good reason, you send a negative message. Following are some of the main forms of bodily communication.

Facial expressions are perhaps the main vehicle for sending body messages. Ekman, Friesen and Ellsworth (1972) have found that there are seven main facial expressions of emotion: happiness, interest, surprise, fear, sadness, anger, and disgust or contempt. Your mouth and eyebrows can convey much information: for instance, 'down in the mouth' and 'raised eyebrows'.

Gaze is an important area of bodily communication. Gaze, or looking at other people in the area of their faces, is both a way of showing interest and also a way of collecting facial information. Speakers look at listeners about 40 per cent of the time and listeners look at speakers about 70 per cent to 75 per cent of the time. Gaze is useful for coordinating speech: for example, speakers look just before the end of utterances to collect feedback about their listeners' reactions. Women are more visually attentive than men in all measures of gaze (Argyle, 1994). *Eye contact* is a more direct way of sending messages, be they of interest, anger or sexual attraction.

Gestures are physical movements that can frame or illustrate words coming before, during or after what is being said. An example of using a gesture to display and emphasise an emotion is clenching your fist to show aggression. Gestures may also illustrate shapes, sizes or movements, particularly when these are difficult to describe in words. How you gesture can vary according to your sex. Sometimes men's gestures are larger, more sweeping and forceful, while women's gestures are smaller and more inhibited.

Gestures can also take the place of words: for example, nodding your head either up and down or sideways for saying 'yes' or 'no', respectively. For people from Western cultures, a brief activity that highlights the power of your conditioning is to alternate between shaking your head sideways as you say 'yes' and nodding your head up and down as you say 'no'. How did you feel and what did you think about doing that? However, remember that cultures differ in what they communicate through head nodding and head shaking. For instance, Laungani (1999) observes that in India it is not uncommon for 'people to nod and shake or nod *and* shake their heads to mean yes or no' (p. 139).

Your *posture* may convey various messages. Turning your body towards your client is more encouraging than turning away from them. Also, whether you lean forwards or backwards may indicate interest or disinterest. Height tends to be associated with status: for instance, you 'talk down to' or 'talk up to' someone. Women may be at a disadvantage unless another's body posture is changed: for instance, by sitting down.

Posture may also communicate how anxious you are: for instance, sitting with your arms and legs tightly crossed suggests that you are emotionally as well as literally uptight. However, if you are a woman, you may appear too relaxed: some men may mistakenly perceive uncrossed and open legs as a sign of sexual availability whether you wear a skirt, trousers or jeans. Such perceptions manifest a double standard in how people decode body messages.

The degree of *physical proximity* that is comfortable for Britons and Antipodeans is generally the same (Hall, 1966). The zones vary according to the nature of the relationship. In the *intimate zone* (between six and 18 inches) it is easy to touch and be touched. This zone is reserved for spouses, lovers, close friends and relatives. The *personal zone* (between 18 and 48 inches) is appropriate for less close friends and for parties and other social gatherings. The *social zone* (between four and 12 feet) is comfortable for people not known at all well. The *public zone* (over 12 feet) is the distance for addressing public gatherings.

If *clothes* do not make the counselling student, helper or client, they certainly send many messages which may influence how much and in which areas clients reveal themselves. These messages include your social and occupational standing, sex-role identity, ethnicity, conformity to peer group norms, rebelliousness and how outgoing you are. While maintaining your individuality, you need to dress appropriately for your clientele: for example, delinquent teenagers probably respond better to informally dressed helpers than do stressed business executives. Your personal *grooming* also provides important information about how well you take care of yourself; for instance, you may be clean or dirty, neat or tidy. In addition, the length and styling of your hair sends messages about you.

Box 3.1 looks at how your bodily and vocal communication may encourage or discourage clients from talking to you and experiencing and exploring themselves. Which communications are rewarding and give courage or confidence to clients and which are put-downs?

Box 3.1   Encouraging and discouraging vocal and bodily communication

Look at the non-verbal messages below. Imagine yourself as a client. Put an E before all those messages on the part of your helper that you would find rewarding or encouraging, and a D before all those messages which you would find unrewarding or discouraging.

__	1 Picks nose	__	16 Looks alert
__	2 Calm manner	__	17 Smiles when greeting you
__	3 Leans far back	__	18 Sits higher than you
__	4 Head very close to yours	__	19 Half closes eyes
__	5 Tugs at ear	__	20 High-pitched voice
__	6 Looks towards you	__	21 Leans slightly towards you
__	7 Sits on same level as you	__	22 Looks clean
__	8 Bounces a leg	__	23 Comfortable speech rate
__	9 Picks lint off clothes	__	24 Monotonous voice
__	10 Voice easy to hear	__	25 Body posture open to you
__	11 Stares at you	__	26 Flowery arm gestures
__	12 Facial expression matches what you feel	__	27 Has vacant look
__		__	28 Has warmth in voice
__	13 Relaxed seating position	__	29 Pauses for you to continue
__	14 Slouches	__	30 Whispers
__	15 Raises eyebrows		

Culture and communication

Earlier I mentioned that use of language is influenced by the rules of the social context in which it takes place: for example the home, the pub or the helping interview. Extending this comment, all external communication, be it verbal, vocal or bodily, is influenced by cultural considerations. Simply stated, culture is 'the way we do things here'. Most often the term 'culture' refers to patterns of thoughts, feelings and behaviour of different ethnic groupings. However culture can be used more inclusively to include patterns related to different groupings: for instance regional, social class, religious, organisational and minority. Here my focus is on culture as related to ethnic groupings.

In Britain, about 95 per cent of the population are Anglo-Celtic Caucasians. The largest minority groupings are Indian, Pakistani and Afro-Caribbean people. Australia is one of the world's most multi-cultural countries, with about one-sixth of the population having either or both parents born overseas and many others being first generation immigrants. In the 1950s and 1960s most migrants came from conti-nental Europe, especially Britain, Italy and Greece. The white Australia policy ended in the 1970s and now Asians from South-East Asia (Malaysia, Philippines, Vietnam), North-East Asia (China, Hong Kong) and Southern Asia (India, Sri Lanka) are easily the main migrant group. In addition, Australia has about a quarter of a million people of Aboriginal and Torres Strait Islander origin. In New Zealand, Maoris comprise just over 10 per cent of the population.

You cannot use counselling skills independently of your own and your clients' cultural contexts. Also, almost invariably in Australia and frequently in Britain, members of counselling skills training groups come from differing cultural backgrounds. Furthermore, sometimes counsellor trainers' cultures differ from that of students. Being pri-marily culturally British, sometimes during my 13 years in Australia I experienced myself as culturally different from the counselling students I trained. For instance, I experienced mainstream Australian students as communicating less respect for authority and speaking with less understatement than in British culture.

A useful distinction exists between the culture-deficit and culture-sensitive approaches to using counselling skills. The culture-deficit approach assumes that the rules, values and behaviours of the dominant culture are normal and that variations observed in minorities are deficits. Pittu Laungani (1999), who comes from an Indian background, provides an amusing example of Bernie, a previous jack of all trades in his London flat, saying 'You know, Dr Laungani, you are almost a true Brit! Almost one of us.' Meant kindly as a supreme compliment, Bernie was unaware of the implicit culture-deficit assumptions of his statement.

The culture-sensitive approach avoids the assumption that dominant group practices are proper and superior. Helpers show respect for cultural differences and may emphasise positive features of cultural variation. Helpers also show sensitivity to minority group members' different levels of and wishes for assimilation into the mainstream culture. Migrant clients are assisted to develop their own identities rather than either being crudely moulded or more subtly influenced into being 'true Brits' or 'dinky dye Aussies'.

The task of detailing cultural variations is too large and complex for this book. Instead, Box 3.2 tries to raise your awareness of the importance of culture by highlighting aspects of Aboriginal people's verbal, vocal and bodily communication.

Box 3.2   Aboriginal culture and communication

Following are some aspects of Aboriginal people's verbal, vocal and bodily communication.

Verbal communication
- Value is placed on brevity of reply rather than detailed elaboration, so 'yes' or 'no' responses are more common.
- In Aboriginal language there is no word for thank you. People do things as an obligation.
- According to the laws of some tribes, it is unacceptable to speak or use the name of a dead person.
- Terms which are offensive to Aborigines include: full-blood, half-caste, quarter-caste, native and part-Aborigine.

Vocal communication
- There is a greater proportion of silence in Aboriginal than in non-Aboriginal communication. Most of the time these are not awkward silences for Aboriginal people.

Bodily communication
- *Eye contact* – to some Aboriginal people, it is unacceptable to look others straight in the eye.
- *Gaze* – frequently Aborigines listen without looking and feel no strong obligation to look at the person talking to them.
- *Proximity* – some Aboriginal lifestyles do not allow men and women to mix freely.
- *Attendance* – attending interviews at specific times is far removed from the usual Aboriginal lifestyle.

Genuineness: Creating consistent communications

Since counselling students, helpers and clients can create communications in so many different ways, genuineness becomes important.

Sometimes people have poor skills in matching actions to words. When sending messages you can be deceiving others, yourself or both. However, human communication is often more complex than this and involves shades of grey. If you have good skills in sending messages 'loud and clear', your vocal and bodily communication matches your verbal communication. If you fail to send consistent verbal, vocal and bodily messages you make it harder for listeners to decode your overall communication accurately. Also, you increase their chances of their perceiving you as insincere. In general, verbal communication is easier to control than non-verbal communication. Thus you can often pick up important messages about the real meaning of a communication by attending to how things are being said.

Your feelings and physical reactions

Seeing's believing, but feeling's the truth.
Thomas Fuller

To a large extent, you are what you feel. Common feelings include happiness, sadness, anger, anxiety and sexual arousal. Feelings represent your animal nature and are not skills in themselves. Dictionary definitions of feelings tend to use words like 'physical sensation', 'emotions' and 'awareness'. All three of these words illustrate a dimension of feelings. Feelings as *physical sensations* or as *physical reactions* represent your underlying animal nature. People are animals first, persons second. As such you need to learn to value and live with your underlying animal nature. Also, to get it working for rather than against you. The word 'emotions' implies movement. Feelings are processes. You are subject to a continuous flow of biological experiencing. *Awareness* implies that you can be conscious of your feelings. However, at varying levels and in different ways, you may also be out of touch with them.

Physical reactions both represent and accompany feelings and, in a sense, are indistinguishable. For example bodily changes associated with anxiety can include: galvanic skin response – detectable electrical changes taking place in the skin; heightened blood pressure; a pounding heart and a rapid pulse; shallow, rapid breathing; muscular tension; drying of the mouth; stomach problems, such as ulcers; speech difficulties, such as stammering, speaking rapidly and slurring words; sleep difficulties including difficulty getting to sleep, disturbed sleep and early morning waking; and sex difficulties, for instance complete or partial loss of desire. Other physical reactions include: a slowing down of body movements when depressed and dilated eye pupils in moments of anger or sexual attraction. Sometimes you react to your physical reactions. For example, in anxiety and panic attacks, you may first feel tense and anxious and then become even more tense and anxious because of this initial feeling.

Experiencing, expressing and managing feelings

Feelings and physical reactions are central to the helping process. As helpers, you require the capacity to experience and understand both your own and your clients' feelings. However, just because your feelings represent your animal nature this does not mean that you and your clients can do nothing about them. In both counselling skills training and in helping clients, three (albeit overlapping) areas where feelings and accompanying physical reactions are important are: first, experiencing feelings; second, expressing feelings; and thirdly, managing feelings. Sometimes counselling courses mainly focus on experiencing feelings at the expense of the other two areas. In Box 3.3 I illustrate each area with a brief example.

Box 3.3   Experiencing, expressing and managing feelings

Experiencing feelings

Hannah, 32, is a social work student who, in the early sessions of a counselling skills training group, smiled a lot and only gave positive rather than corrective feedback when commenting on fellow students' practical work. Hannah had difficulty experiencing her negative feelings and reservations about their work and acknowledging this both to herself and the group. Now in the later sessions of the group, Hannah is becoming more confident in acknowledging her negative as well as her positive feelings about other students' counselling skills.

Expressing feelings

Jeff, 46, is an out-placement counsellor whose client, Tuan, 42, was made redundant three months ago and has since searched hard for another job. Tuan has struggled to overcome his fears about networking, making cold calls and going for interviews. This session Tuan enters, sits down and announces that he has landed an excellent job with a leading pharmaceutical company. Jeff's face immediately lights up at the news and he smilingly says 'I'm really happy for you.'

Managing feelings

Gerry, 48, was a counsellor trainer recently separated from his wife. A consequence of this was that Gerry only intermittently saw his two young daughters, who were the pride of his life. Around this time Gerry found himself becoming increasingly emotionally and sexually attracted to Julie, 29, a student on the Diploma in Counselling course where he was a staff member. Julie had sent no signals that she was particularly interested in him. Gerry realised that as a professional counsellor trainer he needed to manage his feelings of vulnerability, loneliness and sexual attraction without involving Julie. Consequently, Gerry explored with a trusted supervisor how best to manage his feelings.

Creating how you feel and communicate

A major theme of this book is that your mind significantly mediates or *influences* feelings and communication to the point where they become the consequences or results of what is going on in your mind. Here I provide you with an STC framework for analysing the relationships between mind, feelings and communications or between how you think, feel and act. In this framework, STC stands for Situation–Thoughts–Consequences. In learning counselling skills and helping clients, more often than not how you feel, physically react and communicate in specific situations is mediated by your thoughts at T rather than by a direct response to the actual situation. The same holds true for your clients.

Let us take the example of Hannah, aged 32, the social work student who felt anxious about giving corrective feedback about fellow students' practical work. Assume that the trainer has discussed with the group the benefits of students learning from one another and that all the training group members have agreed they feel comfortable receiving constructive feedback from one another. Box 3.4 provides an example of the influence of Hannah's mind on her feelings, physical reactions and communication.

Box 3.4   Influence of mind on feelings, physical reactions and communication

S1 – Situation   Early in the training group Hannah has the opportunity to give constructive feedback about their practical work to her fellow students.

T1 – Thoughts   Hannah's thoughts include 'I must make a good impression', 'They may get angry with me if I am honest', and 'The trainer is evaluating me all the time'.

C1 – Consequences   Hannah's feelings include timidity and fearfulness. In addition, she fails to experience the full range of her reactions. Hannah's physical reactions include tension in her face and neck, and her mouth going dry. Hannah's communication consequences include giving only positive feedback and smiling nervously.

Now imagine that, by the training group's later sessions, Hannah has acquired some more effective mind skills. She may also have learned some more effective communication skills that help her to think more confidently when giving corrective feedback. Following is Hannah's revised STC.

S2 – Situation   Towards the end of the training group, Hannah has some further opportunities to give constructive feedback about their practical work to her fellow students.

T2 – Thoughts   Hannah thinks 'I can help other students if I give corrective feedback tactfully', 'The other students bear some responsibility for their reactions to my feedback', and 'The trainer wants to help me and the other students develop our skills'.

C2 – Consequences   Hannah now feels moderately relaxed, more confident and happier. Hannah experiences no major physical discomfort. Hannah's communication consequences include giving balanced feedback that points out possible areas for other students to work on. In addition, Hannah listens better when other students provide her with constructive feedback and thanks them for sharing their views with her.

If you can see the relationships between your mind, feelings, physical reactions and communication, you are in a better position to identify and develop appropriate skills to manage a range of situations both in counselling skills training and in helping clients. When you detect self-defeating feelings, physical reactions and communications, you can look for thoughts that may contribute to them. Then, as in the example of Hannah, you can create more skilful thoughts.

The STC framework can be used to analyse and alter your underlying mind skills as well as your various thoughts. For example, when Hannah thought 'I must make a good impression' she was exhibiting the poor mind skill of choosing an unrealistic rule – namely, 'I must be liked by everyone'. Furthermore, when Hannah thought 'The trainer is evaluating me all the time' she was probably exhibiting the poor mind skill of perceiving inaccurately. Hannah may have jumped to this conclusion about the trainer without having any real evidence for it. Often counselling skills students, helpers and clients can exhibit the same characteristic good and poor mind skills in many different situations: for example, situations faced in study, work, leisure and at home.

Summary

You always have choices in how you communicate. Understanding external communication is important both for your helping skills and for assisting clients to communicate better. Try to develop a helping manner that is comfortable for clients. Five aspects of communication are verbal, vocal, bodily, touch and taking action communication. Dimensions of verbal communication include formal and informal language, content, amount, honesty and ownership of speech. Dimensions of vocal communication include volume, articulation, pitch, emphasis and rate (VAPER). Dimensions of bodily communication include facial expressions, gaze, eye contact, gestures, posture, physical proximity and clothing and grooming. You cannot properly understand communication independent of its cultural context. You are more likely to be perceived as genuine if your vocal and bodily communication matches your verbal communication.

Your feelings represent your animal nature and are not skills in themselves. Feelings or emotions are processes at varying levels of your awareness. Physical reactions both represent and accompany feelings. Three important areas of feelings are experiencing, expressing and managing them.

Your mind significantly influences how you feel, physically react and communicate. You can use a simple Situation–Thoughts–Consequences (STC) framework for analysing relationships between mind, feelings and communication. In addition, the STC framework can be used to analyse and alter your underlying mind skills as well as your various thoughts.

Activities

Activity 3.1   Creating verbal communication

Part A   *Creating personal information for getting acquainted*

Training group students and trainer(s) can participate in one or more of the following activities where the object is to allow others to get to know you better. Observe how you create your verbal communication by what you choose to reveal and conceal.

- *Introduce yourself*   Spend one or two minutes describing yourself as a person to the whole training group.
- *Introduce a partner*   Divide into pairs. Partner A discloses to partner B, who listens and may ask a few questions. After a set time period, say two or three minutes, the partners reverse roles. This pairs work is followed by partners introducing one another to the whole training group.
- *Use triads or small groups*   Divide into threes or small groups and introduce yourselves to one another during a set time period.
- *Circulate with personal information visible*   Fill out either an index card or a 'post it' sticker with information about yourself, which you then pin or stick on your front. Then circulate and hold brief conversations with as many people in your training group as you can within a set time period.

Hold debriefing sessions at the end of getting acquainted activities. Explore issues connected with creating, disclosing and withholding verbal information.

Part B   Assessing my verbal communication

Assess yourself on each of the following creating verbal communication dimensions regarding either participating in your counselling skills group and/or helping clients:

- use of formal and informal language;
- content of talk;
- amount of talk;
- honesty of talk;
- ownership of talk;
- cultural considerations in how you verbally communicate;
- other important areas not listed above.

Activity 3.2   Creating vocal communication

Part A   Raising awareness

Your partner talks about a topic of interest to her/him and your job is mainly to listen; however:

- start by using terrible vocal communication when you respond; then
- switch to using good vocal communication;
- then hold a debriefing period in which you discuss what it felt like sending and receiving terrible and good vocal communication;
- reverse roles and repeat the steps above.

Part B   Assessing my vocal communication

Self-assessment
Assess yourself on each of the following creating vocal communication dimensions regarding either participating in your counselling skills group and/or helping clients:

- volume;
- articulation;
- pitch;
- emphasis;
- speech rate;
- use of pauses and silences;
- cultural considerations in how you communicate with your voice;
- other important areas not listed above.

Obtaining feedback
Obtain feedback from the other students in your training group and from your trainer(s) on your good and poor vocal communication skills.

Part C   Changing a specific dimension of vocal communication

Pick a specific dimension of vocal communication that you think you might improve; for instance you may have a tendency to talk too softly. Then hold a conversation with a partner in which you work on improving the specific dimension of vocal communication you have targeted. Either during or at the end of your conversation ask for feedback on how you are doing.

If appropriate, afterwards you and your partner reverse roles.

Activity 3.3   Creating bodily communication

Part A   Raising awareness

Your partner talks about a topic of interest to her/him and your job is mainly to listen; however:

- start by using terrible bodily communication when you respond; then
- switch to using good bodily communication;
- then hold a debriefing period in which you discuss what it felt like sending and receiving terrible and good bodily communication;
- reverse roles and repeat the steps above.

Part B   Assessing my bodily communication

Self-assessment
Assess yourself on each of the following creating bodily communication dimensions regarding either participating in your counselling skills group and/or helping clients:

- facial expression;
- gaze;

- eye contact;
- gestures;
- posture;
- physical proximity;
- clothing;
- grooming;
- cultural considerations in how you communicate with your body; and
- other important areas not listed above.

Obtaining feedback
Obtain feedback from the other students in your training group and from your trainer(s) on your good and poor bodily communication skills.

Part C Changing a specific dimension of bodily communication

Pick a specific dimension of bodily communication that you think you might improve; for instance you may have a tendency to sit with too rigid a posture. Then hold a conversation with a partner in which you work on improving the specific dimension of bodily communication you have targeted. Either during or at the end of your conversation ask for feedback on how you are doing.

If appropriate, afterwards you and your partner reverse roles.

Activity 3.4 Experiencing, expressing and managing feelings

Provide examples that illustrate strengths and difficulties in each of the following areas.

Experiencing feelings
- with respect to yourself
- with respect to a client or someone else

Expressing feelings
- with respect to yourself
- with respect to a client or someone else

Managing feelings
- with respect to yourself
- with respect to a client or someone else

Activity 3.5   Influence of mind on communication, feelings and physical reactions

First do this activity on your own. Then, if appropriate, discuss your answers with another or others.

1   Fill out an STC (Situation–Thoughts–Consequences) Activity Sheet for a either a counselling skills training group or a helping clients situation where you think you may possess unwanted feelings and physical reactions and be communicating less effectively than you would like. See the example of Hannah in the text for guidance in how to do this.

2   Rehearse and practise your new thoughts, for instance by:
- making up a reminder card and then regularly reading your card and thinking your changed thoughts;
- making up a cassette, listening to it regularly and then thinking your changed thoughts.

3   Repeat steps 1 and 2 above for one or more other situations.

STC (Situation – Thoughts – Consequences) Activity Sheet

Situation (State the problematic situation clearly and succinctly.)

Thoughts (1) (Record your thoughts about the situation. Put a plus (+) by helpful thoughts; a minus (–) by unhelpful thoughts; and a question mark (?) if in doubt.)

Consequences (1) (What are the consequences of your thoughts?)

Feelings

Physical reactions

Communication

Thoughts (2) (Keep your helpful thoughts about the situation, but replace your unhelpful thoughts with more helpful thoughts.)

Consequences (2) (What are the consequences of your revised thoughts?)

Feelings

Physical reactions

Communication

4 Helping as a Process

He who does good comes to the temple gate,
He who loves reaches the shrine.
                    Rabindranath Tagore

Chapter outcomes

By studying and doing the activity in this chapter you should be able to:

- *understand what is meant by a helping process model;*
- *understand some of the advantages and disadvantages of helping process models;*
- *gain an overview of the three-stage relating–understanding–changing helping process model; and*
- *gain knowledge of some helper skills and client processes involved in each stage of the model.*

Many counselling skills trainers and students find it useful to think about helping within the framework of helping process models consisting of different stages. Helping process models are simplified step by step representations of different goals and activities at progressive stages of helping (Nelson-Jones, 1999b). Here the word process has two meanings: first, the process of time going by; and second, the processes or procedures that take place in each of the different stages of the helping model across time. Helping process models can encompass both helper processes and client processes at each stage of the model.

Helping models are structured frameworks for viewing the helping process. They provide ways of assisting counselling skills students and helpers to think and work more systematically. Helping process models work on the assumption that the use of helping skills is cumulative:

insufficient application of skills in the earlier stage or stages negatively influences ability to help in later stages.

In Chapter 1, I broke down the use of counselling skills into five different goals: supportive listening, managing a problem situation, problem management, altering poor skills that create problems, and bringing about a changed philosophy of life. Even when presented with broader problems, the most that introductory counselling skills students can often do is focus on specific situations within them. Consequently, here I present a simple three-stage managing a problem situation model which can provide a stepping stone to using more complex models later.

Some readers may be in situations where using a helping process model such as the following may be inappropriate all of the time or most of the time. For example, many nurses may find little opportunity to apply all three stages of the model systematically. Even those of you who are in positions where you can apply the model are encouraged to use it flexibly. For instance, the main focus for someone counselling a recently bereaved parent may be on supportive listening rather than on managing specific problem situations.

The fact that the helping process model is presented in three stages may imply a degree of tidiness inappropriate to the actual practice of helping. Often the stages overlap and sometimes helpers find it necessary to move backwards and forwards between stages. Be careful about applying this or any other helping process model mechanistically.

The relating–understanding–changing (RUC) helping process model

Following are the three stages of the helping process model used in this book (see also Figure 4.1). Each of the three stages is named after its main task for both helper and client.

Stage 1: Relating Here the main helper and client task is to start establishing a working relationship. Clients dissatisfied with the relationship will lessen their participation in or leave helping. Helpers assist clients to tell their stories and, if appropriate, ask them to choose a specific problem situation to work on.

Stage 2: Understanding Here the main helper and client task is to clarify and enlarge their understanding of the chosen problem situation. Helpers assist clients to describe their thoughts, feelings, physical reactions and communications relating to the problem situation and to

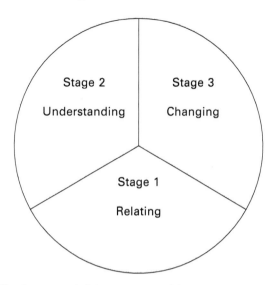

Figure 4.1   The three-stage helping process model

look for ways in which they may be communicating, acting and thinking less effectively than required.

Stage 3: Changing   Here the main helper and client task is for clients to change so that they deal with problem situations more effectively than in the past. Helpers and clients set goals and develop and implement strategies to address problem situations and to communicate, act and think better. Furthermore, they attend to how clients can maintain helpful changes.

I now provide a brief overview of each stage of this helping process model, prior to presenting a case study which shows the model in action. An assumption in describing the model is that of a relatively formal helping context, so those of you training for and/or working in more informal contexts may have to make the necessary adjustments in adapting the model to your particular circumstances. Another assumption is that of very brief helper–client contact, say up to six sessions at most. A final assumption is that the problem situation has a history rather than is one being faced for the first time.

Stage 1: The Relating Stage

The helper in the process
Helping relationships start at, if not before, the point at which helpers first meet with clients. For instance, how you handle a telephone call

may decide whether a client wishes to set up an appointment with you. Also helpers need to calm themselves down and get their helping space ready before they open the door of their offices to meet clients. A preliminary phase of the relating stage is the introductions phase, the purpose of which can be described as meeting, greeting and seating. The session starts with the moment of first contact with the client. When meeting clients in a waiting area, it may be perceived as more friendly if, as well as saying their names, you go over to them and show them into your office rather than just stand at the door. You should politely show them to their seat and help them to feel safe. At an appropriate moment, possibly even in the waiting area, you may greet them along the lines of: 'Hello, I'm . . . a helper here'. The issue of what you and your clients call each other can be handled according to the formal or informal rules of the context in which you help.

How you start the session may vary according to your helping context as well as according to your wishes and those of the client. For example, some helping contexts require some basic information gathering at the start of sessions. Apart from this, the main choice in starting a session is whether first to allow clients to tell their stories and then do some structuring about the nature of your helping contact or the reverse. My preference is for letting clients talk first and 'get their problem(s) off their chest'. Sometimes, clients come with one clearly identified problem situation, for example how to handle anxiety concerning an important exam in a week's time. On other occasions, they may have many or more complex problems. In any event, create an emotionally comfortable helping relationship and use your active listening skills to help clients overview their main reasons for coming to see you. If there is more than one problem area, summarise and identify the different problem areas and ask them which one they want to address. Then, assuming your helping contact is brief, ask them to identify a particular situation within the problem for you to work on together.

The client in the process

Clients wonder whether they can trust their helpers, what is going to happen in helping, whether their secrets will be divulged elsewhere and whether they will be treated with sympathy and respect. They want to be helped to feel comfortable and safe. They may not find it particularly easy to talk about certain aspects of their problems and they want to be able to go at their own pace. They appreciate helpers with calm and reassuring presences, who do not overpower them and who are prepared to hold back and let them say why they have come. Clients can feel overwhelmed by problems. Given limited time for helping, many clients may think it better to try and make progress on just one of them.

Box 4.1   Stage 1: Relating

Main task
The main helper and client task is to start establishing a working relationship.

Sub-tasks
- Meeting and mutual introductions.
- Entering and seating.
- Structuring the helping process.
- Establishing boundaries and constraints.
- Assisting the client to feel psychologically safe and understood.
- Assisting clients to tell their stories.
- Choosing a problem situation to focus on.

Illustrative counselling skills
- Bodily attending skills.
- Structuring and contracting skills.
- Skills for showing sensitivity to difference, e.g. cultural, racial.
- Skills for dealing with reluctance and resistance.
- Active listening skills.
- Summarising skills.
- Basic questioning skills.
- Prioritising skills.
- Mind skills that enhance the above communication skills.

Stage 2: The Understanding Stage

The helper in the process

Both helper and client require a fuller understanding of the specific problem situation the client has selected. Often clients feel at an impasse in problem situations. Getting them to describe the situation more fully in a supportive emotional climate can loosen their thinking, enlighten them and encourage them to think that they may be able to manage it better. Based on the foundation of good active listening skills, helpers use questioning skills that elicit information about clients in relation to their problem situations in such areas as: thoughts, feelings and physical reactions; attempts to cope in the past, including interaction patterns established with significant others; the situation's context; perceptions of personal strengths, resources and support factors; and any other considerations that either clients or helpers consider pertinent. Sometimes, helpers may engage clients in mini role-plays that can go some way to eliciting the actual verbal, vocal and bodily communications employed in situations.

Helpers seek to enlarge as well as to clarify the clients' understanding of situations, including their contribution to sustaining negative aspects of them. Helpers may ask questions that elicit information relevant to the clients' mental processes: for instance, their self-talk, rules and perceptions. Sometimes helpers may challenge client perceptions and provide feedback. Furthermore, at appropriate junctures, helpers may summarise ground recently covered. In addition, at the end of the understanding stage, helpers are likely to summarise all the main points elicited so far and check with clients about the accuracy of their summary and whether they wish to modify, add or subtract anything.

The client in the process

Often clients are glad that they are working on tangible situations. In the past they may have felt stuck in relation to their situations. Clients can still feel the helping relationship is comfortable and that they are not being interrogated, even though helpers question them. Nevertheless, clients may feel vulnerable about some aspects of their situations and not reveal everything. Being able to get many of their thoughts, feelings and physical reactions systematically out into the open helps clients to get in touch with and reflect upon them. Clients can also find it useful to examine specific verbal, vocal and bodily dimensions of their communication rather than just talk in vague terms about them.

Clients can appreciate brief helper summaries along the way that give them pause for thought and reflection. In addition, clients can find final summaries, pulling together what they have been saying about their problem situations, particularly enlightening and thought provoking. As the understanding stage progresses, clients may start thinking that perhaps they can do something constructive about their situations after all.

Box 4.2   Stage 2: Understanding

Main task

The main helper and client task is to clarify and enlarge their understanding of the chosen problem situation.

Sub-tasks

Maintaining the helping relationship
Clarifying helper and client understanding of the situation
Understanding the context of the situation
Expanding helper and client understanding of the situation
Looking for insufficiently effective communications and actions
Looking for insufficiently effective thinking
Maintaining boundaries

Illustrative counselling skills

Attending and active listening skills
Asking questions skills
    e.g. feelings, physical reactions, mind, communication, actions,
    background and context
Identifying strengths and resources skills
Challenging skills
Providing feedback skills
Disclosing skills
Skills for identifying poor communication and actions
Skills for identifying poor thinking
Summarising skills
Mind skills that enhance the above communication skills

Stage 3: The Changing Stage

The helper in the process

Two somewhat overlapping approaches that helpers and clients can take to the changing stage are the problem solving approach and the changing specific communications and thoughts approach. In the problem solving approach, helpers assist clients to clarify goals for problem situations, generate and explore options to attain them, and develop and implement action plans.

In the changing specific communications and thoughts approach, helpers and clients work together to specify communication and thoughts goals and the strategies to attain each of them. They may explore options in regard to which goals to set. Often statements of goals can include not only what clients want to achieve but the communication they want to avoid as well. Helpers can assist clients to develop plans to attain their communication and thoughts goals. Frequently, helpers act as client-centred coaches in assisting clients to develop more effective verbal, vocal and bodily communication for their problem situations. Helpers are careful to keep clients 'owning' their problems and to draw out clients' ideas and resources in dealing with them.

Sometimes coaching includes role-playing. Some helpers incorporate the use of the whiteboard into their coaching: for instance, jointly formulating with a client a clear verbal request for someone to change their behaviour and then pinpointing desirable vocal and bodily communication to back up this request.

In addition, helpers can encourage clients to think more effectively. For instance, once clients have identified useful ways of communicating in their problem situations, helpers can coach them in helpful self-talk for rehearsing and enacting this behaviour in real life. Also, helpers can assist clients to challenge unrealistic rules and perceptions and replace them with more realistic ones.

Helpers can assist clients to rehearse and practise their new ways of thinking and communicating between sessions and then report back at the start of subsequent sessions. They encourage clients to assume responsibility for changing their behaviour both now and in future. Before helping ends, helpers and clients review ways that clients can maintain helpful changes afterwards.

The client in the process
Often clients appreciate their need to think more clearly about what they want to achieve in situations. They also may be very aware of the need to avoid repeating behaviours that have worsened situations in the past. Many clients have never taken a systematic approach to analysing and changing how they communicate and act. They can find it useful to have their communication broken down into its verbal, vocal and bodily elements so that they may improve it bit by bit. Clients who are visually oriented like working with helpers to outline desirable communications on the whiteboard. During the changing stage, many clients start getting more of a sense that they can take control of their communication. In addition, they appreciate helpers who pay attention to how they think, realising that a stronger inner game can lead to a better outer game. In the past, many clients have allowed themselves to be too easily discouraged and distracted from their goals. Most clients recognise the importance of being responsible for their thinking and communication and also for maintaining their gains once helping ends.

Box 4.3   Stage 3: Changing

Main task

The main helper and client task is for the client to change so that the problem situation is addressed more effectively than in the past.

Sub-tasks
- Maintaining the helping relationship
- Exploring options
- Clarifying and setting goals
- Planning for change
- Developing more effective communication and actions
- Developing more effective thinking
- Supporting practice
- Looking for ways to maintain change
- Maintaining boundaries
- Ending the helping contact

Illustrative counselling skills
- Attending and active listening skills
- Facilitating clients in clarifying goals
- Generating options to attain goals
- Translating unhelpful communication and thoughts into goals
- Client-centred coaching skills
- Demonstration skills
- Rehearsing skills
- Skills for assisting clients to develop coping self-talk
- Skills for assisting clients to develop preferential rules
- Skills for assisting clients to reality-test perceptions
- Negotiating between session activities skills
- Conducting post-initial session skills
- Ending helping skills
- Assisting clients to maintain gains skills

Putting the stages of the RUC helping process model together

Box 4.4 uses a case example as an illustration of integrating the different stages of the RUC helping process model. The example takes the changing specific communications and thoughts approach to stage three of the model. The client's problem situation is the fairly common one of wanting to request a promised pay rise that has not been forthcoming. In introductory counselling skills classes, there is much to be said for focusing on common rather than unusual client problems and situations. Most often, complex and unusual problems and situations are best left to more advanced training. Though this case study has a happy ending, sometimes you may use counselling skills competently and still not achieve the degree of change that either you or your clients would wish.

Box 4.4 The RUC helping process model: the case of Tim

Stage 1 The relating stage

Tim, aged 26, came to see Sheila, 32, a counsellor in private practice, looking upset and nervous. Sheila informed Tim that they had another 45 minutes and calmly enquired why he had come to see her. Sheila used her active listening skills to create a safe and comfortable emotional climate for Tim to tell his story. Tim said that he was dissatisfied with himself and that he was too much of a wimp. He was only moderately successful with women. He had a steady girlfriend for two years, but about three months ago they broke up. Since then he has dated but not found anyone whom he really likes. Tim thought he could present himself more positively to women and came over to them as lacking in confidence. Sheila summarised what Tim had said up until then.

Tim then moved on to talk about his work life. A systems analyst, Tim had been employed with a large international financial services company for the last 10 months. He thought that he was competent at his job and had received a good performance appraisal at the end of six months. What Tim had not received was the pay rise that he had been told he would receive if his performance appraisal was satisfactory. He was very annoyed about this. After some further discussion, Sheila summarised the interview so far and asked Tim whether there were other issues of concern to him. When Tim replied that being more confident with women and securing a pay rise were the two main problems for him, Sheila asked him which of the two he would like to address first. Tim replied that obtaining the pay rise was the problem of most concern to him − in particular, handling the specific situation of asking his boss, Mike, for the promised pay increase. Doing something about this was his main reason for coming to counselling. Sheila and Tim were now about 15 minutes into the first session.

Stage 2 The understanding stage

Sheila proceeded to help Tim clarify and expand his understanding of the problem situation of not receiving his pay rise. Sheila asked for more background about what had actually happened to date. Tim responded that he was very afraid to bring the subject up with Mike because he thought that Mike might get angry and refuse his request. About six weeks ago, he had mentioned it to Mike who replied he would get round to it later. Sheila asked Tim to be more specific about how he had communicated with Tim. Tim thought he had been insufficiently forceful, but had difficulty thinking of how to be more specific.

Then Sheila asked Tim if he would mind asking her for the pay rise in the same way that he had approached Mike. During the mini role-play, Sheila was able to observe that: a) Tim was not directly stating what he wanted and why; b) his voice was weak and diffident; and c) he seemed to be making insufficient eye contact with Mike and his posture was a little slouched. After the role-play Sheila asked Tim to evaluate how he had communicated. Tim said he thought he had not been assertive enough, but was not sure why. Sheila then fed back her observations to him. Sheila also explored with Tim what sort of person Mike was. Tim replied that Mike was a workaholic who sometimes blew his stack when under stress, but basically was a good and fair guy whom he respected. Sheila summarised this middle portion of the initial session and checked with Tim whether her summary was accurate and if he would like to add or subtract anything from it. Tim said it was pretty well on target.

Stage 3   The changing stage

Towards the end of the first session, Tim and Sheila discussed what would be a reasonable goal for Tim. Together they decided that within 30 days, Tim would ask Mike again for the pay rise, including back-pay. Having established an overall goal, Sheila and Tim started planning how to obtain that goal. They agreed that they needed to develop Tim's verbal, vocal and bodily communication skills of handling two situations more assertively: first, setting up the meeting with Mike; and, second, participating in the meeting. In addition, Sheila pointed out to Tim that he could use his mind to calm himself down and coach himself in how to communicate better. Furthermore, Tim could make sure to work on any tendencies he had to perceive Mike as more threatening than he really was. Then they ended the first session and arranged to meet the following week.

At the start of the second session Sheila asked Tim how he had got on during the previous week and where he wanted to start today. Tim wanted to get directly into working on how to get his pay rise. Sheila and Tim's first agenda item was setting up the meeting. Sheila went along with Tim's wish to concentrate on communicating better before looking at thinking more effectively. Together they explored verbal, vocal and bodily communication options for how best to bring up the topic with Mike. Then they conducted a number of role-play rehearsals. After each role-play Sheila asked Tim to evaluate his performance before offering her feedback. Sheila and Tim also identified some different ways Mike might respond and developed and rehearsed Tim's communication for these situations.

In addition, Sheila and Tim explored his fears and how he could use his mind to concentrate on his goal, calm himself down, and coach himself in how to behave skilfully when requesting the meeting. Furthermore, Sheila encouraged Tim to challenge his thinking whenever he started getting exaggerated fears about Mike.

Near the end of the second session, Sheila and Tim switched to their second agenda item, how Tim might handle himself during the meeting with Mike. In much of the remaining time, they discussed various scenarios for the meeting. About five minutes from the end of the session, Sheila asked Tim to write down the main points they had covered in this session. Also, they negotiated a between-session activity in which Tim agreed to spend at least five minutes a day mentally rehearsing competent performance in requesting a meeting with Mike.

At the start of the third session, Sheila asked Tim how he had got on the previous week. Tim said that he had thought a lot about how to approach Mike and was becoming increasingly confident that he could do so competently. Then Sheila and Mike concentrated on the situation of the meeting itself. Essentially they repeated the same steps towards improving Tim's communicating and thinking that they had used in the previous session regarding setting up the meeting. They rehearsed how Tim might not only make his salary increase request but also how he might handle different responses from Mike. Sheila made the distinction between having a process success and an outcome success – namely, that Tim might use good skills, but still not get the outcome he wanted. Tim felt this observation helped take the pressure off him since he would be less likely to blame himself if he did not get his pay rise. Sheila and Tim reviewed how he might think more effectively. Tim wrote down the main points covered in the session and agreed to rehearse in his imagination each day both requesting a meeting and performing competently during it. Towards the end of the third session Tim said he would request a meeting with Mike before the next session.

When Tim came in for the fourth session, he said he had faced his fears and set up a meeting with Mike. During the meeting Mike apologised for not having put through the salary increase earlier. Mike said he would recommend Tim's increase immediately, including back-pay. Sheila expressed her pleasure at this outcome. Sheila and Tim spent the remainder of the session concentrating on improving Tim's social life. They ended the session with an agreement to meet again only if Tim thought it necessary.

Some cautions for training groups

Already I have advised those of you using counselling skills as part of other roles to be flexible in adapting the RUC model to suit your particular circumstances. Here I offer three cautions about training counselling skills students in the RUC model.

Trainers should avoid trying to do too much too quickly. Introductory counselling skills courses can range from about 20 to 100 contact hours and their main function is to train students to listen properly to clients. For a training group that has 20 or so contact hours, adapt the RUC model to limited training goals: for example, the bulk of the course might emphasise building good helper–client relationships with active listening skills (stage one). For this group less emphasis would be placed on asking a few well chosen questions to clarify understanding (stage two) and then facilitating clients in finding ways of handling their problem situations better (stage three).

Both trainers and students should be cautious about the dangers of instant expertise. Even if the course lasts for 60 to 100 contact hours, students will still be beginners. Sometimes, I get frightened when I suggest training introductory counselling skills students in clarifying understanding and changing skills. My underlying fear is that students may be too anxious, too arrogant or too poorly trained to understand the importance of holding back, acknowledging their limitations, and of respecting and valuing clients' responsibilities for and contributions to managing their problem situations. Remember to work side by side with your clients as their companions rather than imbue yourself with a mantle of phoney expertise.

Last, trainers should help students to understand that the constraints of introductory counselling skills courses may give them a distorted view of how to help a range of clients. Of necessity, introductory counselling skills courses are likely to focus on brief helping since students do not have the skills or access to clients for extended helping. A possible danger is that students come to think that brief helping is the only form of helping. Students who are learning counselling skills as part of courses to become accredited counsellors may need reminding that their introductory skills based on the RUC model will need expanding so that they can do extended as well as brief helping. Most clients who have been emotionally deprived over a period of years require more than quick fixes. In Chapter 1 I shared my own experience of entering counsellor training and being in counselling. I could never have been salvaged by my counsellor in brief helping. Instead, I needed an extended period of nurturing, healing and caring affirmation.

Summary

Helping process models are simplified representations of different activities at progressive stages of helping. Problem management and altering poor skills that create problems models may be too complex for introductory counselling skills training groups. A basic three-stage relating–understanding–changing (RUC) helping process model for managing problem situations is presented. Like any helping process model, it should be used flexibly.

The main helper and client task of stage one, relating, is to start establishing a working relationship. Helpers assist clients to tell their stories and, if appropriate, ask them to choose a specific problem situation to work on. The main helper and client task of stage two, understanding, is to clarify and enlarge both parties' understanding of the chosen problem situation. In addition, helpers assist clients to look for ways in which they may be communicating, acting and thinking less than effectively. The main helper and client task of stage three, changing, is for the helper to assist the client to change so that the problem situation is addressed more effectively than in the past. Helpers assist clients to set goals and develop and implement strategies to attain them. In addition, both parties pay attention to how clients can maintain desirable changes after helping ends.

Three cautions about training introductory counselling skills students in the relating–understanding–changing model are: avoid trying to do too much too soon; be careful about possessing instant expertise; and remember that later on you may need to adapt your introductory skills for extended helping.

Activity

Activity 4.1   Helping process models

Part A   Helping process models

1   What is a helping process model?
2   What are the strengths and limitations of helpers using helping
    process models?

Part B   The Relating–Understanding–Changing (RUC) helping process model

3   Describe some helper skills and client processes for each stage of
    the RUC helping process model.

The relating stage
* helper skills
* client processes

The understanding stage
* helper skills
* client processes

The changing stage
* helper skills
* client processes

4   What are some strengths and limitations of the RUC helping
    process model for use in introductory counselling skills training
    groups?

5   How applicable is the RUC helping process model to the setting or settings in which you currently help or might help in future? If you consider you need to modify this model, please specify why and how.

5 Learning Counselling Skills

I hear, I forget
I see, I remember
I do, I understand.
Chinese Proverb

Chapter outcomes

By studying and doing the activities in the chapter you should be able to:

- *understand some distinctive features of learning counselling skills;*
- *understand some different approaches to skills training;*
- *gain knowledge about stages of learning counselling skills;*
- *know some of the main methods of learning introductory counselling skills;*
- *identify some skills for managing your learning;*
- *identify some skills for working with your fellow students; and*
- *identify some skills for getting the best from your trainer.*

Many factors contribute to creating a happy and productive environment for learning counselling skills. The professional competence and personal qualities of your trainer or trainers are crucial. The size of your training group makes a difference. For instance, Windy Dryden, Ian Horton and Dave Mearns (1995) recommend a maximum staff–student ratio of one trainer to 12 students.

In addition, the physical resources allocated to your training are important. In both academic settings where I trained counsellors, the University of Aston in Birmingham and the Royal Melbourne Institute of Technology, we were fortunate enough to have both a suitably furnished large group room and two smaller interview rooms available for training. By suitably furnished, I mean that the space was flexible and students could sit in circles, horseshoes, or subgroups.

Counselling skills training is enhanced by easy access to audiovisual aids, for instance video recording and playback facilities. Students may also learn more if supported by good counselling skills library facilities: including books, journals, cassettes and videotapes. Having acknowledged many external influences, my main focus in this chapter is to assist you to get the most out of your introductory counselling skills training group experience.

Counselling skills training is different

Let us look at a few of the ways in which learning counselling skills may differ from the types of learning you have experienced before. Strange as it may sound, much of counselling skills training is about unlearning rather than learning. Many of the ways you have learned to listen and interact in everyday life differ from how skilled counsellors work. For example, social conversations, emphasising meeting both parties' needs, differ from counselling conversations, emphasising meeting clients' needs. As you learn counselling skills a tension exists between the pull of the past and the requirements for present and future skilled helping. For some students a further tension exists between the pull of the counselling approach adopted in your training group and that of approaches you have been or are being exposed to elsewhere.

Another difference in counselling skills training is that you are not learning academic knowledge but practical skills. It is insufficient to know and be able to talk about what to do, you have to be able to do it as well. Furthermore, your trainers need to adapt their teaching styles to incorporate a focus on the transmission of practical 'how-to' 'hands on' knowledge and skills. I review some methods for teaching practical skills later in this chapter.

Counselling skills training also differs in that counselling skills involve you as a person and not just the application of techniques. In Chapter 2 I reviewed some ways that your mental processes might influence your ability both to learn and to use counselling skills. You may need to work through personal agendas before you can be fully present to your clients. Many counselling skills students can gain from both a broadening and deepening of life experience. Students who have led sheltered lives may perform more effectively once they gain insight and experience of other lifestyles: for instance different social classes, cultures and problems. Furthermore, you may need to work on deepening your humanity and on getting more in touch with your potential for compassion and inner strength.

Microskills and holistic approaches to skills training

The microskills approach to counselling skills training is advocated by prominent counselling skills trainers like Allen Ivey (1994) and Gerard Egan (1998). The microskills approach to counselling developed out of the microskills approach to teaching, where the single communication skills units of the process were identified and taught sequentially as separate units. Illustrative counselling microskills include attending behaviour, open and closed questions and reflection of feeling. Ivey proposes a five-step microskills teaching model consisting of : '(1) warm-up and introduction to the skill, (2) examples of the skill in operation, (3) reading, (4) practice, and (5) self-assessment and generalisation' (Ivey, 1994: 20).

The holistic approach to learning counselling skills in its pure person-centred form has reservations about the very concept of skills. Carl Rogers was terrified of person-centred counselling being reduced to mechanistic skills. Instead he preferred to talk about the attitudinal qualities of the counsellor in relating to clients (Rogers, 1975; 1980). However, researchers into person-centred counselling have found it useful to identify counselling skills, such as empathy, congruence and non-possessive warmth. Contemporary person-centred counsellor trainers, like Dave Mearns, acknowledge the concept of skilful behaviour, but are reluctant to break it into smaller units for fear of losing its integrated quality (Mearns, 1997).

If anything, the differences in counselling skills training are differences of emphasis: for example, person-centred training possessing more of a holistic emphasis and trainers like Egan and Ivey possessing more of a microskills emphasis, but also acknowledging the need for integrating skills.

The position I adopt is that counselling skills consist of both external communication and mental processes that enhance or interfere with external communication. I identify both communication skills and mind skills. Communication skills, such as questioning and reflection of feeling, represent separate external activities. However, the mind skills that influence communication skills cut across the different external skills. Possibly, you could say that I have a more microskills emphasis when it comes to communication skills and a more holistic emphasis when it comes to mind skills.

In regard to teaching counselling skills, trainers and students may want to start with looking at the microskills for each stage of the relating–understanding–changing (RUC) helping process. However, at the end of training for each stage it is important that students start feeling comfortable integrating that stage's component skills. By the end of training for the whole model, students should possess competence in integrating the component skills of all three stages.

Personal counselling

When I was in training, I learned more about being a counsellor from being a client observing and experiencing a skilled counsellor at work than I learned from my counselling skills classes. Helper, heal thyself. Possibly, one thing that both microskills and holistic trainers are likely to agree on is that many, if not all, students aiming to become professional counsellors require disciplined personal counselling if they are to release and show more of their full humanity and helping potential to clients. However, such trainers are likely to differ in the counselling approach they recommend to students, for instance cognitive-behavioural, psychodynamic or person-centred. Some trainers may suggest that it is good for counsellors to gain the experience of being a client in more than one approach, though not at the same time.

The relatively brief duration of most introductory counselling skills training groups allows students simultaneously to experience being a client in only one counselling approach. To avoid confusion and support skills training, perhaps students should first seek to become clients in the core theoretical model for their overall helping services course, assuming such a model has been identified. However, many introductory counselling skills students do not seek to become professional counsellors. Often such students are less motivated to undergo personal counselling than those in counsellor training.

Stages in learning counselling skills

In the last chapter I presented a three-stage model of the helping process. You can also think about learning counselling skills in stages.

Box 5.1 illustrates three different ways of looking at the skill development process. The three-stage verbal control model was first proposed by the Russian psychologist Luria (1961) to explain the socialisation of children. I have adapted it to explain the 'socialisation' of counselling skills students.

The four-stage competency framework was first proposed in relation to competent instruction (Robinson, 1974). The competency framework has since been found useful by counsellor trainers, such as Francesca Inskipp (1996), and by trainers of counsellor trainers and supervisors, such as Petruska Clarkson and Maria Gilbert (1991). The three-stage person-centred skill development model was proposed by Mearns (1997).

Box 5.1   Stages of counselling skills learning

Stages of verbal control

Stage 1: Control by the trainer's outer speech
The trainer controls and directs the student's acquisition of a skill.

Stage 2: Control by the student's outer speech or conscious inner speech
The student needs to verbally direct and control her or his behaviour, either out loud or by sub-vocalising.

Stage 3: Control by the student's preconscious inner speech
The student's inner speech becomes automatic and assumes a self-governing role.

Stages of competency

Stage 1: Unconscious incompetence
Students do not know what they do not know.

Stage 2: Conscious incompetence
Students can feel inadequate and deskilled when presented with new requirements for how to think and act.

Stage 3: Conscious competence
Students are knowingly competent, possibly after a struggle to learn their new skills. Some students feel their use of skills is artificial in this stage.

Stage 4: Unconscious competence
With practice and the passage of time, the skill becomes part of the person who can enact it as if automatically.

Stages of skill development

Stage 1: Paralysis
The student feels that there is no way of responding that will not violate some guideline or other.

Stage 2: Portrayal
The student tries to portray the skill being taught. The skill is being used from 'outside in' rather than from 'inside out'.

Stage 3: Congruence
The student uses counselling skills unconsciously, creatively and fluidly in response to whatever clients bring.

The different models overlap and have the central theme of students moving from using counselling skills artificially to using them naturally. However, do not expect miracles from introductory counselling skills training groups: if you attain conscious competency, you are doing well.

Methods of learning introductory counselling skills

Following are some of the main methods of learning counselling skills. Training needs to take place in a supportive yet challenging group learning environment. Within such a group setting students learn what to do, how to do it, do it and then engage in a reflection and feedback process about performance. Put more simply, the processes are those of tell, show and do/reflect.

A cohesive group environment

Skilled trainers recognise that much of counselling skills training is student self-appraisal and student to student rather than trainer to student. Consequently, it is critical to attend to processes that make for a cohesive working group. Many students make big sacrifices to come to counselling skills training groups and they should enjoy coming. The group is likely to be more fun for students if they can get to know one another as persons. Time spent at the beginning on ice-breaking exercises and, possibly, an introductory social event can get the group off to a good start. In these introductory sessions, circulate and try and know and be known to as many members of your group as you can. Programming breaks for coffee, tea or meals in training groups is another way that students can get to feel comfortable with one another.

In any group, rules develop about appropriate ways of thinking, feeling and behaving in the group. Also, there are issues of trust, power and control. Box 5.2 lists possible group rules or norms that make for cohesive and effective counselling skills training groups. Such a list of norms can be openly discussed with students as the basis for a learning contract.

Box 5.2   Illustrative rules for counselling skills training groups

- Though the trainer or trainers have ultimate control of the direction of the group, students participate in decisions about how the group is run.
- Students are expected to focus on their mental processes as well as their external counselling skills.
- Each student accepts responsibility for their own learning.
- The expectation of the group is that students will attend all sessions and come on time.
- Students accept responsibility for participating in the group's training activities to the best of their ability, including carrying out homework assignments.
- Trainers and students accept responsibility for helping one another learn counselling skills.
- Trainers and students treat one another with respect and support and challenge one another as appropriate.
- No student in the training group should feel under pressure to reveal any personal information about which they are uncomfortable.
- No telling tales out of school – students have a right to confidentiality from one another and their trainer(s).
- Students do not expect the trainer(s) to act as a personal counsellor or to participate in a therapy group.
- All students adhere to guidelines about conducting and handing in assignments and do not seek special treatment for themselves.

Tell: Instruction and reading

It is hard to implement skills properly if you do not understand them clearly in your mind. First, it is a good idea for trainers to introduce students to the overall model being taught, so that they can see the different counselling skills in context. Then, as the training group progresses, students require clear instruction in the mechanics of each skill or subskill being trained. Furthermore, along the way, trainers should provide opportunities to tell students how to integrate the skills covered so far.

Instruction in counselling skills is not just a matter of trainers preparing systematic content. In addition, trainers require good teaching skills: for example, verbal, vocal and bodily speaking skills and use of overhead projector skills. Furthermore, students require opportunities for questions, clarifications and discussion.

Students can also receive instruction from skills manuals and books. Again, it is a good idea for students to overview the manual or book that is being used as a training group text before focusing on its individual parts. In many instances, students can be asked to read an introductory text such as this book before the group starts.

Show: Demonstration and case examples

Demonstrating counselling skills can be scary for trainers. At times I have felt I was putting my professional self on the line. Nevertheless, demonstration or modelling is vital to teaching any applied skill. Both the communication and thinking components of counselling skills can be demonstrated. Observational learning can be used in training groups to initiate and develop good skills as well as to release latent potential. Observation can also inhibit or lessen the likelihood of students using poor skills, for instance giving gratuitous advice.

Experienced trainers can model the skill or skills in question either live or prerecorded. Prerecorded demonstrations can be on film, videotape or audio cassette. Though trainers may make videotapes and audio cassettes of skills and subskills, prerecorded material can also be an excellent way for students to observe other counsellors. In addition, students can observe and learn from one another's performances. Furthermore, students can learn from reading case examples and interview transcripts.

Counselling skills students are likely to learn more from demonstrations if they are cued what to look for in advance, see more than one demonstration, can summarise the main points of the demonstration, and get the opportunity to practise the demonstrated skill or skills while still fresh in mind. Sometimes, trainers and students can introduce humour into demonstrations by John Cleese or Rowan Atkinson-like incompetence in showing how not to enact a skill. Imagine being counselled by Basil Fawlty or Mr Bean! However, the main emphasis in all demonstrations should be on competent performance of skills.

Do: Practice

Students can practise counselling skills both during and between training group sessions. Just as demonstrating counselling skills can be scary for trainers, practising them can be scary for students, especially if this practice is in front of trainer and group. Especially early on in training groups, students can do brief activities with one another. A common format is to divide the group into threes, with each student taking turns as client, counsellor and observer. In addition, trainers can do activities either with the whole group: for instance, going round getting all the students to share their responses to different client statements. An alternative is to start doing an activity with part of the group – for example, the trainer role-plays a client who is sequentially counselled by four students in the group while the remaining students observe. Every now and then there is a pause for feedback and discussion from both participants and observers.

As time goes by the activities become longer and require more integration of skills. An issue here is whether students play themselves as 'clients' or role-play other people, or a mixture of both. Advantages of student 'clients' discussing personal material is student 'helpers' are able to respond to real verbal, vocal and bodily communication. This can be very important in learning to respond to feelings, glimpses of feelings, nuances and ambivalent feelings. Furthermore, when being counselled with their own issues, student 'clients' may be more sensitive to good and poor uses of counselling skills than when role-playing third parties. Disadvantages of students as 'clients' include disclosing more than intended and the material revealed being unsuitable for practising targeted skills. However, instructing students to concentrate on specific situations rather than on broader problems should reduce the risks of negative experiences for all concerned.

A major advantage of role-playing is that trainers and students can adjust their roles to illustrate and practise targeted skills (Rennie, 1998). Students can be instructed to adjust 'client' behaviour to suit the purpose of a particular skills training session. In addition, if students think they will experience difficulty with certain kinds of clients, for instance angry clients, trainers can set up appropriate role-plays. Furthermore, students can role-play a range of pertinent problem situations without the risk of disclosing too much. Perhaps, the major disadvantage of role-playing is artificiality, with some students being much better at getting in role than others.

Once students have a basic grounding in counselling skills, trainers can be creative about finding ways for practising skills that are intermediate to working on placements with real clients. At the Royal Melbourne Institute of Technology, for over 10 years I administered an undergraduate volunteer 'client' scheme that had been initiated by a colleague on secondment from the student counselling centre (see Box 5.3).

Box 5.3   A scheme for recruiting 'clients' for supervised counselling skills practice

Getting suitable opportunities to practise can be a big problem on introductory counselling skills courses. At the Royal Melbourne Institute of Technology the counselling course staff looked within the institution for volunteer 'clients'. All undergraduates were required to take some courses outside of their major subject to broaden their education. One of the most popular of these courses was a one-semester unit called Human Communication, which in any given semester could have up to 20 class groups each with up to 25 students. As course coordinator of the Graduate Diploma in Counselling Psychology, with permission from the programme director and lecturers taking the classes, I wrote a letter to undergraduates enrolled in Human Communication inviting them to participate in two videotaped interviews by graduate counselling psychology students.

Those undergraduates volunteering to participate in the scheme were encouraged to bring everyday problems of living to their interviews: for instance, either exam-taking or boyfriend/girlfriend difficulties. They were informed that the videotaped interviews would be scrubbed once their student 'counsellor' had received supervision. Before the end of the semester the undergraduate 'clients' wrote up their experience of being counselled as one of their assessed work options.

Each counselling psychology student received supervision on 14 videotaped interviews in what was an approximately 60-contact-hour (plus supervisions) introductory counselling skills course spread over a year and a half. The interviews started a third of the way through the course.

Do: Feedback and reflection

'How did I do?' and 'How am I doing?' are questions students are likely to ask of themselves, one another and of trainers. You need to develop your skills of evaluating and reflecting upon your use of counselling skills. In the early 1970s at the University of Aston in Birmingham, I had as a colleague for an academic year a well-known American counsellor trainer, Professor Cecil Patterson, who was very reluctant to provide any feedback to students for fear it would interfere with their ability to experience and evaluate themselves. Watching too many demonstrations may also inhibit students from genuinely reflecting on their performance. Throughout your helping life, you have to rely mainly on yourself to monitor and develop your use of counselling skills. Feedback starts at home through your own experiencing, monitoring and reflecting upon how you help.

External feedback can definitely be overdone with the effect of inhibiting rather than releasing students' potential for helping and reflecting upon it. However, most counselling training groups encourage students to provide feedback to one another and to receive it from trainers. As well as skills of providing feedback, counselling skills students require skills of reflecting upon and evaluating feedback. Often, immediately after activities with fellow students conducted in twos or threes, you process the work done together. On occasion, as well as verbal comments, students can be encouraged to provide brief written comments. Especially if the whole group is involved, written comments can save recipients from feedback overload. Later, recipients can process the feedback in their own time.

You can also reflect upon and receive feedback on videotapes and audio cassettes of your use of counselling skills. Audiovisual feedback can be valuable because it provides actual evidence of how you respond rather than relying on memory, perceptions and inferences.

Some counselling skills trainers adapt Norman Kagan's Interpersonal Process Recall method to assist training (Kagan, 1975). Here the role of the trainer, or someone else, is that of 'inquirer' as the student plays back a videotape or audio cassette of a helping session. The student helper is in control of the tape and can stop and discuss it whenever she or he wishes to comment on processes within either helper or client or between them. The inquirer's role is to provide a supportive emotional climate for recall and reflection of both internal and external processes. The inquirer may ask questions to facilitate the student's exploration, but may not make evaluative comments. Clients can also participate in Interpersonal Process Recall sessions and their recalls can sometimes illustrate considerable differences in how helpers and clients processed the same events in their helping sessions (Rennie, 1998).

Getting the best from your training group

Introductory counselling skills students can reframe the question 'What can I get from my training group?' to become 'What can I give to my training group?' Paradoxically, a giving attitude may get you more of what you want than a demanding getting attitude. Below are a few suggestions for how to get the most from skills training.

Use time management and study skills

All counselling skills students require good time management skills. However, some sabotage their learning through poor skills. The time demands on students are real enough. You may be trying to juggle partner, parenting, home maintenance, recreational, work and academic study commitments. However, enrolling in an introductory counselling skills class implies an implicit, if not explicit, contract that you are willing to devote sufficient time and energy to learn and practise the skills. It may be a good idea to develop weekly timetables in which you block out times for training group sessions, practising skills and completing assignments.

Some counselling skills students need to attend to improving academic study skills: for example, reading skills and meeting deadline skills. For instance, procrastinating students who address their problem either inside or outside of counselling can become more effective at studying and therefore have more time to learn counselling skills. If you require study skills counselling, do not hesitate to get it. As a counsellor trainer, I referred many students to the local student counselling service for this purpose.

Develop giving and receiving feedback skills

Ralph Waldo Emerson once observed: 'I pay the schoolmaster, but 'tis the schoolboys that educate my son'. For good or ill, students learn a tremendous amount from one another. Skilled trainers can rely on and use the wisdom and experience of the group. Students in cohesive counselling skills training groups are likely to have developed good skills at tactfully commenting on one another's work. It becomes much easier to receive feedback, when trainers and students are good at giving feedback. Box 5.4 summarises some guidelines for giving and receiving feedback, though vary which guidelines you follow according to circumstances.

Box 5.4   Guidelines for giving and receiving feedback

Giving feedback
- Use 'I' messages rather than 'You' messages:
  'You' message
  'You did . . .'
  'I' message
  'I thought you . . .'
- Be specific and, where possible, state feedback in the positive:
  Non-specific and negative
  'You interviewed poorly.'
  Specific and positive
  'I thought you could use more eye contact and speak in a louder voice.'
- Use confirmatory as well as corrective feedback:
  'I thought your use of eye contact was good, but that you could still speak in a louder voice.'
- Consider emotional as well as behavioural feedback:
  'When you made very direct eye contact and spoke in a loud voice, I felt overpowered by you.'
- Consider demonstrating your feedback:
  'I would like to show you how your eye contact came over to me . . . [then demonstrate]'
- Consider cultural sensitivity feedback:
  'I wonder whether there wasn't a cultural issue [specify which] operating in the helping session.'
- Provide an opportunity for the receiver to respond to your feedback:
  'Would you like to respond to my (or the group's) feedback?'

Receiving feedback
- Where appropriate, consider requesting feedback.
- Listen carefully and, unless absolutely necessary, avoid interrupting.
- If necessary, check the accuracy of your understanding.
- If you consider the feedback helpful, consider thanking the provider.
- Be assertive in stopping any feedback that you consider is being given destructively.
- You can choose either to respond to feedback at the time or to keep silent about it and process it in your own time.

Use empathy and assertion skills to get the best from your trainer(s)

Counselling skills students have both rights and responsibilities in relation to trainers. Rights and responsibilities intertwine and both trainers and students need to exercise rights responsibly. Here I examine two student skills that can make for good working relationships with trainers: empathy and assertion.

Show empathy to your trainers. The training relationship is a person to person relationship that goes both ways. Some counselling skills students are excellent at taking the perspective of trainers. However, a minority make unrealistic demands for unconditional positive regard and empathic understanding from trainers at the same time as showing little empathy themselves.

If working in an educational institution, your trainers are likely to be in a position of trying to fulfil multiple roles: administrator, teacher, researcher, skills trainer and professional counsellor. On top of this, you are seeking certification or some form of official acknowledgement that you have successfully completed your introductory counselling skills training group. Thus, your trainers face the further role conflict of both training and evaluating you. In addition, very possibly your trainers are working in the wider context of an academic research culture that undervalues professional training. Furthermore, in all academic departments and institutions there is competition for resources. Almost certainly, the counselling skills staff is having to justify the extra expenses attached to practical skills training over traditional classroom teaching. On the one hand, the student contact provided by counselling skills training is very rewarding. On the other hand, partly due to contextual factors, being a counselling skills trainer can be very stressful. Trainers appreciate students who understand this.

Be assertive about getting the best from your training. My assumption is that your trainers are both suitably qualified and conscientious. Nevertheless, during the course of a training group, situations may emerge requiring improvement. One example might be that you have a relatively new trainer who is not doing enough demonstrating. This may be more a matter of insufficient confidence and teaching experience than incompetence. Here students can use feedback skills to bring to the trainer's attention that they would appreciate more demonstration. If the trainer then makes an effort to fulfil the request, this change is more likely to be maintained if you show your appreciation.

Another situation might be that of inadequate training facilities: for instance poor, but not terrible, accommodation. Students are quite within their rights to request a room change. However, whether the change gets made may be outside the control of the skills trainer, who probably also wants better accommodation. Students will maintain better working relationships with trainers if making such requests assertively rather than aggressively and if accepting realistic limitations on what trainers can do.

Summary

Ways in which learning counselling skills differs from learning academic knowledge include unlearning rather than learning, focusing on 'how to' practical skills and involving you as a person. Whereas a microskills approach focuses on specific units of counselling skills, an holistic approach focuses more on integrated skills. You may learn both counselling skills and how to become a more effective human being and helper if you undergo personal counselling.

Three approaches to looking at stages in counselling skills development are: from outer to inner verbal control; from unconscious incompetence to unconscious competence; and from paralysis to congruence. Methods of learning practical counselling skills include: building a cohesive training group environment with rules enhancing learning, instruction, demonstration, practice, feedback and reflection.

You may get more from your training group if you focus on giving rather than getting. You can help yourself by developing your time management and study skills. You can help both yourself and your peers by developing and using good giving and receiving feedback skills. You are more likely to maintain good working relationships with trainers if you use empathy and assertion skills.

Activities

Activity 5.1   Developing counselling skills training group rules

Look at the illustrative counselling skills training group rules listed in Box 5.2.

(a) How applicable are these rules to your training group?
(b) Develop a list of rules for your counselling skills training group.

Activity 5.2   Methods of learning introductory counselling skills

Assess the advantages and disadvantages of each of the following methods of learning counselling skills

- *Cohesive group environment*
  advantages
  disadvantages
- *Verbal instruction*
  advantages
  disadvantages
- *Written instruction*
  advantages
  disadvantages
- *Demonstration*
  advantages
  disadvantages
- *Written activities*
  advantages
  disadvantages

- *Brief training group activities*
  advantages
  disadvantages
- *Interviews with students as 'clients'*
  advantages
  disadvantages
- *Role-played interviews*
  advantages
  disadvantages
- *Interviewing volunteer 'clients'*
  advantages
  disadvantages
- *Feedback from others*
  advantages
  disadvantages
- *Reflection*
  advantages
  disadvantages
- *Personal counselling*
  advantages
  disadvantages

Summarise your conclusions in respect to your current counselling skills training group.

Activity 5.3   Getting the best from counselling skills training groups

Discuss the relevance of, assess yourself on and, if necessary, make a plan to develop each of the following skills for getting the best from your introductory counselling skills training group.

- *Time management skills*
  relevance
  self-assessment
  plan
- *Study skills*
  relevance
  self-assessment
  plan

- *Giving feedback skills*
  relevance
  self-assessment
  plan
- *Receiving feedback skills*
  relevance
  self-assessment
  plan
- *Empathy to trainer skills*
  relevance
  self-assessment
  plan
- *Assertion about training skills*
  relevance
  self-assessment
  plan

Are there any other skills you think it necessary to develop so that you can get the best from your introductory counselling skills training group? If so, please specify.

PART 2

THE RELATING STAGE

6 Helping Relationships

It is better to light a candle than to curse the darkness.
Chinese Proverb

Chapter outcomes

By studying and doing the activities in this chapter you should be able to:

- *describe some key issues in defining helping relationships;*
- *understand differing ways of viewing the importance of the helping relationship;*
- *acknowledge external and internal dimensions of helping relationships;*
- *know what the term working alliance means;*
- *describe some core conditions for helping relationships;*
- *understand some key characteristics that helpers and clients bring to their relationships; and*
- *acknowledge some reasons for flexibility in how helpers relate to clients.*

What are helping relationships? Helping relationships are the human connections between helpers and clients both face to face and in one another's minds. Connection is the essential characteristic of any relationship. People in helping relationships exist in some connection or association with one another, be it in counselling, health care, human resource management, teaching or voluntary agency work. In addition, any person to person contact, however brief, offers the prospect of a relationship which may continue in the minds of the parties both between their meetings and even long after they stop meeting.

In the context of this book, helping relationships are those in which helpers use counselling skills face to face to assist clients in any or all of the following ways: to feel supported and understood, to clarify and expand their understanding, and to develop and implement strategies for changing how they think, act and feel so that they can attain life affirming goals. As such a helping relationship is not a matching relationship between equals to meet both parties' needs: instead one person is actively using counselling skills to assist the other person to attain her or his goals or, at the very least, to receive psychological comfort. Focusing on your clients is extremely important and easier said than done.

Despite common characteristics to effective helping relationships, there is no single way to describe a helping relationship. Already I have distinguished between being a counsellor and using counselling skills as part of other roles. Many readers of this book are likely to use counselling skills as part of helping relationships connected with other roles. These readers' helping relationships are likely to take place in the context of other primary agendas – for example, health or education. Such helping relationships may well take place outside of office settings: for instance talking with patients in hospital beds or with secondary school students between classes.

In addition, though all counselling approaches stress the importance of the helping relationship, they differ in how much they emphasise, perceive and use it. For example, in person-centred counselling, the quality of the helper–client relationship is both necessary and sufficient for change. In the cognitive-behavioural approaches, the helping relationship is regarded as necessary, but insufficient to bring about desired changes. In addition to offering good relationships, cognitive-behavioural helpers require counselling skills that focus on assessing and changing clients' specific thoughts and behaviours. In the psychoanalytic approach, the nature and use of the helper-client relationship differs again in that it can become a source of content to be talked about. Analysts may examine and interpret any significantly distorted client perceptions towards them.

If using the relating–understanding–changing (RUC) helping process model described in Chapter 4, you adjust the helping relationship for each stage of the process. In the relating stage, you offer a helping relationship that creates an emotional climate in which it is easy for clients to talk and feel understood on their own terms. In the understanding stage, while still offering a supportive helping relationship, you ask more questions and direct the helping conversation more than in stage one. In the changing stage, you may be a coach who uses the helping relationship to assist clients to gain confidence and skills and then to practise at changing.

For those of you using counselling skills as part of other roles, your use of the helping relationship at each stage of the RUC model is likely to be heavily influenced by the contexts in which you work. Some of you may only have the opportunity for brief, but nevertheless important, helping contacts. You may be faced with difficult decisions about whether you just offer supportive helping relationships or attempt to use the relationship to foster change as well. In addition, some of you will experience conflicts within your roles: for instance, personnel officers may face conflicts between doing performance appraisals for their organisations and putting their clients' interests first.

My challenge as a writer is to talk about helping relationships in a way that is relevant both to users of counselling skills for other roles and to those training to become counsellors. Your challenge as a reader is to extrapolate from the following review of aspects of the helping relationship, the points most relevant to your particular helping circumstances.

Helping relationships involve mental processes and emotions

Helping relationships take place in the head and the heart as well as face to face. Most obviously, the helping relationship is a public relationship consisting of observable verbal, vocal and bodily communication. Some of this communication is intentional and other parts of it may be unintentional.

The helping relationship is also private and consists of helper and client internal mental processing. Both helpers and clients relate to their perceptions about themselves, one another and their relationship. Another way of stating this is that in relationships each of you develops a *personification* of yourself and of the other person (Sullivan, 1953). These personifications – literally meaning making up or fabricating a person – are the mental maps that guide your helping relationship journeys. Box 6.1 categorises the mental processing involved in helper and client internal relationships into the six mind skills areas introduced in Chapter 2.

Helpers and clients create and edit thoughts both shared and left unshared. These thoughts may be 'there and then', 'there and now' and 'there and in future' thoughts about events outside of helping as well as 'here and then', 'here and now', and 'here and in future' thoughts about events in helping.

Furthermore, the fact that the helping relationship is internal as well as external means that material covered in sessions can be processed between sessions and when helping ends. A consequence is that in successful helping, clients carry round in their minds useful material that they have acquired during their public helping relationships. The knowledge and skills acquired in the public helping relationship have now become the preserve and responsibility of a private self-helping relationship.

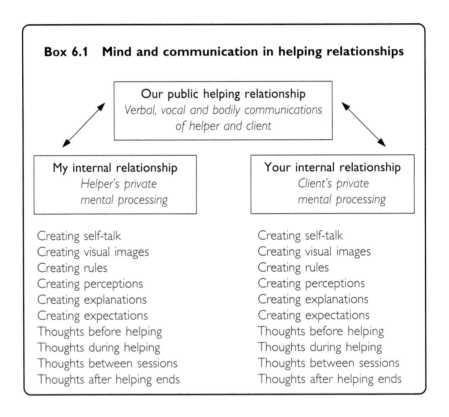

Box 6.1 Mind and communication in helping relationships

Our public helping relationship
*Verbal, vocal and bodily communications
of helper and client*

My internal relationship
*Helper's private
mental processing*

Your internal relationship
*Client's private
mental processing*

Creating self-talk	Creating self-talk
Creating visual images	Creating visual images
Creating rules	Creating rules
Creating perceptions	Creating perceptions
Creating explanations	Creating explanations
Creating expectations	Creating expectations
Thoughts before helping	Thoughts before helping
Thoughts during helping	Thoughts during helping
Thoughts between sessions	Thoughts between sessions
Thoughts after helping ends	Thoughts after helping ends

The helping relationship also consists of helper and client emotions, only some of which may be exhibited. For instance, both helper and client may hold and exhibit different degrees of trust and liking for one another. Furthermore, the helping relationship may be experienced by either or both participants emotionally: for instance, as warm, lukewarm, tepid or cold.

How you think influences how you feel as well as the reverse. Both helper and client feelings may be based on undistorted perceptions of one another as well as on distortions created by such factors as anxiety and reminders of past relationships. In the psychodynamic tradition, in particular, these transfers of past feelings, perceptions and behaviours into the present relationship are called transference if by clients towards helpers. The term counter-transference refers to helper transference towards clients.

Let us take as a transference example clients whose parents have been critical and demanding who then transfer their anxiety about revealing personal information from their parents to their helpers. As time goes by, clients may perceive and feel about their helpers in less distorted ways. Perceiving their helpers less like their parents, clients feel less anxious, reveal more information, still gain acceptance, trust their helpers further and reveal even more personal information.

Sometimes, the above process is seen as a shift from a transference relationship, based on distorted perceptions rooted in the past, to a real relationship, based on accurate perceptions rooted in the present (Gelso and Carter, 1994). The real relationship also consists of the more genuine and appropriate feelings generated by and contributing to clients' more accurate perceptions of their helpers. In addition, the real relationship incorporates clients' more appropriate verbal, vocal and bodily communication.

Helping relationships involve communication processes and patterns

Helping relationships are processes of two-way communication. Helpers and clients are in a continuous process of responding to one another's verbal, vocal and bodily communication. At the verbal level, the process nature of helping relationships was illustrated in the above example regarding clients anxious about revealing personal information to helpers. Helpers assisted their clients to overcome their transference reactions by engaging in a process of responding with acceptance rather than judgementally to client disclosures. Furthermore, their helpers may have demonstrated their accepting attitude not only by verbal but by vocal and bodily communication: for instance, vocal warmth and an absence of any negative facial expressions.

Clients also both try to influence and actually influence how helpers communicate. For example, Robin, aged 47, is a highly manipulative senior executive who uses flattery as a way of trying to influence his helper's perceptions of and communication towards him. Robin knowingly tries to control his helper. On other occasions, clients can unknowingly play nice, unintelligent or dependent as ways of attempting to elicit caring communications from helpers. If successful, such clients may elicit insufficiently challenging helper communication and this enables them to stay stuck rather than to change.

Helpers and clients can establish patterns of communicating in their relationships that may be for good or ill. For example, helpers quietly encouraging their clients to assume responsibility for their lives may get clients communicating in ways that do so. On the other hand, helpers who encourage dependency may have clients who are continually looking for answers outside of themselves. A simple example of a negative communication pattern is that of talkative helpers who wonder why they have quiet clients. A similar negative example relates to how helpers ask questions: those continually asking questions may set up communication patterns in which clients wait for the next question rather than reveal themselves of their own accord.

The working alliance

Helpers and clients can relate and work cooperatively or at cross purposes. Reluctant clients, those who do not want to be in the client role, and resistant clients, those who throw up barriers to being in the client role, are two categories of clients who may be working against or sabotaging the helping process. The term working alliance is a way of perceiving the task-oriented nature of the helping relationship. Gelso and Fretz define the working alliance as: 'the alignment of the client's reasonable and observing side with the counselor's working, or therapizing, side for the purpose of facilitating the work of counseling' (1992: 152). More briefly, the working alliance consists of collaboration between helper and client to achieve the goals of helping.

Research into the working alliance suggests that the stronger the alliance in the first few sessions, the more positive the results of helping. Three factors may be crucial to the strength of the working alliance. The first factor relates to the degree of either implicit or explicit agreement between helpers and clients as to the goals of helping. Another factor relates to agreement about the tasks of the method of helping being employed. For instance, in the RUC helping process model, helper and client need to feel comfortable with their own and one another's task as they engage in each stage of the process. A third factor consists of the emotional bond that forms between helper and client. Here it is important that helpers show understanding and that clients possess or develop a capacity to trust them.

Core conditions for helping relationships

In 1957, Carl Rogers published a seminal article entitled 'The necessary and sufficient conditions of therapeutic personality change'. In this article, Rogers identified six conditions for therapeutic change, three of which – empathic understanding, unconditional positive regard and congruence – are often referred to as the core conditions of helping relationships. Rogers emphasised the client's perception of the helper's communication of the core conditions and not just the conditions themselves. He stressed that it was necessary for clients to perceive, at least to a minimal degree, empathic understanding and unconditional positive regard, though he omitted to mention congruence as well.

Rogers wrote his statement of the necessary and sufficient conditions in relation to client-centred, or what has more recently become person-centred, counselling. Other counselling approaches, for instance cognitive-behavioural and psychoanalytic, attest to the importance of Rogers' conditions but adapt them and use additional skills as well. As mentioned earlier, in the RUC helping process model the nature of the helping relationship differs according to the stage you are in. You are more likely to use the core conditions as Rogers intended in the relating stage and then modify your use of them in the understanding and changing stages.

In this book, I do not use the terms empathic understanding, unconditional positive regard and congruence, but use different terms to break down the counselling skills covered by these concepts. However, here I briefly describe each of the core conditions for two main reasons. First, the concepts provide valuable insights into how to offer genuinely helpful relationships to clients that will strengthen rather than interfere with developing the working alliance. Second, the terms empathy, unconditional regard and congruence are in such common use in the helping professions that you should know what they mean.

Empathy

Clients like to feel understood on their own terms by helpers. Empathy is the capacity to identify yourself mentally with and to fully comprehend your client's inner world. You may possess and be perceived to show empathic understanding in relation to single client statements, a series of client statements, the whole of a helping session, or a series of helping sessions. Rogers thought helpers should possess and show an empathic attitude. He stressed creating an empathic emotional climate in the helping interview rather than using empathy as a set of skills.

Rogers' use of the term 'empathy' particularly focused on the construct of experiencing. He attempted to improve the quantity and quality of his clients' inner listening to the ongoing psycho-physiological flow of experiencing within them. This flow is an inner referent to which individuals can repeatedly turn to discover the 'felt meaning' of their experience. As well as helping a client to get in touch with more obvious feelings, he attempted to help them sense 'meanings of which he/she is scarcely aware, but not trying to uncover feelings of which the person is totally unaware, since this would be too threatening' (Rogers, 1975: 4).

Empathy is an active process in which helpers desire to know and reach out to receive clients' communications and meanings (Barrett-Lennard, 1998). Responding to individual client statements is a process of listening and observing, resonating, discriminating, communicating and checking your understanding. Needless to say, the final dimension is that the client has, to some extent, perceived your empathy. Even better is that your empathy has enabled your client to get more in touch with the flow of her or his experiencing. Box 6.2, taken from a demonstration film with Rogers as the counsellor, illustrates this process. The client, Gloria, is talking about how her father could never show he cared for her the way she would have liked.

Box 6.2   Dimensions of the empathy process

Client's statement:
'I don't know what it is. You know when I talk about it, it feels more flip. If I just sit still a minute, it feels like a great big hurt down there. Instead, I feel cheated.'

Counsellor's responding processes

Observing and listening: Observes and listens to the client's verbal, vocal and bodily communication.

Resonating: Feels some of the emotion the client experiences.

Discriminating: Discriminates what is really important to the client and formulates this into a response.

Communicating: 'It's much easier to be a little flip because then you don't feel that big lump inside of hurt.' Communicates a response that attempts to show understanding of the client's thoughts, feelings

	and personal meanings. Accompanies verbal with good vocal and bodily communication.
Checking:	In this instance, the client quickly made her next statement which followed the train of her experiencing and thought. However, the counsellor could either have waited and allowed the client space to respond or could have inquired if the response was accurate.

Client perception of counsellor's responding

How the client reacted indicated she perceived that the counsellor showed excellent empathy and that she was able to continue getting more in touch with her experiencing.

Though not used by Rogers, a distinction sometimes made is that between cognitive empathy, understanding your client's thoughts, and affective empathy, experiencing and understanding your client's feelings. This distinction is one of differing emphases since the two areas overlap. In terms of the empathy process, resonating provides the basis for affective empathy. Helpers out of touch with their own feelings are unlikely to resonate and communicate their clients' feelings accurately.

Unconditional positive regard

Unconditional positive regard consists of two dimensions: level of regard and unconditionality of regard. Level of regard, or possibly more correctly level of positive regard, consists of positive helper feelings towards the client, such as liking, caring and warmth. Unconditionality of regard consists of a non-judgemental acceptance of the client's experiencing and disclosures as their subjective reality. A key issue in unconditional positive regard is that helpers are not trying to possess or control clients to meet their own needs. Instead, helpers respect clients' separateness and accept their unique differences. Such acceptance gives clients permission to have and fully experience their thoughts and feelings.

Sometimes the notion of helpers possessing unconditional positive regard is criticised because it implies acceptance of clients who exhibit unacceptable behaviours, for instance domestic violence or sexual abuse. Possible rejoinders to such criticism include the following points. Unconditional positive regard can mean accepting the validity of clients' subjective experiencing without agreeing with their behaviours, and in addition, it may be important in creating the conditions of psychological safety whereby they can acknowledge and question unacceptable behaviours for themselves. Furthermore, an important reason why clients may be behaving badly is that they have experienced insufficient unconditional positive regard in their pasts.

Another way of looking at unconditional positive regard is that helpers respect and value the deeper core of clients and identify with their potential rather than with their current behaviours. Unconditional positive regard involves compassion for human frailty and an understanding of universal conditions which lead individuals to become less effective persons than may be desirable. Clients are more likely to blossom and change if loved for their human potential rather than rejected for their human failings. Though I realise that this may be setting very high standards, often the inability of helpers to feel and show unconditional positive regard reflects their own insufficient personal development.

Congruence

Congruence or genuineness has both an internal and an external dimension. Internally, helpers are able to accurately acknowledge their significant thoughts, feelings and experiences. They possess a high degree of self-awareness. This self-awareness may include acknowledging parts of themselves that are not ideal for helping: for example, 'I am afraid of this client; or 'My attention is so focused on my own problems that I am scarcely able to listen to him' (Rogers, 1957: 97).

Externally, helpers communicate to clients as real persons. What helpers say and how they say it rings true. They do not hide behind professional facades or wear polite social masks. Congruent communication is characterised by honesty and sincerity. For example, compassionate and caring helpers live these qualities in their helping encounters. Their verbal, vocal and bodily communication sends consistent caring messages. They are not portraying how they think they should be but communicating how they truly are in those moments.

Congruence does not mean 'letting it all hang out'. Helpers are able to use their awareness of their own thoughts and feelings to nurture and develop their clients. Though congruence may include personal disclosures, these disclosures are for the benefit of clients and in the interest of humanising the helping process and moving it forward.

What helpers and clients bring to helping relationships

Like any relationship, helping relationships do not start from scratch. Both helpers and clients bring many personal characteristics to their helping relationships. Some characteristics may be shared, while others represent differences. Furthermore, helpers and clients bring thoughts about their own and one another's characteristics. Following are some characteristics that helpers and clients bring to the helping relationships. How helpers and clients handle their similarities and differences can work for or against the strength of their working alliance.

Culture

Helpers and clients can come from different cultures and be at differing levels of assimilation to the mainstream culture (Palmer and Laungani, 1999). Even if they both come from the mainstream culture they may have differing levels of adaptation or rejection of its main rules. Helpers and clients who are native-born of migrant parents may experience split loyalties between the pull of parental cultures and personal wishes to assimilate into mainstream culture.

Helpers and clients who are migrants may experience differing levels of repulsion and attraction both to their previous and new home cultures. Migrants always carry around part of their previous cultures in their hearts and heads. Some migrants are never really happy in their host countries. However, migrants idealising previous cultures can get a rude awakening when they go home for the first time.

In addition to the cultures that helpers and clients bring, they each have differing experiences of how accepted they have been within their own and other cultures. Some will have been fortunate enough to have had their cultural differences accepted and cherished, while others will have received feedback that their cultures are inferior.

An important cultural issue relates to expectations about helper and client roles. For example, cultures may differ in their rules about whom they consider appropriate help-givers, the appropriateness of disclosing personal information to strangers, how they exhibit different emotions and symptoms, and the degree of direction expected from helpers. In addition, cultures differ in their attitude to time and to the making and keeping of appointments.

Race

Helpers and clients may come from different races. Whereas cultural differences can be subtle, racial differences are readily observable. Both helpers and clients may have experienced or be experiencing racial discrimination in relation to the majority white host culture. Also, sometimes those from majority cultures can feel suspicion and hostility when they venture into minority cultures. The idea of racially matching helpers and clients (black with black, Asian with Asian etc.) is not universally supported (Roach, 1999). However, many relationships between helpers and clients who are of different races involve working through and moving beyond racial stereotypes.

Social class

Social class is still a big issue in Britain and, to a lesser extent, in Australia and New Zealand. Income, educational attainment and occupational status are currently three of the main measures of social class in Britain, Australia and New Zealand. Other indicators include schooling, accent, clothing, manners, nature of social networks, and type and location of housing.

Helpers and clients bring their social class in to their relationships. You also bring your sensitivity to the effects of others' social class on you and your social class on them. If you are insufficiently skilled, social class considerations may create unnecessary barriers to establishing the working alliance. If you possess feelings of either inferiority or superiority on account of your social class, strive to eliminate them. Being an effective helper is difficult enough without the intrusion of avoidable social class agendas.

Gender

Helpers and clients bring their biological sex to their relationship. In most helping settings, women outnumber men both as helpers and clients. Whether the helping relationship exists between people of the same sex or of different sexes can influence the quality of the communication within it.

Gender also refers to the social and cultural classification of attributes and behaviours as 'masculine' and 'feminine'. Helpers and clients bring their gender or sex-role identities to the relationship – how they view themselves and one another on the dimensions of 'masculinity' and 'femininity' and the importance they attach to these constructs.

Helpers and clients can be categorised on the importance they attach to gender issues: for instance, to what extent and in what ways they are advocates for women's or men's issues. Furthermore, both parties may vary in the extent to which they possess sexist views that assume the superiority of one sex over the other.

Sexual and affectionate orientation

Helpers and clients bring their sexual orientation to the helping relationship, whether they are heterosexual, lesbian, gay or bisexual (Kitzinger, Coyle, Wilkinson and Milton, 1998). I use the term sexual orientation rather than sexual preference. Many, if not most, predominantly lesbian and gay people's sexual orientation is a fact of life, based on genetics and learning experiences, rather than a preference, based on free choice. Sometimes the term affectionate orientation is now used as a way of acknowledging that in same sex relationships, as in opposite sex ones, there are many other aspects than the sexual.

Helpers and clients not only bring their sexual and affectionate orientation to helping relationships, they bring their thoughts and feelings about their own and other people's sexual orientation too. Lesbian, gay and bisexual helpers and clients may be at varying levels of acceptance of their own and other people's homosexuality. In addition, lesbian and gay clients may wonder about the sexual orientation and attitudes of helpers. They may fear that their helpers will have difficulty accepting them.

Probably few helpers are openly homophobic, but many may, in varying degrees, be heterosexist. By heterosexist, I mean that either knowingly or unknowingly such helpers assume the superiority of demonstrating affection towards members of the opposite sex. On the other hand, some lesbian and gay helpers may have difficulty working with repressed heterosexuality or the openly heterosexual components of bisexual clients. Wittingly or unwittingly, they may seek to influence such clients into lesbian and gay moulds.

Age

Immediately helpers and clients meet for the first time they will start making assumptions about and connected with one another's age. Assessment of age is the starting point for other thoughts and feelings about themselves and one another. For example, young helpers may perceive themselves as being out of their depths with older clients since they do not have sufficient life experience. Young clients may fear that older helpers will be unable to understand them on account of the generation or generations gap.

Age is partly a physical concept, but it is also an attitude of mind. Older people can be psychologically alive and vibrant, whereas some young people are mentally rigid. Also, how helpers and clients communicate can reinforce or dispel assumptions based on physical age. For example, youthful helpers can communicate in calm and comfortable ways that reassure older clients, while older helpers can show understanding of their young clients' culture and aspirations.

Physical disability

Either the helper or the client or both may be physically disabled in some way. Many people suffer from mobility, hearing, sight and other impairments. Sometimes these impairments are genetic while others are the result of life events, such as industrial accidents, car accidents or military service. Helpers and clients will also have thoughts and feelings about their own and one another's disabilities. Some helpers may rightly feel inadequately skilled to work with certain physically disabled clients.

Being a physically disabled helper raises many issues. Many physically disabled helpers may have become calmer and stronger people if they have successfully managed to work through the emotional ramifications of their disabilities. Helpers may also be very sensitive to consequences stemming from their physical disabilities. For instance, despite still having a great capacity for sensitive and perceptive understanding, my friend Margaret Robertson took early retirement from her position as Head of the Royal Melbourne Institute of Technology Student Counselling Service partly because she considered her progressive hearing impairment interfered with her counselling effectiveness.

Sometimes helpers may be under pressure to change the nature of the helping relationship because of other agendas connected with disabled clients: for example, pressure from insurers or workers' compensation boards for brief helping or to write reports about clients. Though very much a minority, some disabled clients may allow financial claim considerations to sabotage the integrity of the working alliance.

Religion

Helpers and clients bring their religious beliefs, spiritual yearnings and explanations of the meaning of life to their relationships. Such beliefs can be sources of strength. For example, in Western cultures, many helpers are strongly motivated by the Christian concept of *agape* or unselfish love. Furthermore, sharing the same religious beliefs as clients can strengthen the working alliance.

Helpers differ in their abilities to develop relationships with clients whose attitudes towards religion and spirituality differ from their own. An issue for many religious helpers is the extent to which the values and teachings of their church influence how they work. For instance, Catholic helpers may face value conflicts with clients in areas such as divorce, contraception, abortion and pre-marital or lesbian and gay sex.

In this section I have attempted to personalise helping relationships by pointing to some key characteristics that helpers and clients bring to this relationship. Your own and your clients' personal characteristics come in different permutations and combinations. No relationship exists in a vacuum. As helpers you need to be sensitive to the effect that your own and your clients' personal characteristics have on how you communicate and on how you can best develop your working alliance. You also need to be realistic about your limitations and be prepared to refer clients to other helpers who might understand certain clients' special circumstances better.

Flexibility in helping relationships

Do you relate to all your friends the same way? I very much doubt it. Instead, probably you create distinctive relationships depending upon the interaction of your own and each friend's wants, wishes, interests and personal characteristics.

An important issue in offering helping relationships is that of how flexible helpers should be. Should you offer the same helping relationship to all clients or should you vary it? If you vary the relationship, are you just going to be offering an undisciplined form of helping based on whim? Noted American psychotherapist Arnold Lazarus observes that the first thing students learn in introductory psychology courses is that individual differences are paramount, yet many prominent helpers show very little change in how they work with different clients across different sessions (Lazarus, 1993).

Let us look at clients as customers or consumers of helping services. If they are to be best served, you require some flexibility in how you offer helping relationships. For instance, a timid young teenager who has been dominated at home and is very afraid of any form of intimacy may require a much more gentle relationship than a confident teenager who comes for help in making a decision about which major subject to study at university. Another example is that of a recently bereaved person requiring more space to ventilate feelings than someone who is further along the process of coming to terms with loss. Still another example is that of clients who wish to discuss career decisions rationally and then have their expectations dashed by helpers who insist on focusing on their feelings.

On the assumption of 'different strokes for different folks', you can develop a good standard, comfortable style of relating that you vary when appropriate. Considerations for varying how you offer your side of the helping relationship include whether your role is that of counsellor or as a user of counselling skills as part of performing another role. Considerations for different clients include their interpersonal styles and current emotional states, the nature of their problems and problem situations, what sort of relationship they expect from you, the stage of helping you are in and whether clients would be more comfortable with some variation in the relationship according to personal characteristics such as their culture and biological sex. While you cannot be all things to everyone, nevertheless you can thoughtfully vary the nature of the helping relationship to suit individual clients. All helping relationships, whether counselling relationships or relationships requiring the use of counselling skills as part of other roles, need to be created and lived afresh.

Summary

Connection is the essential characteristic of any relationship. Helping relationships are influenced by whether the helper is a trained counsellor or is using counselling skills as part of performing another role. Helping relationships take place in the head and in the heart as well as face to face. Ultimately all helping relationships need to become client self-helping relationships.

As well as their public helping relationship, both helpers and clients engage in internal mental processing before, during, between sessions and at the end of helping. Helpers and clients influence one another with their verbal, vocal and bodily communication. Furthermore, they can set up patterns of communication: for instance, the talkative helper and the quiet client. An important aspect of the helping relationship is that helpers and clients form a working alliance to perform the tasks of helping.

Despite there being different theoretical approaches to helping, most helpers agree that there are some core conditions to effective helping relationships. Carl Rogers identified three central helper-offered conditions: empathic understanding, unconditional positive regard and congruence. Rogers stressed clients' ability to perceive the communication of these conditions was what really mattered.

Empathy – the ability to identify with and mentally comprehend clients' inner worlds – can be viewed as both an attitude and a set of skills centred round an empathic understanding process. Unconditional positive regard consists of two dimensions: level of regard and unconditionality of regard. Helpers need to prize and accept clients as separate and unique persons. Despite clients' failings, helpers can identify with and attempt to release their human potential. Congruence entails helpers both possessing high levels of self-awareness and being able to communicate with clients sincerely, honestly and without social or professional facades.

Helping relationships do not start from scratch. Both helpers and clients bring many personal characteristics to their relationships as well as their thoughts and feelings about these characteristics. Personal characteristics that can influence helping relationships include: culture, race, social class, gender and gender attitudes, sexual and affectionate orientation, age, physical disability and religion. How successful helpers and clients are in negotiating differences in personal characteristics can affect the strength of the working alliance.

While developing a comfortable basic helping style, be flexible in adapting your side of the helping relationship to take into account client considerations. Such considerations include the different interpersonal styles, emotional states, expectations, problems and problem situations, stage in the helping process and cultures of the clients. Every helping relationship needs to be created and lived afresh.

Activities

Activity 6.1   Defining helping relationships

1   How would you define the helping relationship?
2   Critically react to the notion that helping relationships involve internal as well as external relationships.
3   What is the role of mental processing in helping relationships:
  a)   on the part of helpers
    • in strengthening the helping process
    • in interfering with the helping process
  b)   on the part of clients
    • in strengthening the helping process
    • in interfering with the helping process
4   What is the role of emotions in helping relationships:
  a)   on the part of helpers
    • in strengthening the helping process
    • in interfering with the helping process
  b)   on the part of clients
    • in strengthening the helping process
    • in interfering with the helping process
5   Regarding communication processes and patterns in helping relationships:
  a)   how can helper communication influence client communication?
  b)   how can client communication influence helper communication?
  c)   how can helpers and clients set up patterns of communication that
    • strengthen the helping process
    • interfere with the helping process

6   What does the term working alliance mean? How useful is this term when thinking about helping relationships?

Activity 6.2   Core conditions for helping relationships

1   Critically discuss whether there are some central or core conditions operating in all effective helping relationships.
2   *Empathy*
    a)   What does the term empathy mean?
    b)   Critically discuss the role of helper offered empathy in helping relationships.
    c)   Are there any possible negative outcomes from helper offered empathy?
3   *Unconditional positive regard*
    a)   What does the term unconditional positive regard mean?
    b)   Critically discuss the role of helper offered unconditional positive regard in helping relationships.
    c)   Are there any possible negative outcomes from helper offered unconditional positive regard?
4   *Congruence*
    a)   What does the term congruence mean?
    b)   Critically discuss the role of helper offered congruence in helping relationships.
    c)   Are there any possible negative outcomes from helper offered congruence?
5   *Client perceptions*
    a)   Why did Rogers stress the importance of clients perceiving the helper's communication of empathic understanding and unconditional positive regard?
    b)   Assuming helpers offer good levels of empathic understanding and unconditional positive regard, what factors might influence how well clients perceive this?

Activity 6.3   Influence of personal characteristics in helping relationships

How do or might each of the following characteristics influence how you form helping relationships with clients?

Culture
a)   clients similar to me
b)   clients differ from me

Race
a)   clients similar to me
b)   clients differ from me

Social class
a)   clients similar to me
b)   clients differ from me

Gender
a)   clients similar to me
b)   clients differ from me

Gender attitudes
a)   clients similar to me
b)   clients differ from me

Sexual and affectionate orientation
a)   clients similar to me
b)   clients differ from me

Age
a)   clients similar to me
b)   clients differ from me

Physical disability
a)   clients similar to me
b)   clients differ from me

Religion
a)   clients similar to me
b)   clients differ from me

Other personal characteristics (specify)
a)   clients similar to me
b)   clients differ from me

7 Improving Your Listening

It is as though he / she listened
and such listening as his / hers enfolds us in a silence
in which at last we begin to hear
what we are meant to be.

Lao-Tse

Chapter outcomes

By studying and doing the activities in this chapter you should be able to:

- *understand what the term 'active listening' means;*
- *become better at taking clients' perspectives;*
- *use good bodily and vocal communication to show that you are listening;*
- *improve your paraphrasing skills;*
- *improve your reflecting feelings skills;*
- *help your clients to keep talking; and*
- *understand how you can empower your mind to improve your listening.*

How many people do you know who listen to you properly? Most of us know very few. Quite apart from wanting air time to speak about their own thoughts, feelings and experiences, many people we know will put their own 'spin' on what we say rather than listen accurately and deeply to us.

At risk of repetition, the single most important goal of any introductory counselling skills training course is to improve the quality of students' listening. Even experienced counsellors have to monitor the quality of their listening all the time. In nearly 30 years as a counsellor trainer, I cannot remember a single student who could not become a better listener. Some counselling skills students are good to start with, but many other students have to work long and hard to become relaxed yet disciplined listeners.

Four kinds of listening take place in any person to person helping conversation. Listening takes place between both of you and within each of you. The quality of your inner listening, or being appropriately sensitive to your own thoughts and feelings, may be vital to the quality of your outer listening. If you or your client listen either poorly or too much to yourselves, you listen less well to one another. Conversely, if you listen well to one another, this may help the quality of your inner listening.

Developing your communication

The reason why we have two ears and only one mouth
is that we may listen the more and talk the less.
                                        Zeno of Citium

Active listening

How can you create an emotional climate so that your clients feel safe and free to talk with you? Many of the component skills of creating good helping relationships come under the heading of active listening. A distinction exists between hearing and listening. *Hearing* involves the capacity to be aware of and to receive sounds. *Listening* involves not only receiving sounds but, as much as possible, accurately understanding their meaning. As such it entails hearing and memorising words, being sensitive to vocal cues, observing body language and taking into account the personal and social context of communications. However, you can listen accurately without being a rewarding listener. *Active listening*, a term popularised by Thomas Gordon in his 1970 book *Parent Effectiveness Training*, entails not only accurately understanding speakers' communications, but also showing that you have understood. As such, active listening involves skills in both receiving and sending communications.

Active listening is the fundamental skill of any helping relationship. Nevertheless, throughout the relating–understanding–changing helping process model presented here, you adapt how you use active listening in the different stages of the model. However, if you are unable to listen properly in the first place, you will be poorly equipped to integrate active listening with other skills such as the ability to ask questions well.

Taking your client's perspective

There is an American Indian proverb that states: 'Don't judge any person until you have walked two moons in their moccasins'. If clients are to feel you receive them loud and clear, you need to develop the ability to 'walk in their moccasins', 'get inside their skin' and 'see the world through their eyes'. At the heart of active listening is a basic distinction between 'you' and 'me', between 'your view of you' and 'my view of you', and between 'your view of me' and 'my view of me'. Your view of you and my view of me are both inside or internal perspectives, whereas your view of me and my view of you are both outside or external perspectives.

The skill of listening to and understanding your clients is based on your choosing to acknowledge the separateness between 'me' and 'you' by getting inside your client's internal perspective rather than remaining in your own external perspective. If you respond to what your client says in ways that show accurate understanding of their perspective, you respond as if inside their internal perspective. Such responses do not mean you agree with them, rather that you acknowledge that what they say is their subjective reality. However, if you choose not to show understanding of your client's perspective or lack the skills to understand them, you respond from your external perspective.

Following are examples of responses by helpers from their *external* perspectives:

- 'That wasn't a very helpful thing to say in the situation.'
- 'Let me tell you about a similar experience to yours that I had.'
- 'My advice is to forget about it.'
- 'Don't worry.'
- 'You should show you care more.'

Following are examples of responses by helpers as if from clients' *internal* perspectives.

- 'You feel your marriage is heading for the rocks.'
- 'You have mixed feelings about accepting the job.'
- 'You're frustrated that your business is still not showing a profit.'

- 'You really appreciate how understanding your nurse was when you were in pain.'
- 'You've got so many problems that you don't know where to start.'

Often you can show that you are taking your client's internal perspective by starting your response with 'You'. However, as the statement 'You should show you care more' indicates, helpers can make responses starting with the word 'You' from clients' external perspectives.

Always consciously choose whether or not to respond as if inside your clients' internal perspectives. Think of a three-link chain: client statement–helper response–client statement. Helpers who respond from clients' internal perspectives allow them to choose either to continue on the same path or to change direction. However, if helpers respond from their external perspectives, they can influence clients to divert from trains of thoughts, feelings and experiences that they might otherwise have chosen.

Showing that you are listening

Here I review some of the main bodily communication skills by means of which helpers can demonstrate interest in and attention to what clients say (Argyle, 1992; Egan, 1998). Sometimes the use of these bodily communication skills goes by the term attending behaviour. In varying degrees, these bodily messages reward clients for starting and keeping talking.

Body posture

Important aspects of your body posture include physical openness, being relaxed and your degree of trunk lean. Physical openness means facing the client not only with your face but with your body. You need to be sufficiently turned towards your clients so that you can receive all their significant facial and bodily messages. My preference is to sit at a slight angle rather than directly opposite clients.

A relaxed body posture, provided you do not sprawl, conveys the message that you are emotionally accessible. If you do sit in a tense and uptight fashion, your clients may either consciously consider or intuitively feel that you are too bound up with your personal agendas and unfinished business to be fully accessible to them.

Your trunk lean may be forwards, backwards or sideways. If you lean too far forward you look odd and your clients may consider that you invade their personal space. If you lean far back, your clients may find this distancing. A slight forward trunk lean can both encourage clients and avoid threat, especially at the start of helping relationships.

Facial expressions

A friendly relaxed facial expression, including a smile, initially demonstrates interest. However as your clients talk, your facial expressions need to show that you are tuned in to what they say. For instance, if your client is serious, weeping or angry, adjust your facial expression to indicate that you observe and hear what they communicate.

Gaze and eye contact

When listening, gaze means looking in the direction of the client's face, eye contact means looking at the client's eyes. Good gaze skills indicate your interest and enable you to receive important facial messages. In addition, gaze can give you cues about when to stop listening and start responding. However, the main cues used in synchronising conversations are verbal and vocal messages rather than bodily messages. Good eye contact skills involve looking in the client's direction so that you allow the possibility of your eyes meeting reasonably often. Too much eye contact, including staring at your client, threatens. Looking down or away too often may indicate that you are tense or uninterested.

Gestures

The head nod is perhaps the most common gesture in listening: 'small ones to show continued attention, larger and repeated ones to indicate agreement' (Argyle, 1992: 11). Head nods are rewards for talking. On the negative side, head nods can also be powerful ways of controlling what your partner says and does not say. Then unconditional acceptance becomes conditional acceptance. Arm and hand gestures can also be used to show responsiveness to clients. However, helpers who gesture either too little or too much with their heads and arms can discourage clients from talking.

Physical proximity

In Chapter 3 I mentioned the various spatial zones for different kinds of conversations. Active listening entails respecting these zones. If you move into a client's personal space, they may feel uncomfortable and edge away. As a rough guide, helpers and clients can comfortably sit with their heads approximately five feet apart.

Both *within* your bodily communication and also *between* your bodily communication and your vocal and verbal communication, consistency increases the chances of your being perceived as genuinely listening. For instance, you may be smiling and at the same time either fidgeting or tapping your foot. Your smile may indicate interest but your foot tapping impatience, and your overall message may appear insincere.

Good vocal communication counts

The emotional atmosphere you provide when you listen can be greatly enhanced by your vocal communication. Clients need to feel that you are emotionally responsive to their feelings. One of the main ways you can do this is by using vocal communication that neither adds nor subtracts emotional meaning and emphasis. Respond with a voice level which is both comfortable and easily heard. If you talk too loudly, your clients may feel dominated. If you talk too softly, not only may you be difficult to hear but you may convey weakness and under-confidence. Furthermore, you may be encouraging your clients to speak diffidently too.

Articulate your words clearly, since poor enunciation can interrupt clients' trains of thought. Speak at a middle-of-the-range pitch level, since high-pitched and shrill voices can be disconcerting and harsh tones can be threatening.

Communicate with appropriate emphasis and avoid being monotonous. Allow your voice to be expressive in accurately picking up clients' diversity and shades of feeling. You create a more relaxed atmosphere if you do not talk too fast when you respond, but aim for a medium speech rate. Your use of pauses and silences can enhance your capacity to be a rewarding listener. To make it easy for clients to tell their stories, you can pause after each utterance to see if they wish to continue. Also, good use of silences can allow your clients more psychological space to think things through before speaking and to get in touch with their deeper feelings.

Paraphrasing skills

The next two somewhat overlapping skills, paraphrasing and reflecting feelings, involve helpers feeding back to clients what they have just communicated. Counselling skills students may wonder 'Why bother?' or think 'Isn't this all rather artificial?' Remember, in the relating stage, you are trying to help clients tell their stories without taking them off track. Your responses need to facilitate rather than interfere with this goal.

Helper verbalisations of client statements provide rewards for clients to continue. In addition, Rennie (1998) observes that clients' experiences may seem more real to them if verbalised rather than just thought, and even more real if they hear the experiences verbalised by their helpers. Such helper verbalisations may put clients more in touch with their own thoughts, feelings and experiences. Furthermore, by verbalising what clients communicate, helper and client can engage in a process of exploring and understanding more accurately the meaning of what clients are trying to communicate.

A paraphrase expresses the meaning of a client statement or series of statements in different words. On some occasions, helpers may choose to repeat rather than paraphrase clients' words. For instance, if a client shares a significant insight, it may help the insight sink in if the helper repeats the clients' words. However, more often than not repetition becomes parroting. Clients want to relate to persons, not parrots!

Paraphrasing involves rewording at least the crux of the clients' message. You are trying to tell clients clearly and briefly what they have just communicated from their internal perspective. When you paraphrase, you may sometimes use clients' words, but sparingly. You try to stay close to the kind of language they use. Box 7.1 provides examples of paraphrasing.

Box 7.1 Examples of paraphrasing

Counselling skills student to trainer
> *Counselling skills student:* You know, once I start thinking about all the different skills, I get so much into my head that I wonder if I will ever be able to come over to clients as a real person.
> *Trainer:* There's so much to consider that you're afraid of losing your humanity.

Client to social worker
> *Client:* With my husband unemployed and four kids, it's a struggle to keep our heads above water and there are times when I think we are going under.
> *Social worker:* You're doing your best just to survive.

Secondary school student to teacher
> *Student:* My mum and dad are fighting again. There is no real peace at home. My sister has gone off to live with her boyfriend. I wish I could leave too.
> *Teacher:* You'd really like to follow your sister's example and move out from your domestic war zone.

> *Employee to personnel officer*
>   Employee: Part of me wants to continue in my present department, but another
>   part of me wants a transfer.
>   *Personnel officer:* You're not sure whether you want to stay or leave.

A good paraphrase can provide mirror reflections that are clearer and more succinct than original statements. If so, clients may show appreciation with comments like: 'That's right' or 'You've got me'. A simple tip for counselling students who struggle with paraphrasing is to slow the helping conversation down. This will give you more time to think. Another tip for gaining confidence and fluency is to practise paraphrasing both in and out of class.

Reflecting feelings skills

Most helper responses reflecting feelings are paraphrases that emphasise the emotional content of clients' communications. Reflecting or mirroring feelings is possibly the main skill of active listening. Reflecting feelings entails responding to clients' music and not just to their words. It involves feeling and accurately understanding clients' flows of emotions and experiencing and sensitively communicating your understanding back. When you reflect feelings, you give clients the opportunity to listen more deeply to their own feelings. The safer the emotional climate you can create in your helping sessions, the more likely clients are to be able to experience and share their emotions. Many of us have been brought up to bury and hide our feelings, so we need help in getting them out in the open. Often reflecting feelings is a process of gradual unfolding in which clients are able to get more in touch with their underlying feelings and acknowledge them both to themselves and their helpers.

In the previous chapter I described a five-stage empathy process: observing and listening, resonating, discriminating, communicating and checking. Here I collapse this process into the two stages of identifying feelings and reflecting feelings.

Identifying feelings
Before you can reflect a client's feelings back to her/him, you need accurately to identify or discriminate what they are. Sometimes clients say 'I feel' when they mean 'I think'. For example, 'I feel that equality

between the sexes is essential' describes a thought rather than a feeling. On the other hand, 'I feel angry about sex discrimination' describes a feeling. It is important that you distinguish between clients' thoughts and feelings, if you wish to be skilful at picking up feelings accurately. Following are some ways of identifying feelings.

Bodily communication   You can pick up much about what your clients feel from just looking at them. For example, clients may come for help looking tired, worried or happy. They may slump in the chair or sit upright. I once had a very anxious client who sat facing 90 degrees from me with his hand cupped at the side of his face to avoid eye contact. Occasionally he would take a brief glimpse at me. It was about eight sessions before he felt safe enough to have a normal level of eye contact.

Sometimes clients send mixed messages in which their bodily communication is more important than their verbal communication. For instance, May Lee may say 'It's just great' that, after the break-up of a relationship, she is living on her own again, at the same time as her voice chokes, her face looks sad and the corners of her mouth are turned down.

Vocal communication   Observe how clients communicate with their voices. For instance, sighing or slow speech may indicate a depressed client, whereas talking too fast and too much may indicate a highly anxious client. Many of the messages about the intensity of clients' feelings are conveyed by the degree of vocal emphasis they place on them. Some clients who are very out of touch with their capacity to feel may communicate in rather flat and distant voices.

Feelings words and phrases   A good but not infallible way to discover what a client feels is to listen to their feelings words. Listening to feelings words may seem a simple guideline, but sometimes beginning counselling students do not listen carefully enough and then ask clients 'What did you feel?' after clients have just told them.

Feelings words include happy, sad, angry, lonely, anxious, depressed. Feelings phrases are groupings of words that describe feelings. The following is an example of a client using feelings words and phrases that communicate clearly what she means. Kylie says to her helper: 'I really enjoyed our date last night. It was just great. Even after so little time I feel there is something special between us. I can't wait to meet him again.' Kylie's feelings words and phrases are 'really enjoyed', 'just great', 'something special between us', and 'can't wait'.

Physical reactions words   You can also identify feelings by listening to clients' physical reactions words. Clients may also describe their physical reactions with words like tense, tired, pounding heart and headache.

Feelings idioms   Feelings idioms are everyday expressions or turns of phrase used to communicate feelings. Very often such idioms are expressed in visual images, but their meaning is so well understood that you do not need to conjure up the image to understand the message. For example, 'I'm over the moon' is a feelings idiom describing the emotion of joy; 'I've got the blues', depression; 'I've got butterflies in my stomach', anxiety; 'I'm at the end of my tether', exhaustion and/or frustration; and 'I feel fighting mad', anger.

Feelings imagery   Clients can intentionally use visual images to conjure up and communicate feelings. The visual image provides a frame for understanding the feelings content of their messages. For instance, to describe and illustrate embarrassment, clients might use the images of 'I felt like crawling into a corner' or 'I felt like running out of the room'. Another example is that of clients with low self-esteem describing themselves as 'A small person in a world of giants'.

Reflecting feelings

A simple guideline for reflecting feelings is to start your responses with the personal pronoun 'you' to indicate that you are taking your client's perspective. When reflecting feelings it is cumbersome always to put 'You feel' before feelings words and phrases. Sometimes 'You're' is sufficient: for example, 'You're delighted' instead of 'You feel delighted'. It is even better to paraphrase and find different words to describe clients' feelings.

Whenever you can, try to communicate back a client's main feeling. Even though clients may not start with their main feeling, they may feel better understood by you if you reflect their main feeling at the front of your response.

Try to reflect the strength of clients' feelings. For instance, after a row, the client may feel 'devastated' (strong feeling), 'upset' (moderate feeling), or 'slightly upset' (weak feeling) . Sometimes clients use many words to describe their feelings. The words may cluster around the same theme, in which case you may choose to reflect the crux of the feeling. Alternatively, clients may verbalise varying degrees of mixed feelings ranging from simple opposites, for instance 'happy/sad' to more complex combinations, such as 'hurt/anger/guilt'. Good reflections pick up all key elements of feelings messages. On occasion you can assist speakers to find the right way to express their feelings. Here reflecting feelings involves helping others choose feelings words that resonate for them.

Sometimes you can reflect your client's feelings and the reasons they offer for them. A simple way of doing this is to make a 'You feel . . . because . . .' statement that mirrors their internal viewpoint. Reflecting back reasons does not mean that you make an interpretation or offer an explanation from your own perspective.

You respond to your clients' feelings statements with differing degrees of tentativeness depending on how clearly they have communicated and how confident you are about receiving their messages accurately. If you are unclear about your client's real or underlying feelings, you can check with them. Almost invariably you check by slight voice inflections. On other occasions, you check by asking directly: for instance, 'Do I understand you properly?'

Alternatively, you may make comments like 'I think I hear you saying (state feelings tentatively) . . .' or 'I want to understand what you're feeling, but I'm still not altogether clear'. Another option is to reflect back a mixed message: for instance, 'On the one hand you are saying you don't mind. On the other hand, you seem tearful.' After a pause you might add: 'I'm wondering if you are putting on a brave face?'

An important consideration in picking up feelings is to understand whether and to what extent clients possess insight into their feelings: for example, acknowledging shame, anger, hurt, or betrayal. Be sensitive to how much reality clients can handle at any given moment in the helping process. You can threaten clients by prematurely or clumsily reflecting feelings that they experience difficulty acknowledging.

Box 7.2 provides examples of different ways in which helpers can reflect clients' feelings. I do not mean to imply that there is a single correct way of responding to any of the client statements. Reflections of feelings, such as those offered below, can be stepping stones or bridges to clients further experiencing, expressing, exploring, and understanding their feelings. Feelings, like ocean waves, are in a constant process of movement. Skilled helpers are able to follow and reflect the ebb and flow of clients' feelings.

Box 7.2   Examples of reflecting feelings

Reflecting bodily communication
 Client: [*Weeps when entering the helper's office.*]
 Helper: You feel very upset . . .

Reflecting vocal communication
> Client: [*Sighs deeply after reciting a list of problems.*]
> Helper: You feel overwhelmed . . .

Reflecting feelings words and phrases
> Client A: I feel overjoyed.
> Helper A: You feel delighted *or* You're delighted.
> Client B: I feel more than let down by . . .
> Helper B: You feel betrayed by . . .

Reflecting physical reactions
Here, if the physical reaction is literally named, there is a case for repetition to show that you have clearly registered it. Otherwise, consider paraphrasing.

> Client A: Tension in my neck.
> Helper A: Tension in your neck.
> Client B: I feel butterflies in my stomach.
> Helper B: You feel anxiety in your stomach.

Reflecting feelings idioms
> Client: I've got a bad case of the blues.
> Helper: You feel very depressed.

Reflecting feelings imagery
Because the imagery has personal significance for the client, there may be a case for repetition to show that you have clearly registered the imagery. Alternatively, as in response B, you can build on the client's imagery or, as in response C, express its central feelings message.

> Client: I feel like a bird let out of a cage.
> Helper response A: You feel like a bird let out of a cage.
> Helper response B: You feel you can now spread your wings.
> Helper response C: You feel free.

Reflecting mixed feelings
> Client: It's great when Brian and I are together, but I don't want to be around him all the time.
> Helper: You enjoy Brian's company, but want your own space too.

Searching for feelings that resonate
> Client: I don't know how to express my reaction to the way my father treated me . . . possibly angry . . . upset, no that's not quite it . . . bewildered . . .
> Helper: Hurt, anxious, confused . . . do any of these words strike a chord?

Reflecting feelings and reasons
> *Client*: I'm really delighted that I finally seem to be working with a group of
> people who think the same way as I do about running a company.
> *Helper*: You're thrilled because at last you are working with like-minded
> colleagues.

Checking the accuracy of a reflection
Some possible helper responses might include some of the following.

- Use questioning vocal inflection when ending a reflection.
- Pause to check clients' verbal, vocal and bodily reactions.
- Indirectly ask about accuracy: 'I hear you saying you feel . . .'
- Directly ask about accuracy: 'You feel . . . Am I receiving you loud and
  clear?'

Small verbal rewards

Small verbal rewards are brief expressions of interest designed to
encourage clients to keep talking. Small verbal rewards are continu-
ation messages. The message they convey is: 'I am with you. Please go
on.' Helpers can use small verbal rewards for good or ill. On the one
hand, you can reward clients for sharing and exploring their internal
perspectives. For instance, when a client uses imagery to describe a
feeling, you could say 'Tell me more about your image'. On the other
hand, your use of small verbal rewards may subtly or crudely attempt
to shape what clients say. For instance, you may reward clients for
saying either positive or negative things about themselves – possibly
rewarding them more for negative statements in early sessions and for
positive statements later. Furthermore, you can selectively reward
clients for talking about agendas of interest to you. Box 7.3 provides
some examples of small verbal rewards, though perhaps the most
frequently used, 'Uh-hum', is more vocal than verbal.

Box 7.3   Examples of small verbal rewards

'Uh-hum'	'Sure'
'Please continue'	'Indeed'
'Tell me more'	'And . . .'
'Go on'	'So . . .'
'I see'	'Really'
'Oh?'	'Right'
'Then . . .'	'Yes'
'I hear you'	

Open-ended questions

Helpers may use questions in ways that either help clients to elaborate their internal perspectives or lead them out of their perspectives, possibly into yours. Open-ended questions allow clients to share their internal perspectives without curtailing their options. A good use of open-ended questions is when, in the initial session, you wish to assist clients to say why they have come. In subsequent sessions too, you are likely to find open-ended questions useful. Open-ended questions include: 'Tell me about it?'; 'Please elaborate?'; and, slightly less open-ended, 'How do you feel about that?'

Open-ended questions may be contrasted with closed questions that curtail speakers' options: indeed they often give only two options, 'yes' or 'no'.

Open-ended question: 'How do you feel about your relationship?'
Closed question: 'Is your relationship good or bad?'

Open-ended questions may also be contrasted with leading questions that put answers into clients' mouths:

Open-ended question: 'What do you think about her?
Leading question: 'She's a great person, isn't she?'

I am not suggesting that helpers never use closed questions. It depends on the goals of your listening. Closed questions can be useful for collecting information. However, show restraint if you wish to help others share their worlds. You may also need to use open-ended questions sparingly. Leading questions are best avoided at all times since they show lack of respect for clients as separate persons with their own thoughts and feelings.

Four major listening mistakes

If clients are going to give you the gift of revealing themselves, they need psychological safety and space. Such safety and space are both quantitative and qualitative. Unfortunately, some counselling skills students – and more experienced helpers too – communicate to clients that they are not absolutely free to experience and express themselves.

Though there are many other mistakes, the following are four major ones that you can make when you listen.

The first major mistake is to keep interrupting. You do not allow clients to finish what they are saying. For instance, you may butt in and finish off your clients' sentences. Alternatively, you may change the subject. Interruptions can evoke many negative thoughts in clients who are cut off such as: 'He's not listening to me', 'She doesn't think much of what I have to say', 'He's only interested in hearing himself talk' .

The second major mistake is to be too controlling. You may direct and lead the clients into your own agenda rather than theirs. If you monopolise the helping conversation, your clients have little chance to speak. Also, you may dominate by switching the focus of the conversation back onto yourself. If you are too controlling, you restrict your opportunities for listening. Furthermore, you can be impervious to the negative effect you have on clients, many of whom may have suffered from too much control in their pasts. Controlling helpers breed either openly or subtly resistant clients.

The third major mistake is to be too judgemental. Listening well requires you to possess an accepting attitude that respects clients as separate and unique human beings. Be careful about making judgemental statements concerning clients' thoughts, feelings and actions indicating that they fall short of your standards: for example, 'You should not be so depressed', 'You should respect your parents' and 'You shouldn't have done that'.

The fourth major mistake is to give gratuitous advice. You can take over the ownership of your clients' problems and lives. You may barely listen to what your clients say before you come up with what they should be doing. Your style of responding implies 'I know what's best for you'.

Basic facilitation

You engage in basic facilitation of your clients when you employ the active listening skills discussed so far to a series of statements or to whole sections of helping sessions. To a large extent allow clients to control content. Your role is that of a good companion who makes it easy for clients to reveal their internal perspectives on their own terms and at their own pace.

Box 7.4 is an abbreviated excerpt from a course tutoring contact with a counselling skills student, Mary, who is enrolled in the first semester of a two-year part-time Diploma in Counselling Psychology evening course. Here the helper, Richard, uses basic facilitation skills to provide a supportive environment for Mary to tell her story. Richard does not know in advance what Mary is going to say and does not try to direct the conversation in any way. This excerpt is based on many similar conversations I have held with British and Australian counselling students.

The excerpt illustrates the use of counselling skills as part of another role, that of course tutor, and in an informal helping contact rather than in a formal helping session. The setting for such a helping conversation could be either an office during a lecturer's 'office hour' or even a classroom at the end of a class.

Box 7.4   Example of using active listening skills for basic facilitation

Mary: Hello Richard.

Richard: Hello Mary, please sit down.

Mary: I'd like to talk with you about the pressures I'm under at the moment.

Richard: You're feeling stressed. Go on.

Mary: Yes. There are so many things going on at once and I'm feeling that I'm not coping well.

Richard: You don't feel on top of things.

Mary: When I started the course, I knew I might be busy, but I didn't fully realise how much work was involved.

Richard: So you're wondering whether you have bitten off more than you can chew.

Mary: I think I can probably pull through regarding my studies, but right now I am going through a rough patch.

Richard: Uh-hum

Mary: One of my colleagues at work is off sick and I'm having to make up some of the slack. On top of that my widowed mum has just been diagnosed with terminal cancer. All the family are very worried about this and, being the one that lives nearest to her, I'm going out of my way to go over and support her.

Richard: I'm sorry to hear about your mum. You feel stretched by an accumulation of work and family demands, but there is a good chance that you can still cope with the course.

Mary: I just wanted you to know about these things in case at times I don't seem to be as involved as I would like.

Richard: You're worried that these extra pressures may make it seem that you are not giving of your best.

Mary: Yes. I want you to know that I am committed to the course. I will try to come to all the classes and hand in all the assignments on time.

Richard: I see you as a serious student and will do what I can to support you through this rough patch.

Empowering your mind

Many if not all counselling students' minds interfere with their listening. However, you can use your mind to guide you in listening well. Here I briefly illustrate how each of the mind skills mentioned in Chapter 2 can be used either to support or to sabotage good listening skills.

Creating self-talk

You can create goal self-talk that disciplines you to focus on listening: for example 'STOP . . . THINK . . . I can show my respect for my client by listening well to her/him.' When you feel yourself getting emotionally aroused, for instance anxious or angry, you can create cooling and calming self-talk statements such as: 'Calm down . . . my anxiety is a signal that I need to listen carefully.' You can also create coaching self-talk statements for the skills of listening well: for instance, 'Let's make the effort to understand her/his perspective.' Furthermore, as shown below, you can create corrective self-talk once you realise you are prone to making major mistakes that block your listening.

Examples of corrective self-talk

For interrupting:	'Remember to hear her/him out.'
For being too controlling:	'Helping involves respecting clients as separate individuals and freeing them to develop their unique potentials.'
For being too judgemental:	'Clients are more likely to disclose if feeling safe.'
For giving too much advice:	'I am more helpful if I let clients own their problems.'

Creating visual images

You can use visual images to enter into your client's internal perspective. For instance, when clients describe past or current experiences, you can create imaginary pictures that may help you understand these experiences. Furthermore, when clients describe visual images or fantasies, you can try to visually picture them too. However, be careful to remember that your visual images may contain errors in them. Your imagination may be heavily coloured with your own personal experiences, developmental history and current social and cultural environment (McMillan, 1997). Asking clients to describe their experiences and visual images more graphically is one skill for guarding against your potential to distort images.

Creating rules

I have already mentioned the major listening mistakes of being too judgemental and giving gratuitous advice. Here your rules and personal agendas may intrude on your capacity to care for and nurture the growth and happiness of your clients. For instance, if you are inwardly or outwardly critical of aspects of your clients' thoughts, feelings and experiences, there is a good chance that you possess one or more unrealistic rules that 'drive' unhelpful communication. If this is the case, you can detect, challenge and restate the unrealistic rules so that they become realistic rules that enhance rather than erode your ability to listen.

Creating perceptions

Humility is always in order when contemplating how good a listener you are. Without knowing it, you can easily distort clients' experiences by passing them through a filter of your own experiencing and life history. There may be certain topics and situations where your anxiety interferes with your ability to perceive your clients' communications accurately. For instance, some counselling skills students become anxious when the topic turns to sexuality or suicide. Students, and experienced helpers too, can feel threatened by certain categories of clients: for example, clients of the opposite sex, highly successful clients, very intelligent clients, and clients who hold strong views with which you disagree. Furthermore, when anxious, your mind tricks and self-protective habits can interfere with the accuracy of your perceptions. You may become defensive when clients provide feedback that differs from your picture of yourself: for instance, that you do not listen well.

You can use skills of testing the reality of your perceptions so that your own experiencing, defensiveness and agendas do not distort how you perceive your clients. Furthermore, you can strive to create compassionate rather than judgemental perceptions of clients and their human frailties.

Creating explanations

Assume responsibility for how well you listen. Even if you consider that clients behave unreasonably in their private lives, you still need to assume responsibility for listening to their pain, so that you may help them as much as possible. Being critical/defensive, dominant/controlling, and withdrawn/submissive are three styles of interacting that may interfere with listening. If you possess any of these three styles, you need to assume more responsibility for disciplining your listening. If you are critical/defensive or dominant/controlling, your outward communication shows that you do not listen properly. However, outwardly the effects of being withdrawn/submissive on your listening may be less obvious. If you allow clients to be rude and inconsiderate to you your irritation with them may cause you inwardly to tune out to them. Here, if you are to tune in again, you can create explanations that allow you to be more assertive and set limits on their behaviour.

Creating expectations

An important skill is to avoid mindreading or responding on the basis of unnecessary expectations concerning what your clients think or are about to say. For example, if you rush in to finish off your clients' sentences, your responses can get their trains of thought wrong. Furthermore, even when your clients correct you, you may still erroneously think that your version is best. One skill for creating accurate expectations about what clients may say next is to listen carefully to what has already been said. Ways of testing the reality of your expectations about what your client thinks or will say include holding back and waiting for them to speak again, using active listening skills so that they can disclose further, and tactfully asking them what they are thinking.

Summary

Active listening entails not only understanding clients' communications, but also showing that you have understood. Active listening involves helpers in responding as if from clients' internal perspectives. You can demonstrate interest and attention to clients through bodily communication including: an open and relaxed body posture, slight forward trunk lean, appropriate facial expressions, good gaze and eye contact, appropriate gestures and head nods, and sitting neither too close nor too far from them. Your vocal communication can help create a safe emotional atmosphere and show you are tuned into clients' feelings.

Paraphrasing skills entail rewording at least the crux of clients' communications. Most helper responses reflecting feelings are paraphrases that emphasise the emotional content of clients' communications. You can identify clients' feelings from bodily communication, vocal communication, feelings words and phrases, physical reactions words, feelings idioms and feelings imagery. Whenever you can, try and communicate back clients' main feelings. Pick up the strength of feelings and whether feelings communications contain multiple and/or mixed messages. At times you will search with clients for reflections of feelings that resonate with them. Check out the accuracy of your reflections either indirectly, for instance by vocal inflection, or more directly.

Small verbal rewards are brief expressions of interest designed to encourage clients to keep talking. Be careful not to use small verbal rewards in unhelpful or controlling ways. Open-ended questions allow clients to share their internal perspectives without curtailing their options. Such questions may be contrasted with closed-ended and leading questions.

Four major listening mistakes are interrupting, being too controlling, being judgemental and giving gratuitous advice. You engage in the basic facilitation of clients when you employ active listening skills when responding to a series of statements or to whole sections of helping sessions.

You can use your mind to support rather than sabotage listening well to clients. Create calming, coaching and corrective self-talk to keep you appropriately focused on listening. Your visual images can increase your understanding of what clients are saying. Create rules that are accepting of clients and enhance rather than erode your ability to listen. Perceive your listening ability accurately and guard against tendencies to distortion and defensiveness. In addition, assume responsibility for listening well and for correcting your listening errors. Furthermore, avoid mind-reading mistakes that involve incorrect expectations of what clients will say next.

Activities

Activity 7.1   Tuning into the client's internal perspective

Part A   *Identifying the client's internal perspective*

Below are some statement–response excerpts from formal and informal helping situations. Three helper responses have been provided for each statement. Write 'IN' or 'EX' by each response according to whether it reflects the client's internal perspective or comes from the helper's external perspective. Some of the responses may seem artificial, but they have been chosen to highlight the point of the exercise. Answers are provided at the end of this chapter.

Example: Client to relationship counsellor

Client: 'We are having money problems. It's more a matter of arguing over how to spend it rather than not having enough.'

Relationship counsellor:
EX   (a)   'How do you differ in what you want?'
EX   (b)   'You're lucky not to be short of money.'
IN   (c)   'Your issue is fighting over what to buy.'

1. Student to teacher

Student: 'I've got this big test coming up and I don't seem to be able to concentrate. I'm worried sick.'
Teacher:
___   (a)   'This is a case of test anxiety.'
___   (b)   'You're scared because your lack of concentration prevents you from revising properly.'
___   (c)   'You will be all right on the day.'

2. Patient to nurse

Patient: 'I want to get home as soon as possible.'
Nurse:
___ (a) 'You can't wait to get home.'
___ (b) 'I want to get home too.'
___ (c) 'What's so bad about here?'

3. Employee to human resources manager

Employee: 'I'm unhappy about the performance appraisal I received from my boss.'
Human resources manager:
___ (a) 'You should think very carefully before quitting your job.'
___ (b) 'Many people feel disappointed after performance appraisals.'
___ (c) 'You're upset about your performance appraisal.'

Part B   Practice – summarising one another's internal perspective

Work with your partner.

1   Talking in the first person singular using 'I' messages, partner A talks for at least two minutes about what he/she considers important in a helping relationship (Partner A's internal perspective). Partner B responds with small verbal rewards and encouraging vocal and bodily communication, but does not interrupt.
2   When Partner A finishes, talking in the second person singular using 'You' messages, Partner B summarises the main points of what Partner A was saying. Partner A responds with small verbal rewards and encouraging vocal and bodily communication, but does not interrupt.
3   When Partner B finishes summarising, Partner A comments on how accurate Partner B was in understanding his/her internal perspective. Partner B can respond to this feedback.
4   Then reverse roles and repeat 2, 3 and 4 above.

Part C   Observe how you and others respond

1   Watch and listen to TV and radio interviews and chat shows. Observe when interviewers respond from either the interviewee's internal or from their own external perspectives.

2   Monitor your own communication for a week and become more aware of when you respond to speakers from your own or their perspectives:
   (a)   in helping sessions;
   (b)   in your daily life.

Activity 7.2   Paraphrasing skills

Part A   Paraphrasing client statements

Go to Box 7.1 and provide at least one alternative paraphrase to each of the four client statements.

Part B   Practice in pairs and in a group

1   *In pairs*: You 'feed' each other statements. Listeners paraphrase speakers' statements and speakers provide feedback on their reactions to each paraphrase.
2   *In a group*: Members take turns in making statements – they may write them on whiteboards or blackboards. After each statement, all group members formulate a paraphrase and then share them with the group.

Activity 7.3   Reflecting feelings skills

Part A   Formulate reflections of feelings

Reproduce Box 7.2 providing your own examples of helper's reflecting clients' feelings in each of these areas:

*   reflecting bodily communication;
*   reflecting vocal communication;
*   reflecting feelings words and phrases;
*   reflecting physical reactions;
*   reflecting feelings idioms;
*   reflecting feelings imagery;
*   reflecting mixed feelings;
*   searching for feelings that resonate;

- reflecting feelings and reasons;
- checking the accuracy of a reflection.

Part B   Practice in pairs and in a group

1   *In pairs*: Each of you takes turns to be speaker and listener. The speaker picks a topic about which s/he feels comfortable sharing emotions. When listening, help your speaker to talk about her/his feelings by reflecting them accurately. Pay attention to vocal and bodily as well as verbal communication.

2   *Group exercises*:
   (a)   The group picks a feeling. Then members identify and demonstrate the verbal, vocal and bodily communication required to express that feeling mildly, moderately and strongly. Repeat the exercise for other feelings.
   (b)   This exercise may be done with a beach ball or tennis ball. The group sits in a circle. The student holding the ball (the speaker) expresses a feeling by means of verbal, vocal and bodily communication. He/she pauses to allow all students to formulate a reflection of feeling response and then throws the ball to another student (the listener) who attempts to reflect the feeling accurately. Then the listener becomes the speaker and so on.

Activity 7.4   Using active listening skills for basic facilitation

Divide into pairs or into triads (speaker, helper and observer). One of you takes your turn to be the speaker. For at least five minutes, the helper uses the following active listening skills to facilitate your sharing your internal perspective about one or more problem situations in your helping or private life:

- good attending behaviour;
- good vocal communication;
- paraphrasing;
- reflecting feelings;
- small verbal rewards;
- open-ended questions.

Since this is a training activity, along the way the speaker should 'feed' the helper some feelings statements and pause every now and then to give her/him an opportunity to respond. Afterwards hold a debriefing session and reverse roles. Videotape feedback may add to the value of the activity. If in doubt, see Box 7.4 for an example of how to perform this activity. Speakers can role-play clients if uncomfortable with sharing personal material.

Activity 7.5   Creating self-talk and visual images for listening well

Part A   Creating self-talk

1   Identify an upcoming counselling skills training group or helping situation in which you might listen less well than you would like.
2   Identify any negative self-talk that contributes to your listening less well.
3   Create two each of calming and coaching statements for listening well in the situation. Then, put together self-talk that combines calming and coaching statements.
4   Put your statements on cue cards or on a cassette and rehearse them for as long as necessary to learn them properly.
5   Implement your self-talk in the real life situation and assess its consequences.

Part B   Creating visual images and self-talk

1   Identify an upcoming counselling skills training group or helping situation in which you might listen less well than you would like.
2   Think of the verbal, vocal and bodily communication skills you require that will help you to listen competently in the situation.
3   Visually rehearse yourself listening competently in the situation, including coping with any difficulties and set-backs that occur.
4   Accompany your visual rehearsal with appropriate self-talk.
5   Practise your visual rehearsal plus self-talk skills for as long as you find it helpful, then also practise listening effectively in the real life situation.

Answers to activity 7.1   Tuning into the client's internal perspective

Part A   *Identifying the client's internal perspective*

1 (a) EX   (b) IN   (c) EX
2 (a) IN   (b) EX   (c) EX
3 (a) EX   (b) EX   (c) IN

8 Starting the Helping Process

Although the world is full of suffering, it is also full of the overcoming of it.
Helen Keller

Chapter outcomes

By studying and doing the activities in this chapter you should:

- *know the importance of preparing for helping sessions;*
- *have basic skills at meeting, greeting and seating clients;*
- *be able to make appropriate opening statements;*
- *know how to structure when starting the helping process;*
- *possess some strategies for dealing with clients different from you;*
- *possess some strategies for dealing with resistant clients;*
- *possess basic summarising skills;*
- *possess basic structuring the helping process skills;*
- *assist clients to talk about why they have come for helping; and*
- *understand how you can empower your mind when starting the helping process.*

'How do I start the helping process in a friendly yet functional way?'
This seemingly innocent question begs many other questions about
your use of counselling skills in training and practice. For example,
after training will you be using counselling skills in informal contacts
with clients, as part of more formal interviews conducted in roles other
than being counsellors, or as counsellors? During training, are you on a
short, medium length or longer length introductory counselling skills
course? Also, at what stage of the course are you?

In this and subsequent chapters, I mainly present the relating–understanding–changing (RUC) helping process model as though you are on a longer length introductory counselling skills course as part of training to become an accredited counsellor. However, in all circumstances I urge both trainers and students to use the contents of this chapter according to the goals and stage of your introductory skills courses. Readers, such as teachers, pastoral care workers and nurses, who may not conduct formal helping sessions can adapt the skills described here to the special nature of your helping contacts. The same advice holds for personnel officers, careers workers, speech therapists, and social workers and others who, without being accredited counsellors, may use counselling skills when conducting interviews as part of their roles.

The main task of stage 1 of the model is to establish a helping relationship. By the end of stage 1 clients should have had the opportunity to elaborate on why they have come and to select a problem situation for your work together. This chapter goes beyond the previous chapter, which focused on active listening skills and basic facilitation, to review some more task-oriented skills for getting started in initial helping sessions.

Preparation skills

Good preparation is important. I have known many counselling skills students who have got off to a bad start in helping sessions through poor preparation. Here I discuss preparatory considerations for helping sessions in general as well as make comments designed specifically to help counselling skills students avoid common pitfalls.

Pre-session contact

Helping takes place in settings of varying degrees of formality, for instance, counselling services, social work offices, personnel departments, career services and so on. Initial impressions are extremely important and usually start getting formed before helpers and clients meet. Professional and voluntary helping services send messages about how user-friendly they are in how they advertise, in how the receptionist answers the phone, in what messages are given to clients on answer-phones, and in what sort of follow-up there is to answer-phone enquiries. If prospective clients perceive such messages negatively, they may either never use the service or else come along with potentially avoidable misgivings.

When clients come to helping settings, receptionists and waiting areas also send messages to clients about your service. As I know from experience as a vulnerable client, warm, friendly and efficient receptionists are worth their weight in gold. New clients receive much-needed encouragement from sympathetic welcomes. Tact is vital. Receptionists should always remember that they are in a public area and not ask clients to reveal anything that might cause unnecessary embarrassment. Clients can also receive positive messages from waiting areas decorated in comfortable and quietly tasteful ways. On the other hand, clients receive negative messages from dreary, dirty and impersonal waiting areas.

Getting ready

Some counselling skills students rush into helping sessions with clients at either the last moment or late. Always try to arrive early so that you can get the room ready and compose yourself properly. Preparatory considerations about the room include seeing that the seating is appropriate, coffee tables are clean and show no evidence of previous occupants, whiteboards are clear, and video-recording or audio-recording equipment is working and ready to start at the touch of a switch. If, for instance, you have a volunteer 'client' who is already waiting for you, politely keep them waiting outside while you prepare the room. Allowing clients to see preparatory behaviour can negatively interfere with how competent they perceive you to be.

Arriving early also gives you time to relax yourself. This can be especially important for counselling skills students who get very worried about holding and recording practice sessions. Furthermore, you can familiarise yourself with clients' names and check any records or referral letters about them. Then, when you go to ask your client to come in you are ready to focus solely on helping them.

Meeting, greeting and seating

Your helping session starts at the moment of first contact with the client. Skilled helpers possess good meeting, greeting and seating skills. Box 8.1 illustrates the difference between good and poor skills.

Box 8.1   Meeting, greeting and seating skills

Imagine two helpers, both of whose offices are near the waiting area, wanting to meet and greet clients for the first time.

Poor skills

Helper A, who has just had a emotionally draining session with a client, decides to see the next client without any break. Still feeling distracted by unfinished business from the previous client, Helper A opens the office door, peers out, takes a few steps in the direction of the waiting area and calls the next client's first name and surname correctly but without any warmth. When the client looks up, Helper A offers no further introduction and in a neutral voice says: 'Come this way please.' Helper A goes into the office first and, when the client enters, shuts the door and points to a chair and says 'That's for you'.

Good skills

Helper B calmly comes out of her/his office, goes over to the waiting area, smiles and calls out either the client's first name and surname or the client's first name alone depending on the nature of the helping setting. The client gets up and the helper introduces herself or himself along the lines of 'Hello, I'm ___ (states name). Please come this way' and then escorts the client to her/his office, smiles again as the client enters the office and then, with an open palm gesture, indicates where the client should sit and says 'Please sit down'.

Many counselling skills students require practice at becoming comfortable people for clients to meet from the moment of first contact. An issue that some students raise is whether or not to engage in small talk when first meeting clients. This is partly a matter of individual helper style. As long as the small talk is minimal and does not give the impression of a social relationship, it may humanise the meeting and greeting process. However, be sensitive to clients who are nervous about their conversational ability, those wanting to get straight into helping, and clients in crisis. Some helpers, for instance Dave Mearns and Brian Thorne (1988), consider small talk to be mostly detrimental. Many of the main messages of warmth, welcome and interest are best conveyed by helpers through good bodily communication.

Opening statements

Opening statements can have various functions: indicating the time dimensions of the helping session, checking 'where the client is at', and, if necessary, obtaining permission to record the session. Helpers are not all knowing. Opening remarks, openers or permissions to talk, are brief statements indicating that helpers are prepared to listen. Helpers start initial sessions with opening remarks that build rapport and encourage clients to share why they have come. You can leave until later a statement about how you work. Opening remarks are 'door openers' that give clients the message 'I'm interested and prepared to listen. Please share with me your internal perspective.' You are there to discover information about clients and to assist clients to discover information about themselves.

Be careful about using common opening remarks like 'How can I help you?' or 'What can I do for you?' Such remarks can get initial sessions off to unfortunate starts by connoting that clients are dependent on helpers rather than on helping themselves.

Remember that when making your opening remarks, your bodily and vocal communication is very important in indicating that you are a comfortable and trustworthy person with whom to talk. You are trying to create a safe emotional climate. Speak clearly and relatively slowly. Be comfortably seated yourself and look at your client. Avoid crossing your knees or arms. However, you can still sit with an open posture if you are crossing your ankles.

Good bodily and vocal communication can make it easier to obtain permission to record sessions. Counselling skills students who ask permission in nervous and hesitant ways are more likely to trigger doubts and resistances in clients than students who ask calmly and evenly.

Box 8.2   Opening statements

Acknowledging time boundaries
When the client is seated, you can first indicate the time boundaries of the session by saying something like 'We have about 40 minutes together' and then give a permission to talk.

Permissions to talk:
- 'Please tell me why you've come?'
- 'Please tell me what brings you here?'
- 'Please tell me what's concerning you?'
- 'Please tell me what's the problem?'
- 'Please put me in the picture?'
- 'Where would you like to start?'

Permission to talk acknowledging a referral
- 'You've been referred by __. Now how do you see your situation?'

Permission to talk responding to client's bodily communication:
- 'You seem upset . . . Would you care to say what's bothering you?'
- 'You seem nervous . . .'

Follow-up 'lubricating' comments:
- 'It's pretty hard to get started.'
- 'Take your time.'
- 'When you're ready.'

Permission to record a session:
Before giving a 'permission to talk' remark, you may need to get permission to record the session along the lines of the following statement:

> Would you mind if I videotaped this session for supervision purposes? Only my lecturer [*if relevant add, 'and counselling skills training group'*] will see the tape which will be scrubbed clean when it has been reviewed. If you wish we can turn the recorder off at any time.

Opening statements for use in informal helping include:
- 'Is there something on your mind?'
- 'You seem tense today?'
- 'I'm available if you want to talk.'

Sometimes, helpers may need to complete organisational require-ments for gathering basic information before giving clients permission to talk. However, be flexible: for instance, clients in crisis require psycho-logical comfort before bureaucratic form filling which can come later. On occasion, helpers may need to indicate the limitations of confi-dentiality surrounding the session: for example, the need to report to a third party or any legal limitations. In addition, helpers who take notes may offer brief initial explanations for so doing or even ask clients' permission.

Many readers have informal contacts with clients outside of formal helping sessions, for instance: correctional officers in facilities for delinquents; residential staff in half-way houses for former drug addicts; or nurses in hospitals. Here you may use permissions to talk when you sense that someone has a personal agenda that bothers them, but requires that extra bit of encouragement to share it. Some suggestions for opening statements for informal helping are provided in Box 8.2.

Dealing with difference

Some differences between helpers and clients become immediately obvious the moment they set eyes on one another: for example, race, gender, age and most physical disabilities. Other differences, such as culture, are less immediately obvious. Each case requires judging on its merits: for example, south Asians in Britain and south-east Asians in Australia are at varying degrees of assimilation to the host culture. One clue about whether clients come from different cultures can be found in their accents when speaking English. Still other helper–client differences are not apparent on the surface, for example sexual and affectionate orientation.

Should helpers acknowledge such differences right at the start of helping or wait until helping progresses and/or leave it to clients to bring up such issues? Furthermore, if you raise issues of helper–client difference, how do you go about it? One possibility is to directly acknowledge the difference at or near the start of helping and ask the client what they think about this. However, a risk of acknowledging difference right at the start is that this may not be 'where the client is at'. Such an acknowledgement may reflect more the helper's rather than the client's concerns and, hence, derail clients from revealing and exploring their internal perspectives. Another option is to hold back and see what the client's concerns are before acknowledging differences. However, with some clients and in some settings immediate acknowledgement of difference may be best.

A further option is, as clients start telling their stories, to invite them to assist you in understanding any aspects of their problems that may be influenced by differences between you. For example, a statement inviting attention to cultural issues might be: 'Cultural considerations can be important, so please help me to understand your culture when necessary.' Each client has a unique life history and way of interpreting the impact of their differences on how they function, so be careful not to pigeon-hole clients into your version of what their differences should mean. In addition, clients differ in the extent to which they are or have been victims of others' prejudices and of discriminatory structures and practices within institutions.

Dealing with reluctance and resistance

Resistances may be broadly defined as anything that gets in the way of helping. Resistances are clients' feelings, thoughts and communications that frustrate, impede, slow down and sometimes stop the helping process. Reluctance, which is unwillingness or disinclination on the part of potential or actual clients to enter into the helping process, is an aspect of being resistant about helping. Some clients do not see the need for help. They reluctantly come to meet others' wishes: for instance, children sent by teachers or parents, or substance abusers and perpetrators of domestic violence sent by the courts. At best most clients are ambivalent about coming for help. At the same time as wanting change, many may have anxieties about changing from their safe and known ways and also about the helping process: for instance, revealing personal information. Here my focus is on how to deal with reluctance and resistance right at the start of helping.

Counselling skills students and even experienced helpers can sustain and create clients' resistances through poor listening skills. By using good active listening skills, you can do much to build trust. Some clients manifest reluctance to be in helping by aggression. One approach to handling such aggression is to reflect it back locating the feelings clearly in the client, yet showing that you have picked them up loud and clear. Just showing clients that you have understood their internal perspectives and are not frightened by their negative feelings can encourage participation in helping.

Unlike with helper–client difference where it may be best to hold back, if you detect significant reservations about being in helping it may be best to bring this agenda out in the open and give clients permission to elaborate. For instance, you might say 'It seems pretty clear to me that you do not want to be here. If I'm right I'm wondering what specifically upsets you about coming?' You can then use your active listening skills to help them articulate their thoughts and feelings.

You may lessen reluctance if you can help clients identify reasons for being in helping. For example, you may listen to complaints about others and then help clients to see that, however valid their complaints may be, they are still left with the problem of how best to relate to these people. Questions that encourage clients to think about goals may be useful: for instance, 'What are your goals in the situation?' and 'How is your behaviour helping you get what you want?'

Helpers require sensitivity to the pace at which different clients can develop the trust required for a good working alliance. Clients who feel pressured by helpers may become even more resistant and reinforce rather than lower their defences. Flexibility, realism and tact are important attributes for dealing with reluctant and resistant clients.

Summarising skills

Summaries are brief helper statements about longer excerpts from helping sessions. Summaries pull together, clarify and reflect back different parts of a series of client statements either during a discussion unit, at the end of a discussion unit, or at the beginning or end of helping sessions.

Here I focus on helper summaries in the relating stage. Where possible, helper summaries serve to move the session forward. Such summaries may mirror back to clients segments of what they have said, check and clarify understanding, identify themes, problem areas and problem situations. Summaries may serve other purposes as well. If clients have had a lengthy period of talking, helpers can summarise to establish their presence and make the helping conversation more two-way. Furthermore, if clients tell their stories very rapidly, helpers may deliver summaries at a measured speech rate to calm clients down.

When clients tell why they have come for helping, you may use summaries that reflect whole units of communication. Such summaries tie together the main feeling and content of what clients say. Basic reflection summaries serve a bridging function for clients enabling them to continue with the same topic or move on to another. Other functions include making sure helpers listen accurately, rewarding clients and clarifying your own and their understanding. A variation of the basic reflection summary is the reflecting feelings and reasons summary that links emotions with their perceived causes.

Another useful summarising skill for early in helping is to be able to provide an overview of different problem areas. Imagine that a client comes to seek your assistance and starts describing a number of different problems. Identification of problem area summaries can provide clients with clearer statements than they managed on their own. Furthermore, such summaries can provide a basis for asking clients to prioritise either which problem is most important or which they want to focus on first. Box 8.3 provides examples of summarising statements.

Box 8.3   Examples of summaries

Basic reflection summary

Teacher to student: You hate being bullied both physically and verbally. You think the other boys are ganging up on you and pushing and shoving you around. You don't like their snide taunts and you also think they gossip about you behind your back. Your relationship with that group of boys has got to the point where you speak to them only if absolutely necessary. You don't think it a good idea to complain to the staff, because that might only make matters worse.

> **Identification of problem areas summary**
> *Relationship counsellor to client:* You started talking about your problems with Mohammed over his being reluctant to spend time with your parents. You then moved on to talk about the effects of your recent redundancy on your relationship – your having less money as a couple and how you do not like being so dependent on him. You then moved on to talking about how, for some time, your sex life together has been less than satisfactory for both of you. You also expressed some dissatisfaction with Mohammed not being prepared to pull his weight around the home even when you still had a job.

Who summarises can be an issue. Generally, in the relating state of helping it is probably better for the helper to do the summarising. Clients are still finding their feet and appreciate helpers making it as easy as possible for them to share their internal perspectives. In the understanding and changing stages, there may be occasions where clients can be invited to summarise: for instance, when checking their understanding of a helping strategy.

Structuring skills

Helping sessions are new experiences for many clients. Helpers can try to make the helping process more comprehensible and less threatening. Structuring entails explaining the helping process to clients. Structuring is conveyed by bodily and vocal as well as by verbal communication. It can occur in each of the three stages of the RUC helping process model. However, here I only cover structuring statements pertinent to the relating stage.

The relating stage may only last the first 10 to 15 minutes of an initial helping session. Nevertheless, it is probably best to structure in two statements, an opening statement and a follow-up statement, rather than do it all at the beginning. If you offer the whole explanation at the beginning, you may fail to respond to clients who want emotional release or to share information with you.

In phased structuring, your opening statement provides the first occasion for structuring. Here you can establish time boundaries and the understanding that the client's main role for the time being is to talk and your main role is to help the client to do this.

Your second or follow-up structuring statement comes after clients have had an initial chance to say why they have come. Here you briefly and simply explain the helping process to them. Box 8.4 provides two follow-up structuring statements providing a framework for the helping process model used in the book. The first statement is where the client clearly has only one main problem and the second statement is where the client has presented with more than one problem. If a specific situation has not already emerged, your follow-up statement requests clients to identify a situation within a main problem area for your work together.

Box 8.4   Examples of structuring statements

Opening statement:

> We have about 40 minutes together, please tell me why you've come?

Possible follow-up statements:
(a) Single problem

> You've given me some idea why you have come. Now since time is limited, I wonder if together we can select a specific situation within your problem (specify) that we can work on. I will help you to understand the situation more fully and then we can examine strategies for dealing better with it. Is that okay with you?

(b) More than one problem
After making an identification of problem areas summary, the helper says:

> Which of these would you like to focus on? [The client states her or his choice.] Good. Now I wonder if we can identify a particular situation within this problem that it is important for you to manage better. Then we can explore this situation more fully and perhaps come up with some useful strategies for dealing with it. Is that all right with you?

Structuring can strengthen the helper–client working alliance by establishing an agenda or goal for the helping process as well as obtaining agreement on how to proceed. You may need to help clients choose a particular situation to work on that is important for them. You may also need to respond to questions. However, do not allow yourself to be seduced into an intellectual discussion of the helping process. If you make your structuring statements in a comfortable and confident way, most clients will be happy to work within the framework that you are suggesting.

Starting the helping process

We have now covered many of the skills for beginning the initial session. The last chapter covered active listening skills such as good bodily and vocal attending behaviour, paraphrasing, reflecting feelings and using small verbal rewards and open-ended questions. This chapter has reviewed opening statements, dealing with difference, reluctance and resistance, summarising and structuring. Box 8.5 puts many of these skills together in an abbreviated example of the relating stage of the RUC helping process model. The helper assists the client to tell his story and then selects a problem situation for their further work. The setting is a college counselling centre.

Those counselling skills students training in counselling skills as part of other roles or in informal helping are asked to alter the way the relating stage is presented so as to be maximally useful for your future helping work. Furthermore, even students training to be counsellors should start by conducting mock 10 to 15 minute interviews just focusing on the relating stage.

Box 8.5   Example of the relating stage

Helper: We have about 40 minutes. Would you please tell me why you've come?

Client: Well it's not an easy thing for me to talk about . . .

Helper: Take your time . . .

Client: My friend suggested I come to the counselling service.

Helper: Your friend made the suggestion, but why did you choose to come?

Client: My problem is that I'm extremely shy.

Helper: Can you tell me more?

Client: That's my problem . . . I have difficulty opening up to people.

Helper: So it's hard letting people get to know you, including me.

Client: Yes . . . but I want to change. My mum is a shy person and I think I am rather like her. Dad's more hearty, but he is away on business much of the time.

Helper: You'd really like to become more outgoing.

Client: I'm getting worried now that my shyness is going to hold me back in life. Right now I get very lonely because I'm living away from home and find it difficult to make friends.

Helper: You feel isolated now and concerned about your future if you stay withdrawn.

Client: I'm 20 and want to have a girlfriend.

Helper: You think it's high time for you to be dating.

Client: That's it. I see girls that I fancy, but just don't see how any of them could be interested in me.

Helper: So you have doubts about your attractiveness to women.

Client: Yes. It's not as though I'm bad looking, but I just lose confidence around women.

Helper: You feel your courage deserts you round women you fancy.

Client: I also have difficulty talking with my classmates.

Helper: Uh-hum . . . Can you say more?

Client: It's both when we are in the canteen and in class. I just seem to clamp up. I do have things I'd like to say, but get frightened about what others will think.

Helper: You feel terrified about saying the wrong thing and so keep a low profile. Can I summarise the ground we have covered so far?

Client: Okay.

Helper: Right now you're lonely and worried that your shyness will cause you to miss out in life. You have difficulty socialising with your classmates, hold back on participating in class, and are bashful and under-confident with women. You want to change to become more outgoing. Is that about right?

Client: Yes . . . but can you help me?

Helper: You mentioned three problem areas: dating, socialising with classmates and participating in class. Are there any others?

Client: Those are the main ones.

Helper: Well let's select a specific situation that it is important for you to manage better in one of these areas. Then we can explore this situation more fully and perhaps come up with some useful strategies for dealing with it. Is that all right by you?

Client: But where to start . . .

Helper: Pick a situation that you can work on in the near future that may not be too difficult for you.

Client: Okay, I'd like to start with participating more in class.

Helper: Can you identify a specific situation?

Client: Yes. I hold back in my tutorial group.

Empowering your mind

At the start of practice helping sessions, some counselling skills students put much extra pressure on themselves by creating unhelpful as contrasted with helpful thoughts. Here I review three common mind skills deficiencies of beginning students.

Creating self-talk

When you are feeling a little unsure of yourself it is very easy to feel even more unsure if you start telling yourself negative statements. For example, when starting helping sessions with 'clients' you may tell yourself: 'I am going to make a mess of this', 'I don't know enough to perform competently' and 'My counselling skills are poor'. In addition, if you start getting more anxious, you may tell yourself that: 'The situation is going to get out of control', 'The client will notice how anxious I am', and 'My anxiety is going to make my counselling skills even worse'.

Already I have suggested that you come for your helping sessions early so that you give yourself time to get prepared. During this period, you can create statements that calm you down: for instance, 'calm down', 'take a few slow deep breaths' and 'take it easy'. Such calming statements have value in their own right and not only as correctives to negative self-talk.

In addition, you can coach yourself in listening skills that help take the pressure off you. Many students find instructing themselves: to 'Speak slowly and clearly' useful since this self-talk creates both a relaxed atmosphere and more time to think. You can also coach yourself to 'Give the client space to tell her/his story' rather than pressure the client because I am anxious.'

Creating rules

Counselling skills students can stress themselves if they possess perfectionist rules along the lines of 'I must perform perfectly', 'I must be as good as all my classmates' and 'I must learn counselling skills immediately'. In addition, some students create rules demanding others' approval like 'My clients must approve of me' and 'My peers must approve of me' and 'My trainer must approve of me'.

Like the counselling skills trainers mentioned in Chapter 2, you can have either demanding rules or preferential rules. I encourage you to detect and challenge any demanding rules. Illustrative questions you can ask yourself include: 'Is there such a thing as perfection?', 'Why should I as a learner of counselling skills expect that I exhibit a high level of competence right away?' and 'Why is it vital that my clients approve of me?' You can then substitute a preferential for a demanding rule: for instance, 'The perfect is the enemy of the good' might be substituted for the rule 'I must perform perfectly'. Such a mental change can contribute to your feeling and communicating in a more relaxed way in helping sessions.

Creating explanations

Another way that counselling skills students pressure themselves is by assuming too much responsibility for the success of helping. The late Carl Rogers had great faith in the client's intrinsic tendencies towards personal growth if given the right helper-offered conditions. Even if you are not so optimistic about human nature as Rogers, you can still acknowledge that clients have both a right and a responsibility to make the most of their lives. Your job is to help clients develop their potential and cope better with their problems and problem situations rather than to take over their lives.

Sometimes, I have had to help very well-intentioned counselling skills students to see the limits of their responsibility to clients. Students can relax and help clients more when they acknowledge that helping is a cooperative endeavour in which the best that helpers can do is to offer competence rather than guaranteed results. Clients have to help themselves too. Also, there are many environmental factors in clients' lives that may influence the success of helping.

Summary

Starting the helping process varies according to whether you use counselling skills informally, as part of other roles, or as counsellors. Good preparation is important. Many messages are sent out about how user-friendly helping services are in their advertising and how they respond to phone calls. Friendly and efficient receptionists and welcoming waiting areas are important. Take time to set up interview rooms and relax yourself before greeting clients. Go over to clients, use their names, escort them to your office, and politely show them where to sit.

Opening statements can indicate the time available and invite clients to say why they have come. Helpers working in informal settings can also develop opening statements that give clients the chance to talk. Helpers can deal with obvious differences between them and their clients either immediately, after waiting to see whether clients are concerned about them, or by inviting clients to assist them in understanding how their differences impact on their problems. One option for helpers with reluctant and resistant clients is to bring this out into the open and give clients permission to elaborate. Helpers require sensitivity to the pace at which clients are comfortable working so as not to create unnecessary resistances.

Summaries pull together different parts of a series of client utterances during or at the end of a discussion unit. In the relating stage, helper summaries can reflect feelings and identify problem areas. Structuring entails explaining the helping process to clients. It is probably best to structure in two statements, an opening statement and a follow-up statement, rather than do it all at the beginning. In meeting, greeting and seating clients, making opening statements, summarising and structuring, good bodily and vocal communication contributes greatly to creating safe emotional climates for clients. In the relating stage helpers use active listening and getting started skills to assist clients to tell their story and then select a problem situation for their further work.

At the start of practice helping sessions some counselling skills students put extra pressure on themselves through poor mind skills. Students can empower their minds by creating calming and coaching self-talk rather than negative self-talk, preferential rather than demanding rules, and by acknowledging the limits of their responsibility for the success of helping. More realistic thinking can contribute to students feeling and communicating in helping sessions in more relaxed ways.

Activities

Activity 8.1   Starting helping sessions

If appropriate, readers who work in informal settings should please adapt this exercise to suit your circumstances. In addition, those training to use counselling skills for roles other than as counsellors, can adapt the exercise for maximum relevance.

Part A   Meeting, greeting and seating

Role-play with a partner meeting a client in a waiting area, showing them to your office, and getting them seated – see Box 8.1 for suggestions. Then hold a feedback and discussion session and, if necessary, do more role-plays until you feel confident about your performance. Afterwards, reverse roles.

Part B   Making an opening statement

Role-play with a partner making an opening statement – see Box 8.2 for suggestions. Then hold a feedback and discussion session and, if necessary, do more role-plays until you feel confident about your performance. Afterwards, reverse roles.

Part C   Combining meeting, greeting and seating and making an opening statement

Role-play with a partner meeting a client in a waiting area, showing them to your office, getting them seated and making an opening statement. Then hold a feedback and discussion session and, if necessary, do more role-plays until you feel confident about your performance. Afterwards, reverse roles.

Part D   Issues for discussion

- the role of small talk when first meeting clients;
- how best to deal with clients different from you;
- how to handle reluctant and resistant clients.

Activity 8.2   Practising relating stage skills

Work with a partner. Each of you thinks of an area in your personal or work life that you are prepared to share in role-playing the relating stage of an initial session. Alternatively, you can role-play a client with a genuine concern. One of you acts as client. The helper conducts an interview of up to 15 minutes using the following skills:

- preparation skills, for instance setting up the room and any recording equipment;
- meeting, greeting and seating;
- making an opening statement;
- active listening;
- as appropriate, dealing with difference, reluctance and resistance;
- structuring; and
- summarising.

By the end of this relating stage section of the interview, the helper should have assisted the client in identifying a specific situation for your future work together (see Box 8.5). After the relating stage session, hold a feedback and discussion session, possibly illustrated by going through a videotape or audio tape of the session. After a suitable interval, reverse roles.

Activity 8.3   Empowering my mind for starting helping sessions

Part A   Creating self-talk

1   Identify any negative self-talk that you may use when starting an initial helping session with a new client.

2   Create two each of:
    • calming self-talk statements;
    • coaching self-talk statements.
3   Rehearse and practise putting together your calming and coaching self-talk statements so that you feel more comfortable when getting started with a new client.

Part B   Creating rules

1   Identify any unrealistic or demanding rules you may be creating that put extra pressure on you when starting an initial helping session with a new client.
2   For each of these rules:
    • challenge and question it;
    • create a preferential rule which you substitute for the demanding rule.
3   Rehearse and practise telling yourself your preferential rule(s) so that you feel more comfortable when getting started with a new client.

Part C   Creating explanations

1   Do you tend to assume too much of the responsibility for the success of helping when starting an initial helping session with a new client?
2   If so:
    • challenge and question your explanation(s) for the success of helping;
    • replace any unrealistic with more realistic explanations about why helping may or may not be successful.
3   Rehearse and practise telling yourself your more realistic explanation(s) so that you feel more comfortable when getting started with a new client.

PART 3

THE UNDERSTANDING STAGE

9   Clarifying Understanding

A matter that becomes clear ceases to concern us.
Friedrich Nietzsche

Chapter outcomes

By studying and doing the activities in this chapter you should be able to:

- *know some purposes for clarifying understanding;*
- *be aware of some cautions about using questions in helping;*
- *realise the importance of ensuring that clients retain ownership of problem situations;*
- *possess better skills at asking questions about feelings, physical reactions, thoughts and communication/actions;*
- *understand the importance of interspersing active listening with questions; and*
- *develop some skills of empowering your mind for clarifying understanding.*

Welcome to stage 2 of the relating–understanding–changing (RUC) helping process model. In stage 1, the relating stage, you lay the foundation of your working alliance with clients. You build your relationship with clients by allowing them to tell their stories and share their internal perspectives. During this process you act as a comfortable companion who reduces the threat inherent in initial helping sessions and informal helping contacts so that clients feel more confident about 'levelling' or sharing their real agendas with you. You are in a receptive listening mode and hold back on probing clients to any great extent. Even if they come with just one problem situation, you make it easy for them to talk about this rather than get them responding to questions from you. If clients come with multiple problems, you ask them to choose in which area they want to focus and then encourage them to identify a specific problem situation in it for your future work.

In stage 2, the understanding stage, you maintain your emphasis on maintaining good relationships with clients. An axiom throughout helping is RELATE OR PERISH. However, in stage 2, helpers move the helping process forward by clarifying both the client's and their own understanding of the targeted problem situation. Staying in clients' internal perspectives, you help them to develop fuller pictures of problem situations than they would have developed alone.

Frequently clients only look at part of the picture when thinking of problem situations. Emotions may cloud thought processes. In addition, sometimes significant others in clients' lives have vested interests in preventing them from formulating their own versions of reality. Clients may gain approval only if they anaesthetise or distort how they truly view situations. On their own, clients may find it difficult to gain the kind of detached perspective they can often attain with skilled and supportive assistance. In stage 2, helpers can calmly and fairly systematically assist clients to think more clearly about problem situations.

Cautions about questioning clients

One of the hardest tasks of most introductory counselling skills trainers is to ensure that students remain focused on meeting their clients' needs rather than their own. There is a great danger that, when students are given permission to question clients, they revert to previous modes of relating and lose some if not all of their active listening skills. Students may fall into one of a number of traps, two of which I mention here. In the social trap, counselling skills students go back to dealing with clients' problems in the same way that they might deal with friends' problems by both asking questions and giving advice from their own perspectives. In the medical trap, counselling skills students mimic a physician 'help set' that puts clients in passive receptive positions (Brammer and McDonald, 1996). Students ask questions to form diagnoses about clients' problems which may then be followed by treatment suggestions.

Questions have the potential to damage helping relationships, sometimes beyond repair. Clients resent being interrogated from helpers' frames of reference rather than understood from their own. For example, insufficiently skilled helpers may ask a series of questions, scarcely listen to the answers, and then go off on another tangent whether or not clients see this as relevant. In addition, clients resent intrusive questioning about sensitive personal material. Furthermore, by clumsily taking control helpers can create resistances and anger. Even if clients appear acquiescent, helpers may have encouraged their dependency rather than helping them assume responsibility for their lives.

Sometimes questioning can make the helping process too intellectual. Helping is often messy and virtually all clients' problems are emotionally tinged. Trying to tie everything up into neat little bundles is highly inappropriate. Another risk in questioning is that of failing to adjust the nature of the questions to the client. For example, emotionally expressive helpers, often women, require sensitivity in probing emotionally inexpressive clients, often men, about their feelings. Conversely, inexpressive helpers may pay insufficient attention to the feelings of expressive clients. In addition, helpers always require sensitivity to cultural differences regarding who can ask questions to whom and about how to do it.

The relevance of the above cautions to counselling skills training is that students should start by questioning clients sparingly and never engage in unnecessarily intrusive questioning. Whatever the length of the introductory skills course, it is imperative that students learn to keep the focus of helping relationships on clients. Trainers should be ready to rein students' tendencies to question too much and listen too little. In addition, trainers should help students to realise that, if they can create safe emotional climates, clients will reveal more and deeper information, often without having to be asked.

Who 'owns' problem situations?

In the last chapter I mentioned that sometimes counselling skills students assume too much of the burden for the success of helping and are at risk of taking over clients' problems and lives. Ensuring that clients continue to 'own' their problems and problem situations is a major way that students can minimise the dangers of too much or too clumsy questioning. Ownership entails clients in retaining the main responsibility for doing something about their situations. Students and helpers can assist clients to fulfil this responsibility, but they cannot and should not do it for them. Box 9.1 illustrates the difference between helper and client ownership of a problem situation. In the negative example I use exaggeration to make the point about using questions to control and dominate clients.

Box 9.1   Helper and client ownership of problem situations

The problem situation

The client Pat, a single mum, comes to helping about her uneasy relationship with Andy, her 15-year-old son. One area of the problem is that Pat wants Andy to do more household chores. The specific situation that the client wishes to work on is how to ask Andy to mow the lawn once a week. Pat has recently made an unsuccessful request for Andy to do this job.

Helper owns the problem situation

Bossy Boots Bobbie/Bob is a helper whose attitude towards clients is 'Don't worry. I know what's best for you.' Bobbie/Bob fires off a series of questions at Pat emphasising the word 'why', including: 'Why doesn't Andy do what you want?', 'Why should you do so much for him?', 'Why don't young people these days show more gratitude?' and 'Why don't you tell Andy that if he does not cooperate with you, you are going to stop giving him his pocket money?' When Pat attempts to provide answers to the questions, Bobbie/Bob gives the impression that both her answers in the helping session and her performance at home are just not good enough. Bossy Boots Bobbie/Bob wants to make sure Pat follows her/his advice on dealing with Andy.

Helper assists client to own the problem situation

In the relating stage, Helpful Harriet/Harry allowed Pat to share her concerns over how Andy is turning out. Now, in the understanding stage, Harriet/Harry acts as a companion to Pat as she explores her feelings, physical reactions, thoughts and communication in relation to asking Andy to mow the lawn once a week. Harriet/Harry attempts to create a safe emotional climate in which Pat can volunteer information without having to be asked all the time. Many of Harriet/Harry's questions to Pat emphasise the words 'how' and 'what': for instance, 'How did you feel when Andy refused?', 'How did you make the previous request?', 'What goes through your mind when you make requests of Andy?' and 'What strengths do you have for dealing with the situation?' Harriet/Harry intersperses active listening responses with her/his questions. All of Helpful Harriet/Harry's verbal, vocal and bodily communications show respect for Pat's right to find her own solution to handling the situation.

Questioning skills

How do you go about assisting clients to get a fuller understanding of problem situations? Without being too regimented, you and the client engage in a process of systematic inquiry about different aspects or 'angles' of the situations. However, when learning how to question, I urge students to err on the side of asking too few rather than too many questions. Once you get more skilled at asking a few well-chosen questions within the context of comfortable helping relationships, then you can gradually build up the number of questions you ask, but never to the point where you overwhelm and depower clients. On short introductory counselling skills courses, the most you will probably have time for is to become skilled at asking a few good questions that clarify and elaborate clients' internal perspectives.

If you learn to use questions to clarify problem situations skilfully, clients may feel more understood by you than if you had only used active listening skills. Clients may also think that they understand themselves and 'what's going on' in problem situations better. Of course, the reverse is also true if you question clumsily.

Types of questions

Below are some types of questions helpers can use to clarify problems in addition to open ended questions.

Specific detail questions
When clients mull over problem situations alone they may think in vague terms and miss out significant aspects of the overall picture. Specific detail questions aim to collect concrete information about the how, what, when and where of clients' problem situations. You can also ask for specific examples.

'How' questions   are very useful for eliciting details of how clients feel, physically react, think, communicate or act: for example, 'How do/did you feel/think/act?' When examining communication, remember to ask 'how' questions about vocal and bodily as well as verbal communication. In addition, you can ask how questions that highlight patterns of communication: for example, 'When you say that, how does s/he react?'

Especially for clarifying communication, *show me how* questions can illuminate what actually happened: for example, 'Would you mind showing me how you actually spoke to . . .?' Alternatively, you can suggest a mini role-play: for instance, 'Imagine I am . . . show me how you behave to me in the situation.'

'What' questions   are often similar in purpose to 'how' questions: for example, 'What do/did you feel/think/do?' is virtually the same as 'How do/did you feel/think/act?' 'What' questions can also have value in their own right: for example, 'What happened?' or 'What were the consequences of doing that?'

'When' questions   try to pinpoint temporal aspects of problem situations: for example, 'When did it last happen?' and 'When will it next happen?'

'Where' questions   are useful for eliciting details about the physical context of problem situations: for example, 'Describe where it happens?'

'Specific example' questions   can clarify problem situations by eliciting specific instances rather than talking in circular terms around situations: for instance, 'Can you give me a specific example of . . .?'

Personal meanings questions

You can relate more deeply with clients if you go beyond facts to search for their interpretations and perceptions. The information clients provide often has personal or symbolic meanings for them. For example, partners who do not receive flowers on their birthday may or may not think that this symbolises lack of love. Eliciting personal meanings questions should be open and tentative since clients should, but not always will, know the answers better than anyone else. Illustrative questions include: 'I'm wondering what the meaning of . . . is for you?', 'What do you make of that?' and 'Why is . . . so important for you?'

Identifying strengths questions

Often clients with problems lose sight of their strengths and coping resources. In addition, they may have difficulty remembering and mobilising the help of supportive people. Helping interviews can become overly negative. Allen Ivey (1994) observes that clients grow from their strengths. He uses the term positive asset search to describe searching for clients' strengths. Illustrative identifying strengths questions include: 'What do you see as your strengths?', 'What are your assets?', 'What skills could you bring to this situation?' and 'Are there any people who might be supportive of you?'

Areas for questions

In the relating stage, whether or not clients come with specific problem situations, you use active listening skills to give them considerable space to tell their stories. Then you can make a structuring statement that allows you to examine the chosen problem situation in more detail. For instance, you can say that you will help the client to understand the situation more fully prior to examining strategies for coping better with it. The relating stage may have generated some information about the situation since the boundaries between the relating and understanding stages can be fluid. However, in the understanding stage, you move from a main emphasis on active listening to a main emphasis on fairly systematic inquiry. I insert the word fairly before systematic because you are not taking clients through a set interview protocol, but rather ensuring you and the client possess information about the main dimensions of situations.

When questioning, flexibly adapt the order and wording of your questions. For instance, six important categories of questions are: background information, feelings, physical reactions, mind, communication/actions, and a catch-all category for other questions that seem relevant in the circumstances. As long as you and your client cover the ground, you can do it in the order that seems most appropriate at the time. My own inclination is to start with asking questions about clients' feelings to enhance their sense that I understand them, but this is not a hard and fast rule.

Four areas of questions always worth asking relate to clients' feelings, physical reactions, mind and communication/actions in regard to problem situations. Box 9.2 lists some possible questions you might ask in each of these areas. In addition, if not covered already in the relating stage, you can ask questions about the background of the problem situation, such as 'Since when has it been bothering you?' and 'Have you ever sought help for this problem/problem situation before?' In the catch-all category, if relevant, you might ask such questions as: 'Are there any current stresses in your life that impact on the situation?' and 'Are you taking medication?'

Box 9.2   Examples of clarifying understanding questions

Feelings:
- 'How do you feel in the situation?'
- 'When you say you get ___ [specify feeling], how exactly do you feel?'

- 'On a scale of 1 to 10, how strong is the feeling?'
- 'When do you feel ___? Is it before, during or after the situation?'
- 'How confident are you about handling the situation?'

Physical reactions:
- 'What happens to your body when you feel ___ [specify feeling]?'
- 'Can you describe how you react physically more fully?'
- 'Where exactly do you feel the tension in your body?'

Mind:
- 'What goes through your mind before/during/after the situation?'
- 'Can you take me in slow motion through your thoughts regarding the situation?'
- 'What are you afraid of?'
- 'How frequently do you get those thoughts?'
- 'How do you see the situation?'

Communication/actions:
- 'How do you communicate when in the situation?'
- 'What do you actually say?'
- 'What happens to your voice?'
- 'What body language do you use?'
- 'How have you attempted to cope in the past?'
- 'How do you back up your words with actions?'

At the end of a series of questions such as those in Box 9.2, both helpers and clients should have fuller and clearer pictures of the nature and key dimensions of problem situations. Helpers might ask further questions depending on the answers clients provide. In addition, during the clarifying understanding process, both helpers and clients should start getting some ideas about how to approach problem situations differently. Helpers can ask additional exploratory questions to confirm or negate ideas about how clients may be sustaining problems.

Interspersing active listening with questions

Sometimes in counselling skills classes, I would seat helper and client side by side to indicate the kind of working together relationship desirable in helping. In the understanding stage you are both moving toward the common goal of helping one another understand the problem situation more fully. You are detectives on the look out for relevant information and clues concerning what makes situations into problems for clients.

Helpers require clients' cooperation to conduct the understanding stage. If you can establish a safe and comfortable emotional climate clients are likely to reveal much more both in answer to your questions and of their own accord. Not only will they feel freer with you, they will also be more comfortable about acknowledging to themselves their own thoughts, feelings and experiencing.

Clients feel interrogated when helpers ask a series of questions in quick succession. You can greatly soften your questioning if you pause to see if clients wish to continue responding and then reflect each response. Interspersing active listening has the added advantage of ensuring that you check the accuracy of your understanding. Box 9.3 illustrates the difference between interrogation and interspersing active listening with questions. Though these are only short excerpts, the first shows the helper controlling and dominating the client. In the second excerpt, the helper facilitates Beth's description of her internal perspective. The emotional climate in the first excerpt is 'in the head'. In the second excerpt Beth is encouraged to share her experiencing of her feelings and physical reactions.

Box 9.3 Interspersing active listening with questions

Problem situation

Beth, a 34 year old mature student, comes to her helper worried about failing her undergraduate psychology course. The particular situation that she chooses to focus on is an upcoming statistics exam in two weeks' time.

Interrogation

Beth: I'm getting very anxious over my upcoming statistics exam.
Helper: What makes you so anxious?
Beth: The fact that I may fail.
Helper: What makes you think that you will fail?
Beth: I find the subject difficult and boring. I'm bad at maths too.
Helper: Why are you so afraid of failing?
Beth: Because then it will be harder to get a counselling job.
Helper: What sort of counselling job do you want?

Interspersing active listening with questions

Beth: I'm getting very anxious over my upcoming statistics exam.
Helper: You're increasingly worried about your stats exam . . . Can you tell me more about how you're experiencing your anxiety?
Beth: Yes, I get tense just thinking about it, especially in my chest.
Helper: Tension in your chest . . . how bad is this on a scale of 1 to 10?
Beth: It fluctuates. It started around two or three, but as the exam gets closer sometimes it's six or seven.

Helper: So the tension is getting really uncomfortable. Are there any other feelings or physical reactions connected with the exam?

Beth: I'm not sleeping well and listless much of the time. I've never felt this anxious before.

Helper: It's really getting to you and affecting your sleep and energy level too.

Note that the interrogating helper in Box 9.3 engages in jack-rabbiting or quickly hopping from one topic to another. Always listen carefully to and respect what clients have just said. Frequently, your next question can follow on from and encourage clients to build upon their last response. Questioning that is logically linked to clients' responses creates, a feeling of working together rather than of the session being directed by you.

How you question is very important in addition to what you say. For example, clients may feel overwhelmed if your voice is loud and harsh. If you use little eye contact and have a stiff body posture, they may also feel less inclined to answer your questions. When questioning use good volume, articulation, pitch, emphasis and speech rate. Furthermore, have your body messages clearly showing your interest in clients' answers.

Summarising information from questions

In the understanding stage, helper questions seek to 'flush out' details of clients' problem situations. For instance, in addition to her feelings, physical reactions and thoughts, relevant information for clients like Beth with statistics exam anxiety include: what statistics background she has prior to joining the course, how much she understands the concepts, how caught up she is on course assignments, what revision she has done, how good her revising and exam taking skills are, what her skills at getting help from lecturers and fellow students are, how strong a student she is in this and other subjects, and what other course and personal stresses she is under.

Helpers can choose to summarise information along the way: for instance, a summary each for feelings/physical reactions, thoughts and communication/actions. In addition, they can provide a clarification of problem situation summary that pulls together significant information that they and clients have generated. Box 9.4 provides an example of summarising a client's problem situation, namely that of client Pat in relation to her son Andy first introduced in Box 9.1.

Box 9.4   Summarising a client's problem situation

The problem situation
The client Pat, a single mum, comes for help about her uneasy relationship with Andy, her 15-year-old son. One area of the problem is that Pat wants Andy to do more household chores. The specific situation that the client wishes to work on is how to ask Andy to mow the lawn once a week. Pat has recently made an unsuccessful request for Andy to do this job.

Summary to clarify understanding
Well Pat, I think it might be helpful if I tried to pull together the ground we have covered so far. Basically you love Andy, are proud of him and think he's a good kid. However, you get very anxious over asserting yourself with him by requesting that he does jobs like mowing the lawn. You tense up before you ask him and feel resentful when he does not cooperate. You also tense up because you are afraid that you might lose some of his affection to his Dad who gives you no support in disciplining him. When you tense up you feel this in your neck and get red flushes in your neck and face. You want Andy to behave more like an adult and think that the time has come to stop mollycoddling him. You think Andy is afraid that if he gives a little ground in doing jobs for you he will be overwhelmed by more requests.

When we looked at how you actually communicated with Andy, it seemed as though rather than make a direct request along the lines of 'Please mow the lawn once a week', you blurred it by saying 'Why don't you mow the lawn?' Your voice was not particularly firm and you probably made insufficient eye contact. Then, when Andy turned you down, you sulked and whiningly told him he did not appreciate how much you did for him. Is that about right?

An issue that will almost invariably arise is how it is possible to remember significant information generated by questions for summarising at the end of the understanding stage. One option is to take brief notes discreetly throughout the asking questions process. For instance, you could take an A4 pad and put four subheadings – feelings, physical reactions, mind, communication/actions – at intervals down the page, and when relevant information emerges write it down.

Many counselling skills students dislike taking notes since they fear it blocks their relationships with clients. Probably it is best to start learning how to question without the added burden of learning how to take notes. If on a short introductory counselling skills course, you will have little time to learn about taking notes. Furthermore, if you see clients in informal contacts, taking notes is probably inappropriate.

Note-taking in initial helping sessions enables many experienced helpers to be more, not less, psychologically present to clients since it relieves pressure on them to memorise information. For example, when the time comes to discuss strategies for change, then they have a written record to which they can refer back.

Develop skills of taking notes unobtrusively and of knowing when it is important to show clients undivided attention with your bodily communication. For those of you doing mock interviews on medium-length to longer introductory counselling skills courses, once you have had some experience of questioning without taking notes, give jotting down important points a try, rather than dismissing it out of hand.

Empowering your mind

Thinking skilfully is critical to questioning skilfully. I now illustrate how your mind can interfere with or enhance how you clarify under-standing.

Creating self-talk

Some counselling skills students become tense when it comes to the understanding stage. In the relating stage, clients' statements feed them material with which to respond. In the understanding stage, students have to initiate as well as respond. To counteract tension, you can create calming self-talk statements like 'Relax' and 'Take it easy' to ease the pressure you are putting on yourself.

Creating coaching self-talk statements can also assist you both to feel more relaxed and to question more competently. For example, statements like 'Remember to intersperse active listening with ques-tions' and 'Draw out clients and build on their contributions' may each be helpful. Sometimes, coaching self-talk can become cautionary self-talk: for example, 'I need to resist my tendencies to adopt a medical approach to questioning'. You can also create coaching self-talk that focuses on specific aspects of your vocal and bodily communication: for example, 'Speak calmly and clearly' and 'Avoid staring at clients during and after asking questions'.

Creating visual images

Imagine a jackbooted helper interrogating a client and saying 'Ve have vays of making you talk!' A more profitable alternative to imagining cruel incompetence is to visually rehearse yourself as a helper asking a client clarifying understanding questions with calm and relaxed verbal, vocal and bodily communication. Focus on imagining competent performance rather than on being perfect.

Many of your clients' responses to questions will generate in your mind visual impressions of their lives outside helping. Your mental pictures may be of varying degrees of accuracy and may be heavily coloured by your own prior experiencing. You may jump to erroneous pictorial conclusions about clients' behaviour. When clarifying understanding, obtain as clear a picture of clients' communication in problem situations as possible. 'Show me how . . .' questions are useful for this purpose. By observing demonstrations, you are likely to form better pictures of actual verbal, vocal and bodily communication than if relying on verbal description alone.

Some material clients describe cannot be role-played in helping sessions, for example a description of poor accommodation. Here you can ask follow-up questions that encourage clients to fill in your picture of poor accommodation rather than construct a pictorial fantasy that may be wrong. Just becoming aware that you create visual images about clients' outside lives and problem situations is a starting point for being more rigorous about the accuracy of these images.

Creating rules

Counselling skills students and helpers can possess demanding rather than preferential rules relevant to clarifying understanding. Examples of unhelpful rules concerning questioning include: 'I must be the expert', 'I must be in control of the session at all times' and 'I must discover everything about the client's problem situation'.

A challenge to being the expert is that the clients are more likely to be the experts on details of their thoughts, feelings and experiences than you. Furthermore, as an introduction to counselling skills student you are a beginner rather than an expert. A challenge to being in control of the session at all times is that you may block clients from working with you and revealing valuable information for both of you. Challenges to needing to discover everything about clients' problem situations are that this is: unnecessary, in that you should distinguish between the wheat and the chaff; counterproductive, in that it is time consuming and may alienate clients; and impossible, in that even clients do not know everything about their problems.

You can create a preferential rule like 'I would prefer to ask questions competently' to replace the demanding rule 'I must be an expert'; a rule like 'I am likely to form stronger working alliances and gather more information if I share control with clients' instead of 'I must be in control of the session at all times'; and a rule like 'If possible, the client and I should clarify the main factors affecting the problem situation' for 'I must discover everything about the client's problem situation.'

Creating perceptions

When clarifying problem situations, helpers and clients can collaborate to create accurate perceptions of what is really going on. Skilled questioning involves a process of reality-testing rather than jumping to conclusions and allowing your own agendas to cloud how you see your clients. As you clarify problem situations, suspend judgement and adopt the principle that you do not know anything unless clients tell you. Even then, what clients tell you will be their perceptions of reality which may require further exploration. In addition, be careful about distorting your own perceptions through mind-reading and filling in gaps in information with your own fantasies.

Attempt to perceive accurately the effect of your questions on clients. For instance, carefully observe how questions are answered. Much of the art of questioning lies in decoding clients' answers. Observe what is left unsaid or only partially said, and vocal and bodily communication. You can use these clues to guide you both in the direction and the pacing of your questioning. For example, by accurately perceiving vocal communication you may glimpse that an area is emotionally threatening for a client. Then you can decide whether to try to explore the area further or to back off.

Creating explanations

Towards the beginning of this chapter I mentioned the issue of how important it is for helpers to encourage clients to own their problems and problem situations. Helpers can create much unwanted client behaviour by creating explanations of the helping process that cause them to take over their clients' problems.

Another important issue is that of how you explain the origins of your questions: for example, 'Where do my questions come from?' and 'For whose benefit are my questions?' The reason behind asking feelings, physical reactions, mind and communication questions in the understanding stage is that greater clarity about clients' problems often provides a springboard for their doing something about them. Furthermore, greater clarity can lessen threat and increase confidence.

A more general point is that the explanation for the kinds of questions helpers ask is closely tied to the counselling approach they follow: for example, cognitive helpers will emphasise questions about thoughts, behavioural helpers will raise questions about overt behaviours, and analytic helpers will focus on dreams.

Explanations for the origins of questions can take into account helpers' personal agendas. Some of these agendas may be below the level of their awareness. For example, I once worked in a health setting with a charismatic helper about whom it was said that 'All roads lead to Rome', which in his case was questions about clients' sex lives. In addition to having favoured topic areas, helpers may ask questions to bolster their own feelings of security, control and certainty.

Creating expectations

The way you make structuring statements and use questions to clarify understanding creates expectations for clients about their role in the process: for example, whether they be active or passive participants. Beginning helpers need to be very careful to avoid creating false expectations about their abilities to help clients change. Most students do not have a large repertoire of helping strategies on which to draw. Consequently, beware of putting yourself in a spurious position of expertness and then not being able to 'deliver the goods'.

Students can possess false expectations about clients' abilities and willingness to reveal information. Skilled and experienced helpers adjust their questioning to the pace at which clients are willing to go. Furthermore, they are good at 'sniffing out' areas for questioning that highlight problem situations. So long as you are conscientiously trying to learn counselling skills, do not be too hard on yourself if sometimes clients inadequately participate in clarifying both your and their own understanding of their problems.

Summary

In the understanding stage helpers need to maintain good relationships with clients. Questions have the potential to damage helping relationships. Counselling skills students are cautioned against asking questions as if in personal or doctor–patient relationships. When questioning be sensitive to clients' personal styles and cultures. In addition, remember to allow clients to keep 'owning' problem situations rather than take over ownership of them yourself.

Questions that elicit information about specific details include those starting with the words 'how', 'what', 'when' and 'where'. The statement 'Give me a specific example . . .' is also useful. Two further important types of questions are those exploring the clients' personal meanings and those encouraging clients to identify their strengths.

Four basic areas in which to ask questions are feelings, physical reactions, mind and communication/actions. Good questioning skills include interspersing active listening with questions, asking questions that build on clients' previous responses, and using appropriate vocal and bodily communication. In addition, helpers need to develop skills of summarising the details of clients' problem situations.

Thinking skilfully is critical to questioning skilfully. You can create self-talk and visual images that help you ask questions calmly and competently. In addition, you can ask 'show me how' and other questions that allow you to develop more accurate visual images. Identify any unrealistic rules you possess connected with clarifying problem situations: for instance, those connected with being an expert, being in control, and needing to know everything. Then challenge and substitute more realistic rules for them.

Clarifying problem situations entails you and the client striving to create fuller and more accurate perceptions of what is going on. Beware of jumping to conclusions and observe carefully how clients answer your questions. Think about how you explain the origins of your questions and whether your questions really are of benefit to clients. In addition, create realistic expectations about clients' willingness and abilities to reveal information and about your ability to help them to do this.

Activities

Activity 9.1   Forming questions

Part A   Types of questions

Provide two examples of each of the following types of questions:

- open-ended;
- specific detail:
    - (a)   how question
    - (b)   show me how question
    - (c)   what question
    - (d)   where question
    - (e)   when question
- eliciting personal meanings;
- identifying strengths.

Part B   Areas for questions

Look at Box 9.2 and see if you can add one or more clarifying understanding questions in each of the following categories:

- feelings;
- physical reactions;
- mind;
- communication/actions.

Activity 9.2   Interspersing active listening with questions

Part A   Pairs activity

- Each partner picks a problem situation.
- Imagine that you are at the start of the understanding stage.
- Partner A acts as helper and Partner B acts as client.
- Partner A spends 10 to 15 minutes interspersing questions with active listening as together you clarify Partner B's problem situation.
- At the end Partner A summarises the main details covered so far.
- Hold a sharing and feedback session.
- Reverse roles and go through the activity again clarifying your understanding of Partner A's problem situation.
- As appropriate, hold a whole group sharing and discussion session.

Part B   Group activity

- Each student picks a problem situation that they feel safe in revealing to the group.
- A volunteer acts as client who presents her/his problem situation to the group who, as helpers, sit in a semi-circle facing the client.
- After an opening statement by one helper, go around the semi-circle and take turns in responding to the client, first by reflecting her/his previous response and then by asking a question to clarify her/his problem situation. When the client answers, the next helper reflects the answer and then asks a question and so on.
- The trainer can stop the activity along the way and get the group discussing the ground covered so far and where to go next.
- When finished, hold a sharing and discussion session.
- Students can take turns as the client.

Activity 9.3   Empowering my mind for clarifying understanding

Part A   Assessing mind skills

In regard to clarifying understanding, assess your good and poor skills in each of the following mind skills areas:

Creating self-talk:
- good skills
- poor skills

Creating visual images:
- good skills
- poor skills

Creating rules:
- good skills
- poor skills

Creating perceptions:
- good skills
- poor skills

Creating explanations:
- good skills
- poor skills

Creating expectations:
- good skills
- poor skills

Part B   Improving mind skills

Select at least one of the above mind skills areas where you would like to improve your mind skills. For each mind skills area you select:

- identify any negative thinking that could interfere with your clarifying understanding competently;
- if appropriate, question and challenge your negative thinking;
- substitute realistic thinking for negative thinking; and
- rehearse and practise your new thinking.

10 Expanding Understanding

The real alchemist is one who learns the secret of turning everyday situations into gold, who learns how to make every situation serve him.

John Kehoe

Chapter outcomes

By studying and doing the activities in this chapter you should be able to:

- *possess some skills for challenging clients' perspectives;*
- *have some basic feedback skills;*
- *have some knowledge and skills for talking about yourself;*
- *assist clients to monitor themselves between sessions;*
- *understand more about when and how to refer clients; and*
- *understand more about how to identify unhelpful thinking.*

The previous chapter focused on using questions combined with active listening to clarify understanding of problems and problem situations. These skills are the 'bread and butter' skills of the understanding stage of the relating–understanding–changing helping process model. This chapter reviews some additional skills counselling skills students and helpers can use to expand clients' understanding and their own.

Despite introductory counselling skills courses differing in length and purpose, I hope all readers survey this chapter. However, some trainers and students may wish to move on to the next chapter after spending little or no time developing the skills reviewed here. In helper training less can be more. Trying to do too much can be positively harmful, since it confuses students. However, since there are so many purposes people have for running and enrolling on introductory counselling skills courses, I do not want to prescribe the skills to focus on or avoid. Certain skills in this chapter may still be highly relevant to the goals of some short courses. However, on such courses trainers need to teach skills like challenging in a basic and simple fashion that minimises the chances of students getting out of their depth.

Challenging skills

'Challenging' is perhaps a more gentle word than 'confronting', which conjures up images of clients sitting in hot seats having their self-protective habits remorselessly stripped away by aggressive helpers. Challenges come from helpers' external perspectives with the aim of helping clients develop new and better perspectives about themselves, others and their problem situations. Skilled challenges invite clients to examine discrepancies in their feelings, thoughts and communications about which, for various reasons, they remain insufficiently aware. The challenges I advocate here have two distinctive characteristics: first, they tend to be fairly close to clients' existing perspectives; and second they are given in a relatively non-threatening manner. As Box 10.1 illustrates, challenges can come in many shapes and sizes.

Box 10.1   Examples of challenging inconsistencies

Inconsistency between verbal, vocal and bodily communication

On the one hand you're saying you're all right but I catch a note of pain in your voice and your eyes look a little weepy.

Inconsistency between words and actions

You say that your kids are the most important thing in the world to you, but you're also behind on your child support payments.

Inconsistency between values and actions

You say you believe in equality between the sexes, but you also feel uncomfortable about asking a man for a date.

Inconsistency between goals and actions

You say you want to get a job and gain financial independence, however you're also telling me you've done little about looking for one.

Inconsistency between earlier and present statements

A moment ago you said you hated your hospital training supervisor, now you're saying she's not all that bad.

Inconsistency between statements and evidence

You said your husband never appreciates you, but now you've just told me that he cooked a special meal on your birthday.

Inconsistency between thoughts, feelings and actual communication

You get extremely tense about speaking in public, but you're also saying that you manage to perform so that no one in the audience notices how uptight you get.

Inconsistency between own and others' evaluations

I'm getting two messages. You feel that you are generous, but the feedback from your friends seems to be that you are tight and not paying your way.

How to challenge

Verbal messages for challenges include: 'On the one hand . . . on the other . . .', 'On the one hand . . . but . . .'; 'You say . . . but . . .' and 'I'm getting two messages . . .' or 'I'm getting a mixed message . . .' Your vocal and body communication should remain relaxed and friendly. Beginning students should restrict themselves to making mildly threatening challenges to clients. I see only disadvantages and dangers where inexperienced students make strong challenges.

When challenging it is important to keep clients' ears open to your viewpoint. Offer your challenges as an equal and avoid talking down to clients. Remember, challenges are invitations for exploration. A major risk in challenging clients is that they perceive what you say as put-downs.

Use a minimum amount of 'muscle'. Only challenge as strongly as your goal requires. Strong challenges can create resistances. Although sometimes necessary, even with skilled helpers such challenges are generally best avoided – especially in initial sessions where rapport and trust is not yet established. Strategies that clients can use to resist challenges include: discrediting challengers, persuading challengers to change their views, devaluing the issue, seeking support elsewhere for views being challenged, and agreeing with the challenge inside helping but then doing nothing about it outside (Egan, 1998).

Leave the ultimate responsibility for assessing the value of your challenges with clients. They can decide whether your challenges actually help them to move forward in their explorations. Often your challenges are only mildly discrepant to clients' existing perceptions. If well timed and tactfully worded, such challenges are unlikely to elicit a high degree of defensiveness.

Lastly, be careful not to overdo challenging. Nobody likes being persistently challenged. With constant challenges you create an unsafe emotional climate. If you challenge skilfully, you can help clients enlarge their understanding and act more effectively. However, if you challenge too often and too clumsily you can block clients and harm the creation of a good working alliance.

Feedback skills

Feedback skills and challenging skills overlap. However, challenging skills are used in response to clients' inconsistencies, whereas there is no assumption of inconsistency in this section on feedback skills. Here I distinguish between observational feedback, 'I observe you as . . .', and experiential feedback, 'I experience you as . . .'.

Observational feedback

Helpers as observers of clients' communication may see it differently and possibly more accurately than clients themselves. When helpers and clients are truly working together to try to understand clients' problem situations, there may be occasions where helpers may decide to provide feedback to clients based on their observations. Take clients who have just shown you how they communicate in specific situations. After mini role-plays, clients may show some insight into their communication. However, as an observer, you wish to bring something else to their attention.

In Chapter 5, I reviewed giving and receiving feedback in counselling skills training groups. Many of these same skills are relevant to giving feedback to clients: for example, using 'I' messages; being specific and, where possible, stating feedback in the positive; using confirmatory as well as corrective feedback; considering demonstrating your feedback; and providing opportunities for clients to respond to your feedback.

After a mini role-play my preference is to ask clients to evaluate themselves before providing any feedback. Reasons for this include keeping clients as active participants, reducing the need for feedback from me since clients may have noticed my points anyway, building clients' skills of self-observation, and sensing that clients are more likely to be receptive to feedback from me if they have first had the opportunity to assess themselves. For instance, after inviting clients to comment on their performance and listening to their responses, I might summarise what they have said, enquire 'Would you mind if I added one or two observations . . .?' and then, if given permission, succinctly provide my feedback.

Experiential feedback

Feedback can also involve you in using your experiencing of clients as the springboard for making observations about both the client and the helping process. To an extent helping sessions are microcosms of outside life. Clients can bring to the sessions the same patterns of communication that create difficulties for them outside helping. However, helpers have to be very careful not to let personal unfinished business interfere with how they experience clients.

You may not need to engage in role-plays to experience how clients may come across to others in their problem situations. For example, I once had a very bright and able businesswoman client, Louise, who was repeatedly getting turned down at interviews. I used questioning and active listening to explore what might be going on in these situations. However, the most powerful information I received came from my own feelings of being overpowered by Louise's bombastic and lecturing interpersonal style. My first decision was 'Should I share this experientially based information or sit on it?' Having decided I might try to share the information, my second decision was 'How do I provide this experiential feedback to Louise, who has shown limited insight so far?'

I tentatively suggested to Louise that I experienced her as coming over rather strong as she talked with me and that this might be relevant to panel members' reactions at her interviews. Furthermore, I fed back to her that she had a fairly booming voice. I could have done this more tactfully if I had remembered a comment that she had made that possibly she was 'too educational' at interviews. I could then have introduced my feedback about her booming voice as a hypothesis to clarify an aspect of her comment about being 'too educational'. Had I done this my feedback would have been closer to her own perspective and less from my own.

Instances where helpers' experiencing of clients' interpersonal style may throw light on their problems outside include: not coming on time for interviews, speaking in distant ways, being aggressive, and disparaging themselves. Giving positive experiential feedback to clients with low self-esteem can sometimes be helpful: for example 'I experience you as having some strength to deal with the situation' or 'I experience you as having much to offer a friend'. Such comments need to be genuine feedback rather than superficial reassurance.

Helpers can also provide experiential feedback concerning the helping process. For example, if a client is repetitively going over the same ground, the helper might say: 'I experience you as having taken that topic as far as you can go at the moment and it might be profitable to move on. What do you think?' Another example is that of a helper sharing her or his experiencing of a client who uses humour as a distancing device whenever topics become too personal: for instance 'I get the sense that this topic is getting too close for comfort and so you're starting to act the clown to avoid dealing with it directly'. Needless to say, tact and good timing is very important if clients are to use such experiential feedback to move forwards rather than backwards.

Disclosing yourself skills

Should you talk at all about yourself in helping sessions? How can you show genuineness and humanity if you stay as a blank screen to your clients? Helper self-disclosure relates to the ways in which you let yourself be known to clients. Usually the term refers to intentional verbal disclosure. A useful distinction exists between disclosures showing involvement and sharing personal experiences.

Helper self-disclosure, even in brief helping, can be for good or ill. Possible positive consequences of disclosing yourself include: providing new insights and perspectives; demonstrating a useful skill; equalising, and humanising the helping relationship; normalising clients' difficulties; instilling hope; and reassurance (Edwards and Murdoch, 1994; Knox, Hess, Petersen and Hill, 1997).

There are, however, grave dangers in inappropriately disclosing yourself. You may burden clients with your problems and shift the focus of the helping conversation to yourself. You may come across as weak and unstable when clients, feeling vulnerable themselves, want helpers who have 'got their act together'. In addition, helpers may either intentionally or unintentionally use self-disclosure to manipulate clients to meet their own needs for approval, intimacy and sex.

Showing involvement

Disclosures that show your involvement can humanise helping so that clients feel they relate to real people. There is a 'here-and-now' quality in showing involvement by sharing your reactions to clients. Three areas for disclosing your involvement are responding to specific client disclosures, responding to clients as people, and responding to clients' vulnerability. Box 10.2 provides examples of helper statements for each area.

Showing your involvement can help clients feel you genuinely care. Positive self-involving statements, expressing positive rather than negative feelings about clients, can draw favourable reactions (Watkins, 1990). However, be careful about being too gushing and nice. Clients want detached involvement rather than involvement with psychological hooks attached. Furthermore, some clients may need tough alongside tender love.

Sharing personal experiences

Sharing personal experiences may help your clients feel that you understand what they are going through. For instance, unemployed people might feel differently about helpers who share that they too have been unemployed. In some types of helping, disclosure of shared experiences is an important part of the process: for instance Alcoholics Anonymous and some drug addiction programmes.

Helpers have many choices in sharing personal experiences. Included among these are: whether to mention them or not; whether to restrict yourself to past experiences or discuss current experiences; how honest to be; whether to go beyond disclosing facts to disclosing feelings, for instance not only having been unemployed but then having to struggle against feelings of depression and uselessness; how you coped with your experience; and how you feel about it now. In the kind of brief helping assumed by the relating–understanding–changing helping process model you will not have the opportunity to develop the 'relational depth' that some helpers achieve with some clients later in a series of helping sessions (Mearns, 1997).

Below are some guidelines for appropriate sharing of personal experiences. See Box 10.2 for examples.

- *Talk about yourself* Do not disclose the experience of third parties whom you know.
- *Talk about past experiences* You may not have sufficient emotional distance from current experiences, for instance going through a messy divorce.
- *Be to the point* Your personal disclosures should follow similar client disclosures. Avoid slowing down or defocusing the helping session through lack of relevance or talking too much.
- *Be sensitive to clients' reactions* Have sufficient awareness to realise when your disclosures might be helpful to your client and when they might be unwelcome or a burden.
- *Share personal experiences sparingly* Be careful not to switch the focus of helping from clients to yourself.

Box 10.2   Examples of helper disclosures

Showing involvement
Illustrative responses include:
- *Responding to specific disclosures*   'I'm delighted', 'That's great', 'That's terrible', 'I'm really sorry to hear that.'
- *Responding to clients as people*   'I admire your courage', 'I appreciate your honesty.'
- *Responding to clients' vulnerability*   'I'm available if you get really low', 'I'm very concerned about what you're going through.'

Sharing personal experiences
- *Poor examples (humorous)*   'You think that you have problems in bed, let me tell you about mine!',
  'Ross, I too am the most terrible procrastinator when it comes to doing assignments for my course. Right now I have a workbook to complete for my counselling skills class and I've just not been able to get started.'
- *Potentially helpful example*   'Maria, at one stage in my life I was unemployed too and found it a very scary and difficult time. Though clearly our experiences differ, I think I do have some idea of what you're going through.'

Monitoring skills

As helpers you may need to encourage clients to gather more information to clarify and expand your understanding of their problem situations. In initial sessions, clients are likely to provide useful information, but you may still want to gather even more. Here I review some simple monitoring methods and how helpers can assist clients to use them.

Monitoring methods

Following are some methods whereby clients can monitor their feelings, physical reactions, mind and communication/actions in problem situations. You can also tailor make recording sheets to the particular needs of clients.

Diaries and journals
Some clients keep diaries and journals anyway. Clients can pay special attention to writing up specific instances of their problem situations. Although diaries and journals may be useful to some clients, others are likely to find this approach too easy to ignore and too unsystematic.

Frequency charts
Frequency charts focus on how many times clients think a thought or enact a specific behaviour in a given time period, say each day between the first and second helping sessions and overall during this period. For example, in regard to thoughts, clients may tally how many times they engage in negative self-talk about a problem situation. In regard to actions, unemployed executives who are frightened about making cold calls to prospective employers can record each time they manage to make a call.

Situation, thoughts and consequences (STC) logs
Filling in three-column STC logs can highlight clients' thought processes and help them to see the connections between what they think and how they feel, physically react, and communicate. See Box 10.3 for an example.

Verbal, vocal and bodily communication logs
Frequently clients possess a low awareness of their vocal and bodily communication. During the understanding stage, helpers and clients may become aware of some areas that may be important to understanding clients' problem situations. For instance, a helper works with a teenager, Indira, whose problem situation is difficulty setting limits on her mother, Dina, who repeatedly wants to discuss her separated

father's shortcomings. Box 10.3 contains a possible format for a log to collect information about how Indira communicates. Indira could be cued in advance to observe specific aspects of her vocal and bodily communication.

Box 10.3   Examples of monitoring logs

Situation, thoughts and consequences log

Situation (What happened and when?)	Thoughts (What I thought)	Consequences (How I felt and communicated/acted)

Verbal, vocal and bodily communication log
Situation 1 (*provide basic details including when*)

My words

My voice

My body language

Consequences for myself and others

Situation 2 (*provide basic details including when*)
(as for Situation 1)

How to assist clients' monitoring

Clients are not in the habit of systematically recording observations about how they feel, physically react, think and communicate/act. You may need to motivate them to do so. For instance, you can explain to Indira: 'Systematically writing down how you communicate with your words, voice and body each time your mother attempts to draw you into her marital struggle provides us with information to develop useful strategies for setting limits on her.'

Always either supply monitoring logs yourself or, before the initial session ends, supervise clients in setting up the format for a log. Do not expect clients to make logs on their own. Clients may not do so in the first place and, if they do, they may get them wrong.

Clients are not naturally accurate self-observers. Consequently, helpers may need to train them in discriminating and recording specific behaviours. Clients require clarity not only about what to record, but about how to record it. In addition, clients require awareness of any tendencies they have to misperceive or selectively perceive their actions: for instance, being more inclined to notice deficiencies than strengths.

Remember to reward clients with interest and praise when they fill in logs. This guideline is based on the basic behavioural principle that actions that are rewarding are more likely to be repeated. Furthermore, always reward clients for their efforts by debriefing them.

Referral skills

After mock helping sessions with peers in skills training groups you can discuss referring 'clients' you have interviewed with your trainer and, possibly, fellow students. Introductory counselling skills students seeing volunteer clients under supervision should refer those who have genuine problems for appropriate help. You may need to act before having a chance to discuss a referral with your supervisor. For example, in Chapter 5 I mentioned a scheme at the Royal Melbourne Institute of Technology in which Graduate Diploma in Counselling psychology students counselled undergraduate volunteer 'clients'. There the counselling students were instructed to make referrals of undergraduate 'clients' as appropriate to the Student Counselling Service.

Since making referrals continues to be important once you finish your introductory counselling skills course, I discuss the topic in a more general way here. In initial sessions, and also in subsequent sessions, you may face decisions about referring clients elsewhere. Even experienced helpers have types of clients with whom they feel more competent and comfortable and others less so. Arnold Lazarus states that an important helping principle is to 'Know your limitations and other clinicians' strengths' (Dryden, 1991: 30). He considers that referrals should be made where other helpers have skills that the helper does not possess or have more appropriate personal styles for particular clients. Important ethical issues surround referral, especially where other helpers are more expert than you with specific problems, for instance sexual abuse or substance abuse problems.

Referral may not be an either/or matter. Sometimes helpers continue working with clients but also refer to other helpers or helping professionals. Alternatively, helpers may be the recipients of referrals from other helping professionals who continue working with them. In Melbourne, I worked as a sessional counselling psychologist for a leading Australian careers out-placement company. All my clients were referred by other professionals who continued seeing them for job search counselling. I acted as a 'back-stop' for clients whose problems were more severe or different from their normal clientele.

Sometimes you can refer clients to gain additional knowledge about their problems. For example, refer clients with thought blocking problems or sexual dysfunctions for medical checks. Then, depending on the outcome of these checks, you have relevant information about whether or not to continue seeing them.

On other occasions you can refer the client's problem rather than the client to other helpers and helping professionals. For example, you can discuss with colleagues or supervisors how best to assist certain clients. Occasions when you may refer the client's problem rather than the client include: when you are the only helper available in an area; when clients state a clear preference for continuing working with you; and when clients are unlikely to follow through on referrals.

How to refer

Following are some considerations and skills for making referrals. Avoid unnecessary referrals. You may be too ready to refer clients. Sometimes it is better for clients to continue working with you. Tune into your own anxieties and fears about seeing certain clients. You build your confidence and skills by expanding the range of clients with whom you can work. However, wherever possible ensure that you have adequate supervision and support.

As time goes by try and develop a good feel for your strengths and limitations. Be realistic about the kinds of clients with whom you work well and those with whom you are less skilled. Also, be realistic about your workload and set appropriate limits on it.

Good referrals are more likely to be made to people whom you know and trust rather than 'blind'. Get to know the resources available in your area so that you can avoid making referrals to helpers about whose competence you are unsure. In addition, even if you do know the helper, it may be wise to check if they have time available to see your client.

Where possible, refer early on. If you defer referrals longer than necessary, you waste clients' and your own time. Furthermore, it is preferable to refer clients before they emotionally bond with you.

When making a referral calmly explain to clients why this may be a good idea. You should be able to support your explanation with what they have told you already. Make sure that clients are absolutely clear about how to make contact with the other helper. You can hand out that helper's card or write down their address and phone number.

Spend time discussing any queries and emotional reactions clients may have to your referral suggestions. If the clients are in crisis, you may need to accompany them to the other helper's office. Another consideration is whether and what information you should provide for the next or different helper. You can discuss such issues with your client and, if necessary, ask permission to share information.

Lastly, build a support network. Your support network provides professional support for you when you want to refer clients' problems rather than the clients themselves. Your support network is likely to overlap with your referral network, but some members' roles are different. For example, you can discuss clients' problems with supervisors and trainers, but you are less likely to refer clients to them.

Identifying unhelpful thinking

In Chapter 2, I reviewed how both helpers and clients create their minds. In the understanding stage helpers can be on the look out for clues that clients may be creating negative or unhelpful thoughts. In this section I briefly review some key indicators that clients may possess unhelpful thoughts in three mind skills areas: creating self-talk, creating rules and creating perceptions. Often you will need to infer negative thinking since clients are unlikely to tell you directly 'I have this particular problem with how I think . . .' and then specify it.

Another point to remember is that negative thinking is rarely an either/or matter. Clients mix helpful with unhelpful thinking and it may only be the 20 or 30 per cent of a client's thinking that is unhelpful. For example, 80 per cent of a client's thinking may be about attaining realistically high levels of competence, whereas the remaining 20 per cent is about attaining unrealistically high levels of perfection. It is changing this 20 per cent that helpers and clients need to address.

Creating self-talk

When you ask clients what is going through their minds before, during and after specific problem situations, you can look out for self-talk that increases the likelihood of harmful feelings and self-defeating actions. For example, anxiety arousing self-talk may include the following elements: emphasising mastery rather than coping; catastrophising or imagining the worst; adversely reacting to physical symptoms or getting anxious about getting anxious; and being overly self-conscious about what others think. Anger arousing self-talk may include jumping to negative conclusions about others' intentions, focusing on other people's shortcomings, and feeling sorry for yourself. In addition to presence of harmful self-talk, look out for absence of helpful self-talk, for instance absence of calming and of cooling self-instructions.

You can also look out for absence of or insufficient coaching self-talk. Clients may not realise the importance of coaching themselves in how to communicate and act appropriately in problem situations. They may insufficiently clarify their goals, fail to think in terms of a step by step approach to situations, and insufficiently focus on coaching themselves in sending good vocal and bodily communication.

Clients can also lower their self-esteem by talking to themselves as if they were their own worst enemies. For instance, they may tell themselves how stupid, incompetent, uninteresting and ugly they are. In addition, they may fail to remind themselves of their strengths and of supportive people in their lives.

Creating rules

Following are some indicators or signals for demanding rather than preferential rules. You can pay attention to signs of inappropriate language. For example, demanding rules tend to be characterised by 'musts', 'oughts', 'shoulds' and 'have tos': for example, 'I must have approval' or 'Others should do what I want'.

Persistent inappropriate feelings can signal that clients possess a demanding rule. The dividing line between appropriate and inappropriate feelings is not always clear. Life can be difficult, so appropriate feelings cannot simply be equated with 'positive' feelings like happiness, joy and accomplishment. Some 'negative' feelings like sadness, grief, fear and anger can be entirely appropriate for the contexts in which they occur. You have to ask yourself questions like: 'Is this feeling appropriate for the situation?' and 'Is keeping feeling this way helping or harming the client?' Physical reactions may also signal demanding rules: for instance persistent muscular tension could signal clients putting pressure on themselves for perfection or universal approval.

Inappropriate feelings, physical reactions and communications/ actions are interrelated. If clients feel excessively angry because of a demanding rule, their physical level of arousal can impair their judgement to the point where they act violently and worsen rather than help their position. Relevant questions for helpers to ask themselves, and possibly clients too, include: 'Are clients' communications or actions helping or harming themselves or others?', 'Are they over-reacting?' and 'Is their behaviour self-defeating?'

Creating perceptions

In Chapter 2, I mentioned the importance of being able to distinguish fact from inference and guarding against tendencies to jump to unwarranted conclusions. Helpers can closely observe how much evidence clients provide to support assertions about how they and others behave. When clients make statements like: 'I have no friends', 'I'm no good at maths', 'S/he never does anything for me', and 'My boss hates me' helpers can ask clients to generate evidence to support or negate their statements.

Helpers can also look out for characteristic tricks of the mind that might indicate clients are creating insufficiently accurate perceptions (Beck, 1988). Especially when feeling under stress, clients are likely to perceive inaccurately. Using the STC framework, following are six mind tricks clients may use at T that lead to negative feelings, physical reactions and communication consequences at C.

Making unsupported inferences
Drawing conclusions without adequate supporting evidence.

Using tunnel vision
Narrowly focusing on only a portion of the available information in a situation rather than taking into account all significant information. For example, clients focus mainly on the positive aspects of a new girlfriend or boyfriend and select out potentially negative information.

Thinking in black and white terms
Perceiving in all or nothing terms: for example, a client gives the impression 'Either my relationship with my supervisor is a total success or a total failure'.

Magnifying and minimising relevant information
Seeing things as far more important or less important than they really are. For instance, magnifying minor upsets into disasters or minimising

negative events – for example, exaggerating or downplaying the implications of being diagnosed with a heart disease.

Overgeneralising

Making general comments that clients probably would not be able to support if they bothered to check the evidence. For example, 'My partner *never* appreciates me' and 'I *always* try to understand my partner's viewpoint.'

Being overly negative

Attaching unduly negative and critical labels to yourself and others. Overemphasising the negative at the expense of the positive or neutral. Going beyond useful ratings of specific characteristics to devaluing your own or another's whole worth as a person.

Summary

Challenges come from helpers' external perspectives with the aim of helping clients develop new and better perspectives about themselves, others and their problem situations. Included among client inconsistencies that helpers can challenge are those between: verbal, vocal and bodily communication; words and actions; values and actions; goals and actions; and earlier and present statements. Challenge inconsistencies with tact and not too often.

Feedback can be observational and experiential. Observational feedback entails sharing your assessments of how clients are using verbal, vocal and bodily communication when role playing problem situations. Experiential feedback involves using your own experiencing and feelings about clients as a springboard for commenting on how they communicate and think. Often how clients communicate inside helping provides insights into their problems outside helping.

Helpers can disclose themselves by showing involvement and sharing personal experiences. Three areas for showing involvement are responding to specific client disclosures, responding to clients as people and responding to clients' vulnerability. Guidelines for appropriate sharing of personal experience include talking about past experiences, being to the point and doing it sparingly.

Helpers can expand clients' understanding by assisting them to monitor systematically their feelings, physical reactions, thoughts and communications. Monitoring methods include: diaries and journals; frequency charts; situation, thoughts and consequences logs; and verbal, vocal and bodily communication logs. Provide or supervise clients as they draw up monitoring logs and ensure that they are clear as to how to record observations.

Helpers may need to refer clients. However, avoid unnecessary referrals. Skilled helpers build up referral networks and clearly and tactfully explain reasons for suggesting referrals. Often, rather than referring the client, you can refer the client's problem to a supervisor or trusted colleague and then discuss how best to proceed.

Unhelpful thinking is rarely an either/or matter; rather people mix helpful and unhelpful thoughts. Look out for presence of self-talk that increases the likelihood of harmful feelings, self-defeating actions and lowered self-esteem. In addition, look out for absence of calming coaching and affirming self-talk.

Signals for demanding rules include language emphasising words like 'must' and 'should', persistent inappropriate feelings and distressing physical symptoms, and communication and actions that are harmful to self and others. Helpers can identify potentially inaccurate perceptions by assessing how closely clients' inferences fit the facts and looking out for characteristic tricks of the mind such as tunnel vision, thinking in black and white terms, magnifying and minimising relevant information, overgeneralising, and being overly negative.

Activities

Activity 10.1   Challenging skills

Part A   *Challenging skills*

1   What does the concept of challenging clients mean to you? What
are the advantages and disadvantages in initial helping sessions of
challenges to clients:
- by counselling skills students;
- by experienced helpers.
2   Using Box 10.1 as a guide, formulate a challenging response in
each of the following areas:
- inconsistency between verbal, vocal and bodily communication;
- inconsistency between words and actions;
- inconsistency between values and actions;
- inconsistency between goals and actions;
- inconsistency between earlier and present statements;
- inconsistency between statements and evidence;
- inconsistency between thoughts, feelings and actual communication; and
- inconsistency between own and others' evaluations.

Activity 10.2   Feedback skills

Part A   *Observational feedback*

- Work in threes, Partner A as 'client', Partner B as 'helper' and
Partner C as observer. Partner A selects a problem situation

involving another person where s/he thinks s/he might communicate better.

- Partners A and B conduct a mini role-play in which Partner B plays the other person and Partner A shows how s/he currently communicates in the situation.
- Afterwards, Partner B invites Partner A to comment on her/his own communication. Then Partner B gives observational feedback to Partner A.
- Next hold a discussion in which Partner C first asks Partner B to evaluate her/his giving feedback skills and then gives observational feedback to Partner B on her/his use of feedback skills.
- Then change roles until everyone has had the opportunity to be client, helper and observer.

Part B   Experiential feedback

1   What does the concept of experiential feedback mean to you? What are the advantages and disadvantages in initial helping sessions of experiential feedback to clients:
   - by counselling skills students;
   - by experienced helpers.
2   Formulate one or more experiential feedback statements.

Activity 10.3   Disclosing skills

Part A   Showing involvement

1   With respect to your present or future helping work, write down the sorts of situations in which it might be appropriate for you to show involvement to clients in initial helping sessions.
2   Using Box 10.2 as a guide, formulate one or more *disclosures showing involvement* in each of the following areas:
   - responding to specific client disclosures;
   - responding to clients as people;
   - responding to clients' vulnerability.

Part B   Sharing personal information

1   With regard to your present or future helping work, write down the sorts of situations in which it might be appropriate for you to share personal information with clients in initial helping sessions.

2   Using Box 10.2 as a guide, for each situation formulate one or more *sharing personal information* statements.

Activity 10.4   Referral skills

In regard to either your current or future helping work:

- When might you refer clients to other helpers?
- What categories of helpers do you require in your referral network?
- What categories of helpers do you require in your support network – when you refer problems but not clients?
- What are some considerations in making good referrals?
- When might you be at risk of making unnecessary referrals?

Activity 10.5   Identifying unhelpful thinking

Part A   Creating self-talk

For a specific problem situation in either your own or a client's life, deliberately formulate unhelpful self-talk statements that might:

- cause you/the client to feel anxious;
- cause you/the client to feel angry; or
- coach you/the client in self-defeating communication or actions.

Part B   Creating rules

For a specific problem situation in either your own or a client's life, how might you be able to identify the presence of one or more unhelpful rules:

- by attending to inappropriate language;
- by noticing persistent inappropriate feelings;
- by noticing unwanted physical reactions; or
- by becoming aware of self-defeating communication/actions.

Part C   Creating perceptions

For a specific problem situation in either your own or a client's life, how might you be able to identify the presence of one or more inaccurate perceptions:

- by observing how much evidence you/the client provide(s) to support assertions about your/their behaviour; and
- by observing the following characteristic tricks of the mind:
    - using tunnel vision;
    - thinking in black and white terms;
    - magnifying and minimising relevant information;
    - overgeneralising;
    - being overly negative.

PART 4

THE CHANGING STAGE

11 Setting Goals and Planning

It is not enough to take steps which may some day lead to a goal;
each step must be a goal and a step likewise.

J.W. Goethe

Chapter outcomes

By studying and doing the activities in this chapter, depending on the type of
introductory course you are on you should be able to:

* *understand the difference between a problem solving and a changing*
  communications and thoughts approach to the changing stage;
* *facilitate clients in clarifying goals in problem situations;*
* *facilitate clients in generating and exploring options;*
* *facilitate clients in action planning;*
* *assist clients to state changing specific communications and thoughts as goals;*
* *understand about planning strategies to attain communications and thoughts*
  goals; and
* *understand the importance of good helper skills for delivering helping strategies.*

Welcome to the changing stage of the relating–understanding–
changing (RUC) helping process model for problem situations. The
preceding stage probably ended with a summary of the main ground
covered so far. In the changing stage, the focus moves from 'What's
going on in the situation?' to 'What can I constructively do about it?'

Throughout the book I have emphasised that introductory counselling skills courses differ in purpose and length. In relating and

understanding stages, students on short courses or at the beginning of longer courses in particular should concentrate on developing good active listening skills, even if it means asking fewer questions and covering fewer skills.

In this chapter I present two approaches to the changing stage: (1) a problem solving approach and (2) a changing specific communications and thoughts approach. To some extent the two approaches overlap. However, in the problem solving approach, counselling skills students are encouraged to stay close to clients' internal perspectives and mainly draw upon clients' suggestions for change. For this reason, the problem solving approach lends itself to short introductory courses and for the beginning phases of longer courses. Later on in longer introductory courses, students can develop some basic skills in stating communications and thoughts sub-goals and in assisting clients to plan strategies to attain their sub-goals. Here, to a greater extent than in the problem solving approach, students are more active in assessing clients and in delivering helping strategies to them. The role of helpers in the problem solving approach to stage 3 is mainly that of facilitators. The role of helpers in the changing specific communication and thoughts approach is both that of facilitators and user-friendly coaches.

Problem solving approach

The problem solving approach to stage three of the RUC helping process model is not restricted to beginning counselling skills students. Experienced helpers can be very skilled at combining active listening skills with probes designed to clarify goals, explore options for attaining them and develop plans to implement a chosen option. Counselling skills students can develop similar skills. Furthermore, once they become more experienced helpers, the problem solving approach to the change stage may remain some students' preferred way of working.

Clarifying goals

Some clients, when they have the various dimensions of problem situations clearly laid out before them, of their own accord clarify goals and then proceed to attain them. Helpers provide such clients with greater understanding and confidence to tap into their own resources and act appropriately in problem situations.

On other occasions, helpers can follow up summaries at the end of the understanding stage with questions at the start of the changing stage that help clients clarify their goals in problem situations. Some clients are so overwhelmed that they lose sight of what they really want to achieve. By the end of the understanding stage many clients will have calmed down sufficiently so that they can take a reasonably rational view of their goals. However, these clients may require your assistance to do this.

You can start the changing stage with a structuring statement along the lines of 'Now we have clarified and summarised many of the main dimensions of your problem situation, perhaps we can try to articulate your goals in it. Do you think this would be helpful?' Many clients will answer 'yes' right away. Some might answer 'What do you mean?' If so you can tactfully explain to them that clarifying where they want to go makes it easier to decide how to get there.

You can distinguish between outcome goals, 'Where do I want to go?' and process goals, 'What are my sub-goals or steps in getting where I want to go?' Here I focus on outcome goals. Often as a practising counselling psychologist I have found clients insufficiently flexible when thinking about goals for specific situations. Rather than latch on to the first goal that comes to mind, you can help clients generate and consider a range of goals by asking 'What are your options in setting goals?' Such goals can be both positive, 'What do I want to achieve?' and negative, 'What do I want to avoid?' and are often a mixture of the two. Box 11.1 lists some questions that students and helpers can use to assist clients in clarifying their goals in problem situations.

Box 11.1   Some clarifying goals questions

- 'What are your goals in the situation?'
- 'What would you consider a successful outcome?'
- 'What are your options in setting goals?'
- 'What do you want to achieve in the situation:
   - for yourself;
   - for one or more others;
   - for your relationship, if appropriate?'
- 'What do you want to avoid in the situation:
   - for yourself;
   - for one or more others;
   - for your relationship, if appropriate?'

- 'Are your goals specific enough?'
- 'How do you know when you have attained your goals?'
- 'Are your goals realistic?'
- 'What is the time frame for attaining your goals?'

Remember not to bombard clients with questions about goals. In most instances, small is beautiful. A few well-chosen questions that get to the heart of what clients want to achieve and avoid are all that is necessary. However, sometimes you may need to facilitate clients in exploring deeper goals and the values that underpin them rather than surface goals. In all instances, respect clients' rights to set their own goals and remember to intersperse active listening with your clarifying goals questions.

Generating and exploring options

Clarifying goals questions are about ends. Generating and exploring options questions are about the means to achieve the clients' ends. Just as clients can latch on to the first goal that comes into mind, so they can latch on to the first method of achieving a goal that comes into their heads.

Box 11.2 is a case example that highlights the outcomes of using generating and exploring options questions to assist clients to attain goals. Often, once clients set goals, they feel stuck in knowing how to proceed. Skilled generating and exploring options questions help clients to put on their thinking caps and use their minds creatively. Many clients are wiser than they know, but have insufficient confidence and skills to get their wisdom out into the open.

Helpers may need to assist clients to think about the consequences of options. Often it is best to generate options first and then assess consequences afterwards. Prematurely assessing the consequences of options can interfere with the creative process of generating them.

Questions and comments for generating and exploring options include: 'Given your goal of ___ [specify goal] what ways might you attain it?', 'Just let the ideas flow without editing them too much', 'Are there any other ways that you might approach the situation?' and 'What might be the consequences of doing that?' Notice that all of these questions and comments put the onus of coming up with ideas on the client. Helpers resist the temptation to take over and own clients' problem situations.

Box 11.2 Generating options to attain goals: case example

The problem situation

A month ago, Debbie, 64, was diagnosed with terminal cancer and told that her life expectancy was probably another two to three years. In her initial anxiety over the diagnosis Debbie was very dependent on her oncologist, Dr Graham, whom she found overpowering. Debbie adopted a very passive stance about everything he said. Now that Debbie has greater acceptance of her illness, she wants to play a more active role in planning discussions with Dr Graham about her treatment. Debbie has the opportunity to discuss her problem situation with Josie, a social worker, who is part of her health care team.

Debbie's goals

Goals that Debbie wants to achieve within the next month

1 To gain greater knowledge about the prognosis and treatment options for the type of cancer that I have to the point where I can conduct an informed discussion about my treatment with Dr Graham.
2 To become more assertive about participating in discussions about my treatment.

Debbie's options

With the assistance of Josie, her social worker, following are some of the options Debbie generates to attain her goals.

Goal 1: Options for gaining greater knowledge about my prognosis and treatment

- reading relevant books and magazines;
- finding out more about and possibly joining a cancer support group;
- asking more questions of my family doctor;
- involving my husband in the search for information; and
- learning to search the Internet for information.

Goal 2: Options for becoming more assertive in participating in planning discussions about my treatment

In addition to becoming better informed

- speaking up when I do not understand what Dr Graham is talking about;
- letting Dr Graham know that I want to participate more actively in my treatment;
- asking questions assertively to Dr Graham;
- changing to another oncologist either now or if Dr Graham proves uncooperative; and
- making better use of other members of the health care team.

When conducting mock interviews as part of counselling skills training, start by keeping matters simple. For instance, you might focus on exploring options to attain one goal only and then only assist your client to generate a few options. If, later on in training, you and your clients generate many options, you can use a whiteboard. Afterwards you and your client can make a written record of what you have put up on it. Holding in your head the kind of detail I have illustrated in the Debbie case example is well nigh impossible.

Assisting action planning

Once clients have generated options, they need to choose those that they are prepared to implement. Plans are outlines of what clients want to do and the steps involved in doing this. Plans can range from the simple to the detailed. Mock interviews with fellow students may only last for a single session and much of real helping is very brief, say up to three sessions. Consequently, develop skills of identifying key goals, assisting clients to choose realistic options, and helping clients commit themselves to a brief plan consisting of one or more specific actions to implement their chosen options. Box 11.3 develops the earlier example of Debbie to the point where she chooses options to attain her goals and specifies how she will implement them. I have deliberately kept the example simple.

Box 11.3   Action planning to implement options

Problem situation
Debbie, a cancer patient, wants to play a more active role in planning discussions with Dr Graham, her oncologist, about her treatment. Debbie discusses her problem situation with Josie, a social worker.

Plan
Step 1 – Read relevant books and magazines. Within seven days go to the library and search for books written in lay person's language about cancer. Also, within seven days go to some bookshops and search for such books. Read at least one book about cancer within two weeks.
Step 2 – Ask more questions of my family doctor. By the end of two weeks, make a list of questions, set up an appointment with my doctor, and ask my questions.

Step 3 – After seeing my family doctor and before my next scheduled appointment with Dr Graham, my oncologist, update my list of questions about my treatment. At the appointment with Dr Graham, tell him that I want to participate more actively in discussions about my treatment and assertively ask him if he would please answer the questions I have prepared for him.

Helper skills of assisting action planning include: assisting clients to choose options for attaining their goals, encouraging them to be specific about how they can implement the options and, where appropriate, sequencing them into a step by step plan which has a time frame. In addition, helpers can explore clients' commitments to implementing their plans and how to deal with any difficulties and set-backs. Furthermore, helpers can encourage clients to write down plans to make them easier to remember. If clients are returning for subsequent sessions, helpers can assist clients in monitoring progress and in adjusting plans, if necessary.

Changing specific communications and thoughts approach

The second approach to the changing stage of the RUC helping process model requires counselling skills students to develop basic skills of: identifying unhelpful communications and thoughts; translating unhelpful communications and thoughts into goals; and planning and implementing strategies that help clients change how they communicate and think.

Since this second approach, more than the problem solving approach, involves students making comments from outside clients' internal perspectives, there is a greater risk of students falling into the trap of being instant experts. That is why the problem solving approach to stage three of the RUC helping process model may be more appropriate for short courses and for the beginning phases of longer courses. When using the changing specific communications and thoughts approach, students need to realise their limitations and follow the advice that porcupine parents give their offspring about making love, namely 'Proceed with caution!'

Identifying unhelpful communications and thoughts

In the clarifying understanding stage of the RUC model, helpers can go beyond describing the dimensions of clients' problem situations more fully to helping them identify specific communications and thoughts on which to work. Your suggestions about such communications and thoughts should flow easily out of what clients have told you during the relating and understanding stages. Make sure that clients consider the communications and thoughts you identify are relevant and, where appropriate, negotiate which ones they find acceptable.

In Box 9.4, I provided a clarifying understanding summary for Pat, a single mum, whose problem situation concerned how to ask her 15-year-old son Andy to mow the lawn once a week. In Box 11.4, I reword parts of this summary so that the helper's clarification includes a clear identification of unhelpful communications and thoughts.

Box 11.4   Identifying unhelpful communications and thoughts

The problem situation
The client Pat, a single mum, comes for help about her uneasy relationship with Andy, her 15-year-old son. One area of the problem is that Pat wants Andy to do more household chores. The specific situation that the client wishes to work on is how to ask Andy to mow the lawn once a week. Pat has recently made an unsuccessful request for Andy to do this job.

Summary to clarify understanding and identify unhelpful communication and thoughts
Well Pat, I think it might be helpful if I tried to pull together the ground we have covered so far. Basically you love Andy, are proud of him and think he's a good kid. However, you get very anxious over asserting yourself with him by requesting that he does jobs like mowing the lawn. You tense up before you ask him and feel resentful when he does not cooperate. You also tense up because you are afraid that you might lose some of his affection to his Dad who gives you no support in disciplining him. When you tense up you feel this in your neck and get red flushes in your neck and face. You want Andy to behave more like an adult and think that the time has come to stop mollycoddling him. You think Andy is afraid that if he gives a little ground in doing jobs for you he will be overwhelmed by more requests.

When we looked at how you actually communicated with Andy, it seemed as though you may have used a number of possibly unhelpful communications. With your words, you failed to make a direct request. Instead of saying 'Please mow the lawn once a week', you blurred it by saying 'Why don't you mow the lawn?'. Your voice was not particularly firm. Also, you probably made insufficient eye contact. What do you think about this feedback?

[Client has the opportunity to contribute.]

Looking for some possibly unhelpful thoughts, when Andy turned you down, you said you sulked and whiningly told him he did not appreciate how much you did for him. I think your self-talk insufficiently coached you in how to make your request assertively. In addition, you may be creating rules that demand that Andy does what you want and demand that he shows affection. Do any of my comments about your thoughts seem accurate to you?

[Client has the opportunity to contribute.]

Translating unhelpful communications and thoughts into goals

Clients need encouragement to work on communications and thoughts that interfere with their effectiveness in problem situations. You need to assist them into a positive frame of mind. Once helpers and clients agree on what specific aspects of clients' communications and thoughts require addressing, translate these into statements of goals. Statements of goals are the 'flip side' of statements identifying the communications and thoughts on which clients need to work. Such statements assist clients to move from thinking 'This is how I may be communicating and thinking insufficiently well concerning the situation' to 'This is how I can communicate and think much better'.

Basically, there are two main ways to state goals: presenting them verbally and presenting them both verbally and in writing. Box 11.5 is an extension of the case example of Pat and Andy used in Box 11.4. Box 11.5 both illustrates a helper statement of goals and provides the format for a written statement.

Box 11.5   Translating unhelpful thoughts and communications into goals

Verbal statement by helper

Pat, let's move on and see if we can state some possible goals for improving how you communicate and think. Your overall goal is to make an assertive request to Andy to mow the lawn once a week. Looking at communication, when asking Andy to mow the lawn, you could have three goals: one, making a direct request; two, speaking with a firm voice; and three, making good eye contact. What do you think of these goals for communicating better?
[*Client has the opportunity to respond.*]

Looking at thinking, there are two mind areas you could set as goals. First, developing self-talk in which you coach yourself in making assertive requests for Andy to mow the lawn. Second, changing from creating demanding rules, such as 'Andy must do what I want' to stating your wishes as preferences 'I would prefer that Andy does what I want'. What do you think of these goals for thinking more effectively?
[*Client has the opportunity to respond.*]

Written statement to accompany verbal statement
Overall goal:
To make an assertive request to Andy to mow the lawn once a week.

Communication goals:
- Make a direct request;
- Speak with a firm voice;
- Use good eye contact.

Mind goals:
- Develop coaching self-talk
  (about implementing communication goals);
- Develop realistic rules
  (state preferences, not demands).

What are some considerations when translating unhelpful communications and thoughts into goals? Try not to do too much. When first learning, restrict yourself to identifying and then translating into a goal one unhelpful communication and one unhelpful thought. Even when more experienced, keep your statements of goals simple. Always, state communication and mind goals in words with which clients are comfortable. You may need to alter the wording of your statements of goals to suit their preferences.

When stating goals, attend to clients' feelings. Most clients feel positive about statements of goals and see them as motivating. Others, however, may find them threatening. Goals connote the need for effort and change and a degree of ambivalence is inevitable. Pay attention to resistances and reservations. Note voice and body cues of inadequate commitment. Even though clients may verbalise commitment and confidence, their non-verbal messages may indicate otherwise. If possible work through with clients their reservations and commitment difficulties. Some clients feel more comfortable about goals when they become clearer about how to attain them.

Lastly, encourage clients to write the goals down and do so yourself. Both clients' and your own memories are not infallible, so it helps to keep a written record. Furthermore, you can use written records for checking on progress. In addition, clients may wish to post written statements of goals as reminders to change how they communicate and think.

Planning strategies for change

Helping strategies are the ways and means by which helpers assist clients to attain their goals in problem situations. Other terms for strategies are procedures, methods or interventions. All helping strategies need to build clients' abilities to help themselves. Thus helping strategies encompass both helpers and clients. Helpers need to develop a repertoire of strategies to assist clients attain goals. Introductory counselling skills students can develop their repertoire of strategies and the skills of implementing them bit by bit. The next two chapters review some basic ways in which helpers may use strategies to improve clients' communication and thinking.

Plans are overall statements of how to combine and sequence helping strategies for managing problem situations. Let us take the example of planning strategies for change in the example of Pat and Andy, already used in Boxes 11.4 and 11.5 in this chapter. Pat's helper might think that coaching her through role-playing to develop her communication skills is the best strategy to help her attain her communication skills goals.

Regarding Pat's mind skills goals, training in coaching self-talk is the preferred strategy to attain her self-talk goal. The strategy for changing Pat's demanding rule is training in challenging her demanding rule and then stating it as a preferential rule.

Assuming that the client thinks that these strategies might be useful, how do you sequence them? One approach is to ask clients where they would like to work first. A variation of this approach is to ask clients if they would rather focus on their mind goals or their communication goals first. Sometimes, as with Pat, to some degree the sequencing of the strategies is dictated by her goals. For example, Pat can be coached in verbal, vocal and bodily communication skills and then in the coaching self-talk for implementing these skills. Here a focus on communication precedes a focus on mind, though there is obvious overlap.

Pat and her helper still need to sequence in their plan training her in creating preferential rules. Pat's helper can consult with her about when to do this. An advantage of consulting with clients in planning the sequencing of strategies is that they are more likely to be motivated if they have had a say than if not.

The above is a relatively unstructured approach to planning strategies. On some occasions, helpers may suggest a more structured approach: for example, working through a training manual on relaxation skills to combat physical tension. On other occasions, helpers may suggest a semi-structured approach: for instance, a plan for an unemployed client could include a combination of individual helping sessions and attending a group workshop on job-seeking skills.

Usually, when first learning the changing communications and thoughts approach to stage three of the RUC model, counselling skills students can take a relatively unstructured approach. You discuss with clients where to start and where to go next, often as you are going along.

Delivering helping strategies

When at the Royal Melbourne Institute of Technology, I once trained and supervised a counselling psychology student, around 30 years old, called Michael. Michael's daytime job was working as a psychologist in a correctional facility for juvenile delinquents who were serious offenders. Academically, Michael was a respectable rather than outstanding student. However, in his practical skills work Michael possessed a reassuring presence and was particularly good at delivering helping strategies to assist clients in changing communications and thoughts. Allowing clients to retain responsibility for problem situations, Michael would offer simple and clear explanations about how to change, show them what to do, give them practice in doing it, and set simple between-session activities. Without trying to hit winners all the time, Michael played a very steady and methodical game that got results.

In much of helper training the emphasis is on receiver or listening skills rather than on sender or training skills. In the changing communications and thoughts approach to stage three of the RUC helping process model, helpers use relationship and training skills flexibly to assist clients to attain learning goals. My experience is that most beginning counselling skills students are very poor at delivering helping strategies. Unlike Michael, who had learned the hard way in his work with juvenile delinquents, they are insufficiently clear, systematic and thorough.

When discussing learning counselling skills in Chapter 5, I stressed the importance of: (1) *tell*, or learning from clear instruction; (2) *show*, or learning from observing good demonstrations; and (3) *do/reflect*, or learning from practice, feedback and reflection. Students need to develop their skills of being user-friendly coaches to clients. Learn to explain material clearly. Since you are teaching applied skills, always demonstrate them. Then make sure clients know how to enact them. It is not good enough just to ask clients whether they understand the skills and think they can use them. Where possible, ensure that clients enact and practise their changed communications and thoughts until they have some proficiency in them.

In addition, be prepared to negotiate with clients simple between-session activities. Such activities allow clients to rehearse and practise outside of helping what you have been working on in your sessions together. Ways of increasing the likelihood of clients doing between-session activities include: negotiating them rather than imposing them; checking that clients clearly know how to enact the changed thoughts and communications; writing activities instructions and key points down; and discussing with clients any difficulties they anticipate in carrying out the activities.

In coaching clients to change communications and thoughts, remember that a little learned thoroughly is usually preferable to covering more ground superficially. Giving up poor habits is not easy and can be threatening. Almost inevitably, introductory counselling skills courses only allow brief helping contacts of one or two sessions either with peer 'clients' or volunteer 'clients'. Though very brief helping focused on addressing specific problem situations can have positive outcomes, more often than not genuinely lasting changes in how clients communicate and think takes much longer.

Summary

Two somewhat overlapping approaches to the changing stage of the RUC helping process model are: (1) a problem solving approach; and (2) a changing specific thoughts and communications approach. The role of helpers in the problem solving approach is mainly that of facilitators, whereas in the changing specific thoughts and communications approach the helpers are both facilitators and user-friendly coaches.

In the problem solving approach, helpers use active listening and questioning skills to facilitate clients in clarifying goals for desirable outcomes in problem situations. Then helpers proceed to assist clients in generating and exploring options for attaining their goals. The next step is for helpers to facilitate clients in devising step by step plans to implement their chosen options for attaining goals. Such plans should be realistic, have a time frame, and be written down by clients.

In the changing specific communications and thoughts approach, helpers cooperate with clients to identify one or more unhelpful communications and thoughts. Next helpers translate these unhelpful communications and thoughts into communication goals and mind goals. Then helpers plan helping strategies to attain each goal. Helping strategies are methods or interventions for attaining goals. Plans are overall statements of how to combine and sequence helping strategies. Helpers should develop plans in consultation with clients. Sometimes a good approach to planning is to ask clients where they want to start and make decisions about sequencing helping strategies as helping proceeds.

Introductory counselling skills students are urged to acknowledge their limitations and proceed with caution in implementing the changing specific communications and thoughts approach. Furthermore, you need to develop skills of delivering helping strategies including: explaining what to do clearly, showing how to do it; giving clients practice and feedback, and negotiating appropriate between-session activities.

Activities

Activity 11.1   Using the problem solving approach

1   Work with a partner who presents either a problem situation of their own or one based on a client seen elsewhere. You may also have another student in the 'observer' role.
2   Conduct a helping session using all three stages of the RUC helping process model for problem situations. In particular focus on using active listening skills to be a good companion to your client throughout the helping process. For example, in the under-standing stage, just ask a few well-chosen questions and make sure you use good active listening skills when your client responds.
3   When you come to the change stage, take a problem solving approach in which you facilitate your client in:
   • clarifying her/his goals;
   • generating and exploring options for attaining goals;
   • developing an action plan.
4   After the session ends, hold a sharing and feedback session. It can be a good idea to videotape your session and play it back as part of your sharing and feedback session.
5   During a training group, each student should have one or more opportunities to be both helper and client.
6   Excerpts from student videotapes can be shown and discussed with the trainer(s) and the whole training group.

Activity 11.2   Using the changing specific communications and thoughts approach

1   Work with a partner who presents either a problem situation of their own or one based on a client seen elsewhere. You may also have another student in the 'observer' role.

2   Conduct a helping session using all three stages of the RUC helping process model for problem situations. In particular, focus on using active listening skills to be a good companion to your client in the first two stages of the helping process. For example, in the understanding stage, just ask a few well-chosen questions and make sure you use good active listening skills when your client responds.

3   When you come to the change stage, take a changing specific communications and thoughts approach and:
  • identify one important unhelpful communication (you may include verbal, vocal and bodily dimensions) and one important unhelpful thought;
  • translate these unhelpful communications and thoughts into goals; and
  • discuss with your client a plan of helping strategies to attain each goal.

4   After the session ends, hold a sharing and feedback session. It can be a good idea to videotape your session and play it back as part of your sharing and feedback session.

5   During a training group, each student should have one or more opportunities to be both helper and client. Later on, students can identify more than one each of unhelpful communications and thoughts. However, always keep your breakdown of unhelpful communications and thoughts simple.

6   Excerpts from student videotapes can be shown and discussed with the trainer(s) and the whole training group.

Activity 11.3   Assessing my delivering helping strategies skills

Part A   Assessment

Assess your good and poor skills in each of the following delivering helping strategies areas

Offering descriptions to clients:
• my good skills
• my poor skills

Giving demonstrations to clients:
- my good skills
- my poor skills

Coaching clients' practice:
- my good skills
- my poor skills

Negotiating between session activities:
- my good skills
- my poor skills

Summarise your skills strengths and deficiencies.

Part B   Planning

Develop a plan to become more skilled at delivering helping strategies. In your plan include:
- a clear statement of goals;
- what steps you intend taking to attain each of your goals;
- how you will sequence your steps;
- a time frame;
- how you will deal with any anticipated difficulties in implementing your plan; and
- how you will monitor your progress.

12 Strategies for Changing Communication and Actions

Oh . . . stop moaning on about your problems and pull yerself together.
The Bad Samaritan to a man fallen by the wayside.
Steve Best

Chapter outcomes

By studying and doing the activities in this chapter you should be able to:

- *understand the importance of client-centred coaching;*
- *develop your demonstration skills;*
- *develop your rehearsing skills;*
- *develop your setting progressive tasks skills;*
- *develop your skills of designing changing communication and actions experiments;*
- *assist clients to identify and use supports and resources; and*
- *develop your negotiating between-session activities skills.*

The next two chapters are designed to assist you to develop a basic tool kit of strategies for helping clients get from here to there in terms of their specific changing communications and thoughts goals. In addition, you may find these strategies useful when taking the problem solving approach to stage three of the relating–understanding–changing (RUC) model too.

This chapter focuses on helping strategies for changing communications and actions. By communication I mean changing not only the verbal, but the vocal and bodily dimensions of communication. By actions I mean activities that clients can engage in when not in direct contact with others. Though mind and communication/actions intertwine, some basic helping strategies for developing clients' minds are reviewed in the next chapter.

Client-centred coaching

When delivering helping strategies, it is important that you allow clients to retain ownership of problem situations. There is also a risk that helpers become too task oriented and insufficiently oriented towards maintaining the quality of the helping relationship. The urge to teach and instruct can override respect for clients' potentials to lead their own lives and make the decisions that work best for them.

A useful distinction is that between helper-centred coaching and client-centred coaching. Helper-centred coaching essentially takes the jug and mug approach: helpers are the jugs pouring knowledge and skills into clients' mugs (in both senses of the word!). Helpers control the time spent in the changing stage and their comments take the form: 'First you do this, then you do that, then you do that . . .' and so on. Clients are passive receptacles who are allowed to assume little responsibility for the pace and direction of their learning. In reality, very few helpers would work as crudely as I have depicted.

Client-centred coaching respects clients' responsibilities for leading their lives and making the decisions that work best for them when faced with problem situations. Helpers as client-centred coaches develop plans to attain goals in conjunction with clients, describe strategies and obtain consent to proceed, draw out and build upon clients' existing knowledge and skills, allow clients to participate in decisions about the pace and direction of learning, and assist clients in acquiring knowledge and skills for self-helping.

Take the example of providing feedback about clients' performances when rehearsing changed communications. Helper-centred coaches provide the feedback themselves as though they are the experts. Client-centred coaches try to develop the expertise of clients by asking them to evaluate their own performances before providing feedback themselves. Even when they do provide feedback, client-centred coaches are prepared to discuss it and leave clients with the final say regarding its validity for them.

Demonstration skills

Helpers can use demonstrations to develop different and better ways of communicating/acting and thinking. In addition, helpers can demonstrate how to accompany communicating or acting differently with appropriate self-talk. Demonstrations may be used to assist clients in acquiring new responses, strengthening existing responses, and weakening or eliminating self-defeating responses.

Methods of demonstration

Following are some of the ways that you may choose to demonstrate. Introductory counselling skills students are especially encouraged to develop skills of live demonstration.

Live
Probably most helping demonstrations are live. Helpers may use live demonstrations when initially presenting different ways of behaving and when coaching clients afterwards. Live demonstrations have the advantage of here and now spontaneity. In addition, you can interact with clients and modify your demonstrations as appropriate. Unless a recording is made, a limitation of live demonstration is that clients have no copy to watch or listen to on their own.

Helpers can encourage clients to observe live demonstrations in their everyday lives. For instance, shy people can be encouraged to observe and learn from the social skills of those more outgoing.

Recorded
Especially if you are working with client populations who have similar problems, you can make your own recorded demonstrations on videotape or audio cassette. When making recordings, you can erase and correct poor efforts until you get it right. In addition, you can use recordings made by other people, some of which are professionally made: for instance, relaxation cassettes. Advantages of audio cassette and videotape demonstrations are that they can be loaned to clients and be listened to or viewed repeatedly.

Visualised

Helpers can ask clients to visualise or imagine the demonstration scenes that they describe. Clients can be asked to visualise either themselves or someone else performing the targeted communications or actions. Visualised demonstrations are only appropriate for clients who can visualise scenes adequately. A potential drawback is that, even when instructions are given well, there may be important differences in what you describe and what clients imagine. In general clients visualise best when relaxed.

Written

Written demonstrations are more appropriate for helping clients change how they think than how they communicate and act. However, written demonstrations that contain visual images, such as cartoon characters, can convey desirable communications and actions.

Demonstrator skills

You must know your material thoroughly to integrate good demonstrations into helping. For example, if you have a sound grasp of either assertion skills or of showing you care skills, you are more likely to demonstrate these skills adequately than if less sure of your ground. Pay attention to characteristics of the demonstration. One issue is whether to demonstrate incorrect as well as correct behaviours. You may plan briefly to demonstrate negative behaviours as a way of highlighting positive ones. However, make sure not to confuse clients and always have the major emphasis on correct rather than incorrect communications/actions.

Take care how you introduce demonstrations. Your initial demonstration is likely to be part of a 'tell', 'show', 'do/reflect' sequence. You may increase clients' attention by telling them what to look out for and also informing them that afterwards they will perform the communications/actions that you demonstrate.

During and at the end you may ask clients whether they understand the points you demonstrate. Also, clients can summarise the main points of demonstrations. Probably the best way to check clients' learning is to observe and coach them as they perform demonstrated communications/actions.

Box 12.1 provides an example of using demonstration to assist a client to develop the skills and confidence to communicate more effectively.

Box 12.1   Using demonstration skills

Sharon, aged 34, is seeing a helper, Leanne, and the problem situation Sharon wants to work on is how to assertively set limits on men who want to go to bed with her at the end of first dates. In particular, Sharon wants to focus on what to say on her upcoming first evening date with Jim, 41, an attractive man with whom she might like to develop a relationship. In conjunction with Leanne, Sharon develops the following verbal response to a possible request for sex: 'Jim, I'm enjoying our evening together, but I want to get to know you better before answering that sort of question.' With Leanne's help Sharon decides that her vocal communication should be calm and firm. Regarding her bodily communication, Sharon wants to make good eye contact and keep a pleasant facial expression.

Leanne then asks Sharon to be Jim and says she will be Sharon. Sharon role-playing Jim asks Leanne about going to bed together and Leanne responds demonstrating the targeted verbal, vocal and bodily communications. Leanne enquires of Sharon how she experiences this response. Sharon is happy with the response so they reverse roles and Leanne as Jim asks the question. Sharon's response is insufficiently assertive. After asking Sharon to evaluate herself, Leanne uses demonstration to show how she observed Sharon's verbal, vocal and bodily communication. Sharon then tries her response a few more times until she feels reasonably confident that if asked the question by Jim, she can perform competently.

Rehearsing skills

Imagine that you are Stephen Spielberg about to start directing a new film. You have picked your actors and actresses and now want them to become proficient in their roles. Much of your work involves building their communication skills by coaching them at rehearsals in which they try out or role-play their parts.

Some clients become uncomfortable at the idea of role-playing. Feeling shy and vulnerable already, they think they will further expose themselves in role-plays. Possibly 'rehearsing' is a less threatening expression than 'role-playing'. You may need to explain to clients that rehearsing can help them by allowing them to try out communicating differently in an environment where mistakes do not really matter. Doing this can provide knowledge and confidence for communicating effectively in actual problem situations.

One way to start rehearsing is for helpers to demonstrate targeted communications with or without the client playing the other person. For example, in Box 12.1, the helper Leanne demonstrates Sharon's communication goals with Sharon role-playing Jim before inviting Sharon to role-play herself while Leanne plays the part of Jim. Leanne can then coach Sharon through a number of rehearsals in which she assertively sets limits on Jim's amorous request.

You and your client may need to generate and rehearse alternative scripts. Train clients diversely rather than rigidly, so they have the flexibility to communicate well across a range of contingencies. Facilitate clients' contributions to the discussion prior to making your own suggestions. For instance, Leanne could ask Sharon 'What do you think are the main ways in which Jim might respond to your assertive statement?' Then for each of the main ways identified, Leanne could ask 'What verbal, vocal and bodily communication do you need to use to respond effectively?' Then, Leanne and Sharon could rehearse effective communications for different ways Jim might respond.

Helpers and clients need to process each rehearsal. Helpers can ask clients questions like: 'How do you think you did?', 'How were you feeling in that rehearsal?', and 'What difficulties might you face in communicating like that in the real situation?' In addition, helpers can provide both feedback and encouragement. Sometimes, you can audio record or video record rehearsals and use the playback for feedback and discussion.

Box 12.2 provides an example of using audio cassette recording and playback based on my training of a senior executive client Louise who, despite her outstanding qualifications, was repeatedly having unsuccessful interviews for senior positions. An alternative would have been to use video recording and playback, but I did not have this facility available.

Box 12.2   An example of rehearsing a client

When the time came to work on Louise's communication goals for job interviews, Richard and Louise first developed a list of questions that Louise was likely to be asked or that might cause her difficulty. Richard wrote each question down as Louise suggested it. Illustrative questions were:

- 'Why have you applied for this position?'
- 'Why did you leave your previous position?'

- 'How would you go about supplying leadership to professional accountants who work for this company?'
- 'What is your approach toward the supervision of support staff?'

Then, for assessment purposes, Richard and Louise conducted a cassette-recorded mini-interview. When playing back this interview, Richard asked Louise to evaluate her skills along with making some suggestions of his own. As a result of this assessment, Richard wrote six answering question rules on the whiteboard (these were also taken down by Louise):

1   Home in on questions by paraphrasing/repeating their crux/key words.
2   Place conclusion at front of answer.
3   Give reasons for conclusion in point form.
4   Be brief.
5   Voice messages – comfortable, avoid booming.
6   Body messages – smile, look relaxed, use some gestures – but not too much.

Leaving these rules clearly visible on the whiteboard. Louise and Richard then conducted a series of cassette-recorded mini-interviews. When playing them back, Louise first evaluated herself, and then Richard provided her with feedback on her performance and coaching to improve it. Louise rehearsed bodily as well as verbal and vocal communication. These rehearsals, in which Richard represented an interview panel, took place in two subsequent sessions as well.

Setting progressive tasks skills

Knowing how to assist clients to set progressive tasks is a useful skill for beginning counselling skills students to have in their tool kits. Sometimes clients fail either to carry out a task or to succeed at it because they are trying to do too much too soon. Setting progressive tasks in conjunction with clients allows them gradually to build up their confidence and skills to attain communication and action goals. Sometimes progressive tasks are built into plans at the start of the changing stage. On other occasions, helpers and clients formulate progressive tasks to attain specific goals during the changing stage.

In very brief helping, there is limited opportunity for clients to build up desirable communications and actions over a period of time by setting and implementing progressively difficult tasks. All you may have time for is to assist clients to communicate better at relatively simple tasks in a progressively more difficult set of tasks that cluster around a central theme. For example, you may help clients, whose goals are to become more honest, make one or more relatively low-threat disclosures to their partners. Another example is that of helping salespersons afraid of making cold calls start cold calling with relatively non-threatening potential customers.

In setting progressively more difficult tasks, essentially what you are doing is establishing a hierarchy of sub-goals clustered around a theme. Attaining sub-goals allows clients gradually to become more proficient in their targeted communication and action goals. However, even within specific situations, you can break tasks down and train clients progressively: for example, focusing first on verbal communication, then on vocal communication, then on bodily communication and then on putting all three together.

Work closely with clients when listing progressive tasks. Start with small steps that clients think they can achieve. Achieving small first steps motivates clients to persist in attempting more difficult tasks. Be prepared to build in intermediate tasks if clients think the progression of tasks is too steep.

To avoid connotations of failure, you can encourage clients to view attempting each progressively more difficult task as an experiment in which they gain valuable information about themselves. You can also use your demonstrating and rehearsing skills to increase the chances of success in each progressive task. In addition, you can help clients to share feelings and thoughts about attempting graded tasks and train them in relevant mind skills, for instance how to use calming and coaching self-talk.

Usually clients perform progressively more difficult tasks outside of helping. Wherever possible, encourage clients to report back on their progress. Use information about difficulties and set-backs to improve how clients perform in future. If a task on the list genuinely proves too difficult, either change the ordering of tasks or generate different and less difficult tasks to do next.

When clients succeed at tasks, you can reward them with praise, encourage them to acknowledge their success, and help them to realise that succeeding results from willingness to take calculated risks, expending effort and changing how they communicate and act. Repeated success experiences with specific tasks consolidates clients' skills and confidence. Box 12.3 provides brief illustrations of progressive tasks negotiated between helpers and clients to assist clients in changing how they communicate and act.

Box 12.3   Examples of progressive tasks

Public speaking: Sara, a 20-year-old social work student

Changing communication goals
Clear and firm vocal communication, making good eye contact with audience (not reading text).

Progressive tasks
1   Ask questions in tutorials this week.
2   State own opinions in tutorials next week.
3   Give a brief presentation in a small group tutorial within a month.
4   Give at least one brief presentation in front of a larger class by the end of semester.

Becoming and staying fit: Con, a 53 year-old, who has just recovered from a minor heart attack

Changing action goal
Go jogging for a minimum of 20 minutes a day

Progressive tasks
1   Jog for a minimum of 10 minutes a day for the first week.
2   Jog for a minimum of 15 minutes a day for the second week.
3   Jog for a minimum of 20 minutes a day for the third week and thereafter.

Repairing a relationship: Mike and Sandra, a couple in their late 20s

Changing communication goals
A minimum of 30 minutes a day 'happy talk'.
   Verbal communication, talk about non-controversial topics; vocal communication, easy to hear, pleasant pitch; bodily communication, show interest when listening with facial expressions and head nods.

Progressive tasks
1   A minimum of 10 minutes a day of happy talk the first week.
2   A minimum of 20 minutes a day of happy talk the second week.
3   A minimum of 30 minutes a day of happy talk the third week and thereafter.

Assisting identification and use of supports and resources

Counselling skills students and helpers may need to raise some clients' awareness about the importance of identifying and using supports and of lessening contact with unsupportive people. Helpers can assist clients to identify people in home environments who can support their efforts to attain communication and action goals. For example, university students with study skills deficits can seek out sympathetic lecturers and tutors to help them attain action goals, for instance writing more polished essays or preparing well for examinations. Unemployed people can approach friends and relatives who may not only offer them emotional support, but also be sources for job leads. Women working on attaining verbal, vocal and bodily assertive communication goals skills can seek out women's groups where they may find other women with similar objectives. Teachers who feel burned out can associate with colleagues relatively happy with their lot rather than those perpetually complaining. Furthermore, they can attain self-care goals by engaging in recreational activities with people unconnected with education.

An inverse approach to support is for helpers to assist clients in identifying unsympathetic or counterproductive people. Clients are then left with various choices: getting such people to accept, if not support, their efforts to change; seeing less of them; or stopping seeing them altogether. If these people are family members, avoiding them altogether may be difficult, especially if clients are financially dependent on them. Here, helpers and clients may discuss damage control strategies. However, often clients can choose their friendship and membership groups. For example, if juvenile delinquents want to eliminate negative activities like stealing cars and taking drugs, they may need to change the company they keep.

Sometimes, helpers can extend helping strategies into clients' home environments. Helpers may use a variety of people as aides: teachers, parents, welfare workers, supervisors and friends. Some guidelines for using 'non-professional' third parties as helpers' aides include: obtain the permission of clients, identify suitable people, and, where necessary, train them in their roles. An example of using a third party as an aide is asking a teacher to help a shy and lonely pupil to participate more in class.

In addition, helpers can assist clients to identify and use resources for helping them attain and maintain communication and action goals.

Such resources include: workshops and short courses; self-help books and manuals: instructional audio cassettes, videotapes and CD-ROMs; appropriate voluntary agencies; peer support groups and networks; and telephone hotlines and crisis information outlets.

Helpers should familiarise themselves with and establish contact with the human supports and educational and information resources of most relevance to the client populations with which they work. Access to suitable supports and resources may be of tremendous assistance to some clients as they take positive steps towards changing how they communicate and act in problem situations.

Designing changing communication and actions experiments

A major concern of all effective helpers is how best to help clients take the risks of changing their communication and actions. Another major concern is how best to help them transfer knowledge and skills to outside of helping. Working with clients to design experiments in which they change how they communicate and act provide an excellent way to approach both concerns. Clients in conjunction with helpers hypothesise about the consequences of using outside helping the communications and actions they have worked on inside helping. Then clients implement the communications/actions and evaluate the consequences of doing so.

An advantage of viewing changing communication and actions in experimental terms is that it helps clients to gain greater detachment about what they do and its results. When experiments do not work out quite as planned, clients do not have to think they have failed. Rather, each experiment is a learning experience in which clients can gather useful information.

Often experiments simultaneously focus on changing both mind skills and communications. For instance, Greg is a senior consulting engineer who was forced out of a partnership in his previous consultant engineering firm because of his very poor relationships with both partners and support staff, who found him aggressive, demanding and distant. Greg comes for brief helping targeted on not making the same mistakes again in a new consultancy firm he is joining next week. Greg knows that he has been assigned a secretary called Courtney and wants to develop a pleasant working relationship with her.

An experiment focused solely on communication might target Greg's verbal, vocal and bodily communication in regard to showing appreciation to Courtney for work well done. An experiment focused solely on mind skills might target Greg's coping self-talk before, during and after he communicates appreciation. An experiment focused on both communication and mind would target both how Greg communicates appreciation to Courtney and his use of coping self-talk.

In Box 12.4, for the sake of simplicity, I focus on designing an experiment to change only how Greg communicates.

Box 12.4   Example of assisting a client to experiment with changing his communication

Problem situation
Greg, who had serious relationship problems in his previous position, wants to improve how he shows appreciation for work well done to his new secretary Courtney during the first week of his new job.

Communication goals
Verbal communication, make comments like 'Thank-you', 'You've done a very good job', 'I appreciate your work'; vocal communication, firm voice with emphasis on positive feedback words like 'thank' and 'appreciate'; bodily communication, good eye contact and pleasant smile.

Making an 'If . . . then . . .' statement
The 'If' part of the statement relates to Greg rehearsing, practising and then using his changed verbal, vocal and bodily communication. The 'then . . .' part of the statement indicates the specific consequences he predicts will follow from using his changed communication. For example:

If I use the following changed communications [see communication goals] to express appreciation to Courtney during my first week in my new job, *then* these specific consequences (for instance, (a) I will feel better about myself for being positive, and (b) Courtney will feel and act more positively toward me) are likely to follow.

If . . . . *If*
. . . .
then
(a) . . . .
(b) . . . .
(c) . . . .
(d) . . . .

Rehearsing and practising

With assistance from his helper Greg can further rehearse and practise his changed communications to have a reasonable chance of implementing them properly.

Trying out changed communication

Greg implements his changed way of communicating to his secretary during his first week at work in his new job.

Evaluating consequences

Initially Greg can evaluate on his own how he gets on when changing his communication. He can ask himself questions like 'How well did I use my changed verbal, vocal and bodily communications?', 'What were the positive and negative consequences of using my changed communications for myself and for others?', 'Have my predictions been confirmed or negated?', and 'Do I want to use my changed communications in future?' Afterwards Greg's helper can assist him in processing the learnings from his experiment.

Negotiating between-session activities skills

After presenting, demonstrating and coaching clients in new skills, helpers can negotiate relevant between-session activities, like the changing communication experiments just described. Many reasons exist for assigning such tasks (Cormier and Cormier, 1991; Egan, 1998; Hutchins and Cole, 1992). These reasons include: speeding up the learning process; encouraging clients to monitor, rehearse and practise changed communications and actions; helping the transfer of trained communications/actions to outside life; finding out about difficulties in using communications/actions in real life; and increasing the client's sense of self-control and of personal responsibility for developing targeted communications/actions.

Following are some central skills for negotiating between-session activities. These skills can increase the chances of clients' compliance. Counselling skills students and helpers can offer reasons for and explain the importance of doing agreed upon activities. Right from the start of tell, show and do/reflect sequences, you can tell clients that to gain competence in their targeted communications and actions they will need to work on them between sessions.

Be careful to negotiate rather than impose activities. Clients are more likely to comply with activities that they have had a say in designing. Three key aspects of realistic between-session activities are that they: consolidate earlier learning; are of appropriate difficulty; and entail a realistic amount of work. It is preferable that clients commit themselves to a modest amount of between-session activities rather than make vague commitments to a larger amount.

How can clients know precisely what to do? Often I have observed introductory counselling skills students rush through negotiating between-session activities at the end of helping sessions in ways that virtually guaranteed client non-compliance. Mistakes students made included not leaving enough time, inviting insufficient client partici-pation, giving vague verbal instructions, and not checking whether clients clearly understood what they were meant to do.

Helpers can design their own between-session activity forms. Box 12.5 shows four possible formats. Where possible, either you or your clients should write down clear instructions for between-session acti-vities on these forms. Writing instructions on scraps of paper is generally not good enough. Always check what clients write to make sure they have taken down the instructions correctly. Furthermore, always check that clients are absolutely clear about what they are agreeing to do. If you wish clients to fill out forms such as monitoring logs, provide these forms yourself. This practice ensures clear instructions and saves clients the extra effort of having to write out forms before filling them in.

Box 12.5   Formats for between-session activity forms

Format 1
Between-session activities
In order to gain the most from your helping session(s) you are encouraged to engage in the following between-session activities.

Format 2
To follow up
In order to gain the most from your helping session(s) you are encouraged to perform the following tasks.

Format 3
Take away sheet
Use this sheet for writing down (1) your main learnings from helping and (2) any instructions for between-session activities.

Format 4
Learning contract
I make a learning contract with myself to perform the following activities before the next helping session.

Explore with clients their motivation for completing between-session activities. Where possible, identify and help clients work through anticipated difficulties and setbacks. Also, identify with clients rewards associated with completing activities. If you have negotiated realistic amounts, hopefully clients will comply.

Sometimes, changing a way of communicating or acting requires clients to give up long-established habits. Here, it can be especially important not to assign an activity that is too difficult too soon. Furthermore, some clients return to unsupportive, if not downright hostile environments. Here you may need to prepare clients more thoroughly prior to suggesting they implement targeted communications in real-life settings. Such preparation is likely to include devising strategies for coping with negative feedback.

Lastly, signal a joint progress review. Let clients know that at or around the start of the next session, you will review progress with between-session activities together. Clients who know that their helpers are interested in and supportive of their attempts to complete between-session activities are more likely to be motivated to do so.

Summary

In the changing specific communications and thoughts approach to stage three of the RUC model, helpers are client-centred coaches who show respect to clients as they assist them to draw out and develop their resources. Helpers require good demonstration skills. Methods of demonstration include live, recorded, visualised and written. Demonstrator skills include thorough knowledge of the material being demonstrated, cuing clients what to observe and, afterwards, checking with clients that they have understood the points demonstrated.

Helpers can rehearse clients in how to attain communication and actions goals. Remember to focus on vocal and bodily as well as verbal communication and to rehearse clients so that they can respond flexibly to different contingencies. In addition, encourage clients to evaluate their own performance before providing feedback. You can also use audio cassette and videotape feedback as part of the rehearsal process.

Helpers can work with clients to establish progressively more difficult tasks. Start with small steps that clients think they can achieve. Having success experience with easier tasks can provide the confidence and skills to proceed to more difficult tasks. You can use your demonstrating and rehearsing skills to increase the likelihood of clients' success in each progressive task. Encourage clients and help them to own their successes.

Helpers can assist clients to identify and use the support of people who will assist their efforts to attain and maintain communication and actions goals. In addition, helpers can help clients develop strategies for avoiding or limiting the impact of unhelpful people. Sometimes helpers deliberately use third parties as aides in the helping process. Some guidelines for using helper aides include: obtaining permission of clients, identifying suitable people and, where necessary, training aides in their roles. Helpers can also assist clients to identify and use other resources, for instance self-help books, instructional audio cassettes and videotapes, workshops and short courses.

Helpers can assist clients to design mini experiments in which they try out and evaluate using their changed communications and actions. Viewing changing specific communications and actions as experiments allows clients to gain a degree of detachment over their attempts to change.

In addition, helpers can negotiate between-session activities with clients. Considerations for enhancing compliance include: explaining the importance of practice, negotiating rather than imposing activities, allowing enough time at the end of a session to discuss activities properly, writing down clear instructions and signalling a progress review in the next session.

Activities

Activity 12.1   Demonstration skills

Part A   Live demonstration

Work with a partner with one of you taking the role of helper and one taking the role of client. Client and helper hold a discussion to choose a specific communication that the client wants to improve. Do not attempt too much. The helper then goes through the following steps in a demonstration:

- cuing the client what to observe;
- demonstrating each of the verbal, vocal and bodily components of the communication and then putting all three together (your partner may role-play the other person as you demonstrate); and
- asking the client to summarise the main points of the demonstration.

Afterwards hold a sharing and discussion session focused on the helper's use of demonstration skills. If necessary repeat the demonstration until the helper feels s/he has obtained some degree of competence in using demonstration skills.

Then reverse roles.

Part B   Live demonstration with accompanying self-talk

Rehearse and practise a live demonstration in which the demonstrator not only demonstrates observable communication but also demonstrates talking her/himself through the communication sequence. You may use a partner as 'the other person' in your demonstration.

Activity 12.2   Rehearsing and coaching skills

Work with a partner with one of you taking the role of helper and one taking the role of client. Either for a specific communication that was demonstrated in Activity 12.1 or for another specific communication that the client wants to improve go through the following sequence:

- cuing the client what to observe;
- demonstrating each of the verbal, vocal and bodily components of the communication and then putting all three together (your partner may role-play the other person as you demonstrate);
- asking the client to summarise the main points of the demonstration;
- introducing the idea of rehearsing the communication to your client;
- rehearsing and coaching your client to the point where, within the limits of this activity, s/he feels able to perform the communication in real life competently. You may use audio cassette or videotape playback as part of the rehearsing and coaching process.

Afterwards hold a sharing and discussion session focused on the helper's use of rehearsing and coaching skills. If necessary, allow the helper to rehearse and coach some more until the helper feels s/he has obtained some degree of competence in using rehearsing and coaching skills.

Then reverse roles.

Activity 12.3   Setting progressive tasks skills

Work with a partner with one of you taking the role of helper and one taking the role of client. Either for a specific communication that was rehearsed and coached in Activity 12.2 or for another specific communication that the client wants to improve, develop a hierarchy of approximately five progressively more difficult tasks for the client to attain. Observe the following guidelines:

- work cooperatively with your client;
- start with easy small tasks;

- have a gradual progression to more difficult tasks;
- both helper and client write the hierarchy of tasks down.

Afterwards hold a sharing and feedback session and then reverse roles.

Activity 12.4   Negotiating between-session activities skills

Work with a partner, possibly in regard to changing a specific communication for which you rehearsed and coached her/him in Activity 12.2. Now rehearse and practise how to negotiate one or more between-session activities so that your partner can use the time before the next helping session to good effect. To increase your clients' chances of compliance, observe the following guidelines:

- allow adequate time for negotiating between-session activities;
- introduce the idea that between-session practice is important;
- negotiate rather than impose activities;
- ensure that the activities are realistic;
- ensure that your client knows precisely what to do;
- get the instructions written down accurately;
- discuss potential difficulties in completing agreed upon activities; and
- signal a joint progress review.

If appropriate, you and your client can design a changing communication and actions experiment in conjunction with this activity.

Afterwards hold a sharing and discussion session focused on the helper's use of negotiating between-session activities skills. If necessary, allow the helper to practise some more until the helper considers that s/he has obtained some degree of competence in negotiating between-session activities.

Then reverse roles.

13   Strategies for Changing Thinking

The greatest discovery of my generation is that human beings can alter their lives by altering their attitude of mind.

William James

Chapter outcomes

By studying and doing the activities in this chapter you should possess some basic skills in helping clients:

- *create alerting self-talk;*
- *create calming self-talk;*
- *create coaching self-talk;*
- *create affirming self-talk;*
- *use coping self-talk in visualised rehearsals;*
- *question and challenge demanding rules;*
- *create preferential rather than demanding rules;*
- *question and challenge potentially inaccurate perceptions; and*
- *create perceptions that more closely fit the facts.*

This chapter develops the changing specific communications and thoughts approach to stage three of the relating–understanding–changing (RUC) helping process model by focusing on assisting clients to empower their minds so that they can deal with problem situations more effectively. In Chapter 1, I mentioned that counselling skills are essentially mind and communication skills. If clients are to communicate and act effectively they need to use their minds in ways that support rather than interfere with their success. In Chapter 2 I outlined six mind skills areas, namely creating self-talk, visual images, rules, perceptions, explanations and expectations. In that chapter I mainly focused on helping counselling skills students see the application of these mind skills to themselves.

I changed the focus to clients' thinking in the subsequent section in Chapter 10 on identifying unhelpful thinking. Here I narrowed the six mind skills areas down to three areas: identifying unhelpful self-talk, rules and perceptions. In this chapter, I mainly review how you can assist clients to empower their minds in these same three mind skills areas. I emphasise helping strategies for only three mind skills to provide a gradual introduction to a large and increasingly important approach to helping, the so-called cognitive therapies. I want to avoid encouraging introductory counselling skills students to attempt too much too soon.

I have selected the three mind skills to provide a basic tool kit for students to assist clients in empowering their thinking. Each of the chosen mind skills has wide applicability. Students and helpers can focus on self-talk whenever they assist clients to cope with specific situations that they find difficult. Albert Ellis, the founder of Rational Emotive Behaviour Therapy, detects, challenges and attempts to alter the irrational beliefs or unrealistic rules created by every client he counsels (Ellis, 1995, 1996). This indicates how common it is to find clients who think erroneously in this way.

Similarly Aaron Beck, the founder of Cognitive Therapy (Beck, 1976, 1988; Beck and Weishaar, 1995), attempts of get every client he counsels to become better at testing the reality and accuracy of their perceptions rather than jumping to unwarranted conclusions. Think of the many clients who come to helping with relationship problems, including problems in dealing with specific situations. It is difficult to see how helpers can work properly with such clients unless they explore the accuracy of their perceptions of themselves, one another and of the patterns of communication in their relationships.

Working with clients' thinking

Herewith a few suggestions when learning to work with clients' thinking. If you have some skills at working with your own thinking, you will probably have more insight into how to work with clients' thinking. So a good place to begin learning is to use the helping strategies reviewed below to empower your own mind.

Depending on the length of your introductory course, focusing on just one area of thoughts is all you may have time to learn. Probably, even on longer introductory counselling skills courses students can only learn the basic knowledge and skills for at most three areas of thinking.

Creating self-talk is a good mind skills area with which to start. One reason for this is that clients can create self-talk that supports any changed communication or action they target. Another reason is that virtually all counselling skills students and helping clients are aware that they talk to themselves anyway. So requesting that clients do so in a more disciplined way is unlikely to be too strange.

Proceed with great caution when assisting clients to alter specific thoughts. I have witnessed a number of beginning students jump in with faulty analyses of thinking which clients have not had the knowledge or confidence to challenge. In addition, students may not understand the mind skills areas properly themselves and therefore present them in confused ways to clients. Furthermore, sometimes students rush through learning sequences rather than train clients in them thoroughly. Remember that clients have usually built up and sustained their ways of faulty thinking over many years and, consequently, quick fixes are unlikely to succeed.

Students can protect clients if they keep offering good client-focused helping relationships. In addition to using good active listening skills, you can coach clients in changing their thinking in client-centred rather than helper-centred ways. At all costs, avoid being an instant and overbearing version of therapists like Freud, Ellis or Beck.

Assisting clients to create coping self-talk

Despite being an experienced writer, before I start a new chapter for a book or a new journal article I always experience a minor episode of lack of confidence and well-being. As I became increasingly aware that this was the case, I learned to combat and control my pre-writing blues with self-talk like: 'Here we go again. These low feelings happen every time before I write something for publication. Calm down. I know from previous experience that I can cope with the situation by preparing adequately and then getting down to writing. Once I start writing I always get a greater sense of being in control and my usual feelings of optimism and well-being return.' My self-talk is always enough to manage my anxiety and get me started. Others, be they clients, students or academics, may talk to themselves much more negatively before writing than I do. Consequently they need to work much harder at correcting their self-talk.

Dimensions of coping self-talk

In Chapter 2, I distinguished between negative and coping self-talk. Furthermore, I indicated that coping, or 'doing as well as I can', is preferable to mastery, or 'doing perfectly'. Following are some dimensions of coping self-talk.

Alerting self-talk

In the above example of my talking to myself before writing, I used the phrase 'Here we go again' to alert myself that I needed to use my coping self-talk to guide me into commencing writing. Clients may need to change gear from the buzz of their usual thinking into calmer and clearer states of mind. You can help clients to recognise danger signals in problem situations, for instance anxiety, anger or depression, and then consciously alert themselves to use coping self-talk. The basic alerting self-talk instruction is 'STOP . . . THINK!' To be effective, train clients to give 'STOP . . . THINK' self-instructions forcefully and possibly repeat them: for instance 'STOP . . . THINK, STOP . . . THINK!' After 'THINK' they can remind themselves to use their self-talk skills in their problem situations: for instance, 'STOP . . . THINK . . . My anxiety/anger is a signal for me to use my self-talk skills'. Clients can then engage in other forms of self-talk: for instance calming themselves down, coaching themselves in how best to communicate and affirming their strengths and support factors.

Calming self-talk

Creating calming self-talk can assist clients to deal with problem situations in many ways. Before, during and after specific situations, they can calm their minds so that they can better handle unwanted feelings such as harmful anxiety or excessive anger. In addition, clients may wish to calm and relax their mind as a way of managing extraneous stresses that then impact on how they handle problem situations. A third purpose for creating calming self-talk is to become more centred and focused when you wish to think through, or talk through, how best to communicate or act in problem situations. Clients' use of calming self-talk helps them to clear a psychological space for getting in touch with their feelings and thinking more sharply and deeply.

When introducing calming self-talk to clients, I may talk about the concept and then provide an example of a calming self-instruction like 'Relax'. Then I encourage clients to come up with some calming self-instructions of their own. Then we may discuss which calming self-instructions the client prefers to use. In addition, I tell, demonstrate and coach clients in how to use a calm and measured voice when giving calming self-instructions. Sometimes, I highlight the difference by saying a phrase like 'Calm down' in a hurried and self-pressurising way.

Cooling self-talk statements might be regarded as a sub-category of calming self-talk. You can train clients who are prone to angry outbursts in cooling self-talk statements. Box 13.1 provides examples of both calming and cooling self-talk statements.

Box 13.1   Examples of calming and cooling self-talk statements

Calming self-talk statements:
- 'Keep calm.'
- 'Slow down.'
- 'Relax.'
- 'Take it easy.'
- 'Take a deep breath.'
- 'Breathe slowly and regularly.'
- 'I can manage.'

Cooling self-talk statements:
- 'Cool it.'
- 'Count to ten.'
- 'Be careful.'
- 'Don't overreact.'
- 'Don't let my pride get in the way.'
- 'I can choose not to let myself get hooked.'
- 'Problem solve.'

Coaching self-talk

Coaching self-talk is no substitute for possessing the communication skills for achieving a task. The first step in coaching self-talk is to assist clients to break tasks down. You can work with clients to think through systematic approaches to attaining goals in problem situations, including how to handle setbacks. Once plans are clear, then clients require the ability to instruct themselves through the steps of implementing them.

Remember to emphasise self-talk about vocal and bodily as well as verbal communication. When clients develop self-instructions, they can coach themselves in how to put across their verbal messages most effectively. Box 13.2 illustrating coaching self-talk is based on the example of Greg and Courtney from the previous chapter. Helpers can also assist clients to develop coaching self-talk statements to handle different ways other people in problem situations might respond.

Box 13.2   Example of coaching self-talk

Problem situation
Greg, a consulting engineer who had serious relationship problems in his previous position, wants to show appreciation for work well done to his new secretary Courtney during the first week of his new job.

Coaching self-talk statements
Using a whiteboard, Greg's helper assists him to develop the following coaching self-talk statements:

- *Verbal communication*   'Remember to make statements to Courtney like "Thank you" and "You've done a very good job".'
- *Vocal communication*   'Keep my voice firm and emphasise words that show appreciation.'
- *Bodily communication*   'Smile pleasantly and maintain good eye contact.'
- *Verbal, vocal and bodily communication*   'When I say "Thank you" to Courtney, I will use a firm voice, emphasise words of appreciation, smile pleasantly and maintain good eye contact.'

Affirming self-talk
I prefer the notion of affirming self-talk to that of positive self-talk. The danger of positive self-talk is that clients may tell themselves false positives that set them up for disappointment and failure. Affirming self-talk focuses on reminding yourself of realistic factors that count in your favour. Following are some aspects of affirming self-talk.

First, clients can tell themselves that they can cope. Sample self-statements include: 'I can handle this situation', 'My anxiety is a signal for me to use my coping skills', and 'All I have to do is to cope'. In addition, once clients cope with situations better, they can acknowledge this: for example, 'I used my coping skills and they worked'.

Second, clients can acknowledge their strengths. Often when clients are anxious about difficult situations, they forget their strengths. For example, when asking for dates, clients may genuinely possess good points, so they do not have to boast about them. Also, they may have good conversational skills that they can acknowledge and use rather than thinking about what may go wrong. In addition, clients can think about any successful experiences they may have had in the past in situations similar to the one they face.

Third, clients may become more confident if they acknowledge supportive people to whom they have access. For instance, relatives, friends, spouses and helping service professionals might each be sources of support, though not necessarily so. Just realising they have supportive people to whom they can turn may be sufficient to help some clients cope better with problem situations.

Coping self-talk as part of visual rehearsal

Coping self-talk may be used before, during and after problem situations. Often alerting, calming, coaching and affirming statements are combined, though not necessarily all at the same time. Clients need to think through the combinations of self-instructions that work for them. Furthermore, helpers should ensure that clients write down alerting, calming, coaching and affirming statements that they find useful.

Coping self-talk may guide visual rehearsal of targeted communications and actions. For example, Greg can use his coping self-talk to guide him through imaginary units of communication with Courtney, possibly improving them as he practises. Greg might visualise being pleased with some work that Courtney has done. Then he can guide visually rehearsing communicating appreciation with statements like: 'STOP . . . THINK . . . Calm down. My anxiety is a signal for me to use my coping self-talk. When I say "Thank-you" to Courtney, I use a firm voice, emphasise words of appreciation, smile pleasantly and maintain good eye contact. I know I can manage this situation well if I try my best.' Greg could be encouraged to practise guiding himself through such scenes repeatedly. Some of these additional practice runs should include how he might handle different responses from Courtney. Visual rehearsal with accompanying self-talk should make it easier for Greg to attain his altering specific communications and thoughts goals when the real situation with Courtney arises.

Assisting clients to create preferential rules

Unrealistic and demanding rules significantly contribute to many clients having difficulty managing their problems and problem situations. Demanding rules can lay the foundation for creating negative self-talk and inaccurate perceptions. For example, demanding rules like 'I must get approval' and 'I must be perfect' probably underlie my feelings of lack of confidence and well-being before starting a new book chapter or article. I would prefer that readers like what I write and that it is competently written. These preferences are very different to demanding approval from readers and perfection from myself.

Usually demanding rules contain realistic as well as unrealistic parts. For example, it is realistic for me to want to write competently, but unrealistic to strive for perfection. Consequently, when assisting clients to alter their rules, focus on discarding the 20 to 30 per cent of the rule that is irrational rather than getting rid of it altogether.

How can you assist clients to create preferential rules to replace their demanding rules? In Chapter 10, I reviewed some indicators or signals for demanding rules. Reading the signals, you can assist clients to articulate or suggest what might be one or more underlying demanding rules relevant to their problem situations. Then you can help clients question and challenge their demanding rules and restate them as preferential rules.

Questioning and challenging demanding rules

To keep matters simple when first learning to assist clients to alter their rules, students can restrict their focus to clients' use of the following four demanding rules:

- 'I must be liked by everyone.'
- 'I must be perfectly competent.'
- 'Other people must do what I want.'
- 'Life must be fair.'

Albert Ellis considers disputing to be the most typical and often-used method of his Rational Emotive Behaviour Therapy. Disputing means challenging demanding rules. The main skill in challenging is that of scientific questioning. Helpers and clients can use reason, logic and facts to support, discard or amend any rule they consider to be potentially demanding. Box 13.3 provides an example of questions that can be used to challenge demanding rules.

When learning how to question clients' demanding rules, students are encouraged to elicit some questions from clients, if possible: for instance, 'How might you question or challenge that rule?' When you do ask questions yourself, do so gently rather than forcefully and respond to clients' answers the same way. Furthermore, show restraint in the amount of questions you ask and remember to integrate active listening into the questioning and challenging process.

Box 13.3   Example of questions that challenge a demanding rule

Problem situation
Tom, a 17-year-old secondary school student, is shy with girls and wants to ask one for a date.

Tom's demanding rule
'I must be liked by everyone'.

Questions that Tom and his helper can use to challenge this rule
- 'What evidence exists for the truth or falseness of this rule?'
- 'What are the positive and negative consequences of holding this rule?'
- 'Do I expect that the other boys in my class must be liked by every girl?'
- 'Is it realistic to expect every girl to like me?'
- 'Is it absolutely necessary for me to be liked by everyone to be successful in life or to find a girlfriend?'
- 'Are there other reasons why a girl might say 'no' to a date other than that she does not like me?'
- 'If some girl does not like me why does this make me unlikeable?'
- 'Why is it awful if some girl does not like me?'
- What can't I stand about some girl not liking me?'

Creating preferential rule statements

Assisting clients to question and challenge their demanding rules should result in loosening their effect on them. An added way of reducing the hold of demanding rules is to assist clients to restate them succinctly into preferential rules. Their challenges can be too many and varied to remember easily. Help clients to create replacement statements that are easy to remember and recall. Sometimes, when time is very limited, helpers may eliminate time spent on questioning and challenging, and move straight into helping clients restate a demanding rule as a preferential rule.

Helpers and clients can alter characteristics of demanding rules to become characteristics of preferential rules. An example is 'I'd PREFER to do very well but I don't HAVE TO' (Sichel and Ellis, 1984: 1). Clients can replace rules about mastery and perfection with rules incorporating competence, coping and 'doing as well as I can under the circumstances'. Furthermore, assist clients to refrain from rating their whole selves rather than evaluating how useful specific communications and actions of theirs are.

In addition, help clients to avoid making out that the world is absolutely awful by accepting that the world is imperfect and by refraining from exaggerating negative factors and possibilities. You can also assist clients to eliminate an 'I-can't-stand-it' attitude by encouraging them to tell themselves that they can stand the anxiety and discomfort arising from themselves, others and the environment not being as they would prefer them to be. Indeed, even in genuinely adverse circumstances, they may have many strengths to rely on and supportive people to turn to.

When working on restating rules, encourage clients to participate in the process by sharing their ideas. Some helpers use a whiteboard and work together with clients to get the wording just right for them to recall and use in future. Box 13.4 shows examples of restating demanding into preferential rules.

Box 13.4   Examples of restating demanding into preferential rules

Problem situation
Tom, a 17-year-old secondary school student, is shy with girls and wants to ask one for a date.

Tom's demanding rule: 'I must be liked by everyone.'
Tom's preferential rule: 'I would prefer to be liked by almost everyone, but there are many fish in the ocean and I can obtain a girlfriend if only some girls like me.'

Preferential restatements of other common demanding rules

Demanding rule: 'I must be perfectly competent.'
Preferential rule: 'I would prefer to strive towards high standards and to do the best I can.'

Demanding rule: 'Other people must do what I want.'
Preferential rule: 'I would prefer that others take my wishes into account, but I need to be sensitive to their wishes too.'

Demanding rule: 'Life must be fair.'
Preferential rule: 'I would prefer that life be fair, but the world is imperfect and I accept that there may be some aspects of it I cannot change.'

Assisting clients to reality-test perceptions

Clients, like everyone else, live in the world as they perceive it. Clients' perceptions about themselves, others and the environment are their subjective reality. However, when facts are taken into account, these perceptions are of varying degrees of accuracy. In longer-term helping clients can be trained to become much more disciplined about not jumping to unwarranted conclusions but, instead, testing the reality of their perceptions. Even in brief helping for specific problem situations, helpers can assist clients to identify potentially erroneous perceptions, assess their reality and, if necessary, replace them with more accurate perceptions.

Checking the accuracy of perceptions

When faced with problem situations, clients may make potentially erroneous statements about themselves, such as 'I'm no good at that', and about others, such as 'S/he always does . . . .' or 'S/he never does . . . .' Such statements or perceptions influence how they feel and communicate and act. When helping clients check the accuracy of their perceptions, you are asking them to distinguish between fact and inference, and to make their inferences fit the facts as closely as possible. In Chapter 2, I gave the example of 'All Aborigines walk in single file, at least the one I saw did' as being an illustration of how people can leap from fact, seeing one Aboriginal walking, to inference, stating that all Aboriginals walk in single file.

Think of clients' perceptions as propositions that together you can investigate to see how far they are supported by evidence. Beck and

Weishaar (1995) give the example of a resident who insisted 'I am not a good doctor'. Therapist and client then listed criteria for being a good doctor. Then the resident monitored his behaviour and sought feedback from supervisors and colleagues. Finally, he concluded 'I am a good doctor after all'.

As shown in Box 13.5, counselling skills students and helpers can assist clients to check the accuracy of their perceptions in problem situations by asking three main questions:

- 'Where is the evidence for your perception?'
- 'Are there any other ways of perceiving the situation?'
- 'Which way of perceiving the situation best fits the available facts?'

Box 13.5   Example of checking the accuracy of a perception

Problem situation
Sophie, 25, is a junior manager at Macrosoft, a computer software company, where all the other managers are men. Sophie feels inhibited from speaking out at managers' meetings of her division of the company.

Potentially erroneous perception
'If I make contributions at managers' meetings, the men will not take me seriously since my division of the company is really a boys' club.'

Question 1   'Where is the evidence for your perception?'
When asked this question, Sophie says she has no real evidence. She reports having participated very little in meetings and being treated politely when she did. However, she also reports that the men engage in a lot of banter, none of which is sexist.

Question 2   'Are there any other ways of perceiving the situation?'
Sophie and her helper come up with the following different perceptions:

- 'If this division of Macrosoft were just a boys' club, they wouldn't have hired me.'
- 'I've participated very little in meetings, so I do not really know how they would react.'
- 'When I did participate, I did so nervously, and perhaps the men would take me more seriously if I participated more assertively.'
- 'The men really are biased against women managers and are just not showing it openly.'
- 'The men are unused to having a woman manager attend their meetings and are unsure how to react.'

- 'The men are deliberately using banter as a way of making me feel excluded.'

Question 3   *'Which way of perceiving the situation best fits the available facts?'*
After some thought, Sophie decides that the most accurate perception is:

- 'I've participated very little in meetings, so I do not really know how they would react.'

Sophie also likes the perception:

- 'When I did participate, I did so nervously, and perhaps the men would take me more seriously if I participated more assertively.'

Sophie's helper coaches her in communicating assertively at managers' meetings so that Sophie can carry out a changed communications experiment to test whether or not the men will take her contributions seriously.

Helpers may need to assist clients to alter thoughts in more than one mind skills area. For instance, Sophie, the client in Box 13.6, might also challenge and alter a demanding rule such as 'I must be liked by everyone'. Furthermore, Sophie could learn to use calming and coaching self-talk to guide her in communicating assertively at managers' meetings.

In addition, as shown in the example of Sophie, sometimes a good way to help clients challenge their thinking is to encourage them to experiment with communicating and acting differently. Assuming Sophie communicates assertively, she can then collect evidence to affirm or negate her suspicion that her division of Macrosoft is really a boys' club that discriminates against a woman manager.

Remembering, rehearsing and practising

So far I have emphasised assisting clients directly to change how they think. Here I focus on how clients can help themselves when on their own.

Remembering coping self-talk statements, statements of preferential rules, and statements of revised perceptions is vital to implementing them in practice. Ways to enhance clients' memory include: writing the statements down on A4 paper; making reminder cards; and making cassettes. Clients can post written reminders in prominent places. In addition, clients can take reminder cards with them and look at them immediately before difficult situations.

Encourage clients to rehearse their revised thoughts. They can use reminder cards and cassettes for rehearsal. In addition, encourage clients to practise hard at relinquishing unhelpful thoughts and replacing them with helpful thoughts in their actual problem situations. They can modify their revised thoughts if they do not work for them.

Genuine learning rarely occurs without setbacks and difficulties. Clients can use coping self-talk to encourage themselves in handling these. In addition, they can challenge any demanding rules about having to be perfect learners. If clients find using their revised thoughts helps them to communicate and act more effectively, this should help them maintain their revised thinking. Furthermore, if clients can acknowledge their successes, this should help motivate them to persist.

Summary

Working with improving your own thinking can help you become more skilled at assisting clients to alter unhelpful thoughts. When learning how to work with clients' thinking, build your skills gradually, be thorough and use good active listening skills.

Dimensions of coping self-talk include alerting, calming, coaching and affirming self-talk. Cooperate closely with clients to develop self-instructions whose wording is comfortable for them. In addition, encourage clients to use appropriate vocal communication: for instance, forceful for alerting self-talk and calm for calming self-talk. Coping self-talk may be used before, during or after problem situations. Furthermore, clients can use coping self-talk to guide them when visually rehearsing how to communicate and act appropriately in problem situations.

Usually demanding rules contain realistic as well as unrealistic elements. Once potentially unrealistic rules are identified, the main skill of challenging them is that of scientific questioning. Helpers and clients can use reason, logic and facts to support, negate or amend rules. Then helpers and clients can work together to formulate succinct preferential rules to replace the previous demanding rules. Characteristics of preferential rules include: stating preferences rather than making demands, emphasising competence and coping rather than mastery and perfection, and rating the usefulness of specific characteristics rather than making overall judgements about one's self-worth.

Clients' perceptions about themselves, others and the environment are their subjective reality. Think of clients' perceptions as propositions that helpers and clients can investigate together to see how far they are supported by the facts. Three main questions for testing the reality of perceptions are: 'Where is the evidence for your perception?', 'Are there any other ways of perceiving the situation?', and 'Which way of perceiving the situation best fits the available facts?' In addition, clients may challenge the reality of their perceptions by communicating and acting differently and seeing if this generates evidence to confirm or negate them.

Remembering changed thoughts is vital to implementing them in practice. Ways to enhance clients' memory include: writing statements down on A4 paper or reminder cards and making cassettes. Clients should also rehearse and practise their changed thoughts both prior to and in their problem situations. Clients are more likely to persist in changing how they think if they realise that setbacks and difficulties are part of the learning process and if they can acknowledge their successes.

Activities

Activity 13.1   Assisting clients to create coping self-talk

Work with a partner who either uses a personal concern or role-plays a client with a mind goal of creating coping self-talk to manage a problem situation better. Within the context of a good helping relationship and, possibly, using a whiteboard during the process:

- use speaking skills to describe the difference between negative and coping self-talk;
- use demonstrating skills;
- assist the client to identify any current negative self-talk;
- use coaching skills to help the client formulate alerting, calming, coaching and affirming self-talk statements; and
- use negotiating between session activities skills.

Afterwards discuss and reverse roles. Playing back audio or video recordings of rehearsal and practice sessions may assist learning.

Activity 13.2   Assisting clients to create preferential rules

Work with a partner who either uses a personal concern or role-plays a client with a mind goal of creating one or more preferential rules to manage a problem situation better. Within the context of a good helping relationship and, possibly, using a whiteboard during the process:

- use speaking skills to describe the difference between demanding and preferential rules;
- use demonstrating skills;
- cooperate with the client to identify any major demanding rules and put the main one into the STC framework;
- use coaching skills to assist the client to question and challenge the main demanding rule;
- use coaching skills to assist the client to create a preferential rule statement to replace the demanding rule; and
- use negotiating between-session activities skills.

Afterwards discuss and reverse roles. Playing back audio or video recordings of rehearsal and practice sessions may assist learning.

Activity 13.3   Assisting clients to reality-test perceptions

Work with a partner who either uses a personal concern or role-plays a client with a mind goal of creating one or more preferential rules to manage a problem situation better. Within the context of a good helping relationship and, possibly, using a whiteboard during the process:

- use speaking skills to describe the importance of reality-testing perceptions rather than jumping to conclusions;
- use demonstrating skills;
- cooperate with the client to identify current inaccurate perceptions and their consequences;
- use coaching skills to assist your client to reality test the existing evidence for a perception by addressing the questions:
    - 'Where is the evidence for your perception?'
    - 'Are there any other ways of perceiving the situation?'
    - 'Which way of perceiving the situation best fits the available facts?'
- use negotiating between-session activities skills; and
- if appropriate, design a changed communications/action experiment to test a perception.

Afterwards, discuss and reverse roles. Playing back audio or video recordings of rehearsal and practice sessions may assist learning.

14 Conducting Sessions and Ending Helping

If we do meet again, why, we shall smile!
If not, why then, this parting was well made.
                                W. Shakespeare

Chapter outcomes

By studying and doing the activities in this chapter you should be able to:

- *understand the importance of helping with both heart and head;*
- *possess some basic skills for the preparing phase of helping sessions;*
- *possess some basic skills for the starting phase;*
- *possess some skills for the working phase;*
- *possess some skills for the ending phase;*
- *understand some issues about length, frequency and number of sessions;*
- *know some sources of information for when to end helping;*
- *understand different formats for ending the helping process; and*
- *understand some methods for assisting clients to maintain changes.*

This chapter addresses what to do after you conduct an initial helping session. Here I review how to go about conducting second and subsequent sessions and how to end helping skilfully.

Helping with both heart and head

In the change stage of the relating–understanding–changing (RUC) helping process model, students need to be careful not to become 'the horror of the dehumanised helper who goes around with a package of skills but no warmth and no presence' (B. Thorne, personal communication, 20 December 1998). You can get so wrapped up in trying to help clients by doing things to and for them that you lose sight of the critical importance of maintaining a client-focused, humane and compassionate helping relationship. Person-centred counsellors like Carl Rogers view the relationship as the core element in assisting clients to change. Even leading behavioural counsellors like Joseph Wolpe assert that, to a large degree, clients change because of 'non-specific relationship factors' (Wolpe, 1990).

Strive to help clients by using both your heart and your head (Nelson-Jones, 1999c). In his book of sermons entitled *Strength to Love*, the late American civil rights leader Martin Luther King quotes the bible: 'Be ye therefore wise as serpents, and harmless as doves' (Matthew 10:16). He then encouraged readers to develop 'a tough mind and a tender heart' (King, 1963). A tender and compassionate heart will enable you to see more deeply and lovingly behind the facades that clients present, thus enabling you to treat them with respect and non-possessive warmth. Behind the disfigurement sometimes caused by clients' mental pain and anxiety, you can glimpse and prize their potential. In addition, you can acknowledge your shared humanity and capacity for human frailty.

A tough mind will enable you to look behind and work on your own facades so that you can be more present to clients. Furthermore, a tough mind will help you develop the technical skills required for delivering different helping strategies.

As a counselling skills student it can be difficult to keep hold of your humanity when interviewing. So many things can be going on in your head at once. You want to help your clients. You are trying to stay tuned in to them and observe and listen carefully to their various verbal, vocal and bodily communications. You are thinking about what helping strategies to adopt and how to deliver them. In addition, both you and your clients may be mindful of being video recorded or cassette recorded for supervision purposes.

Try not to add to your difficulties by burdening yourself with needing to appear as an expert. Being helped by a concerned and caring human being is much more important to most clients than being helped by a technical expert. As in any relationship, clients will pick up whether you are really interested and concerned about them. In addition, as in any relationship, if your concern gets transmitted the other person will help you to relate to them. In an atmosphere of mutual liking and often with clients' help, you can retrieve many of your mistakes. Furthermore, if you are honest about being a coun-selling skills student, clients will make allowances for your lack of professional technical expertise. However, clients are much less likely to make allowances for your deficiencies as a concerned human being. Remember that many clients have suffered from the phoniness of significant others in their pasts and have a keen sense of smell in sniffing out helper phoniness.

Conducting sessions

The following review focuses more on conducting sessions in the changing specific communications and thoughts approach to changing stage of the RUC helping process model than to the problem solving approach. However, many points are relevant to both approaches. I hope those readers who engage in informal helping contacts rather than conduct formal helping sessions can also find something of value from the discussion.

Helping sessions have four phases: preparing, starting, middle and ending. In Box 14.1, based on the assumption that helping will con-tinue for at least one more session, some relevant skills and issues are presented and discussed for each phase.

Box 14.1   The four phases of helping sessions

1. The preparing phase
Illustrative skills:

- Reflecting on previous and next session(s).
- Consulting with trainers, supervisors and peers.
- Ensuring that you understand relevant helping strategies.
- Practising delivery of helping strategies, if appropriate.
- Preparing and having available relevant handouts and between-session activity sheets.
- Arriving on time.
- Setting up the room.
- Relaxing yourself.

2. The starting phase
Illustrative skills:

- Meeting, greeting and seating.
- Re-establishing the relationship and working alliance.

- Reviewing between-session activities.
- Establishing session agendas.

3. The middle phase
Illustrative skills:

- Actively involving clients in process.
- Client-centred coaching.
- Delivering specific helping strategies.
- Checking clients' understanding.
- Refining session agendas.
- Keeping sessions moving.

4. The ending phase
Illustrative skills:

- Structuring to allow time for ending.
- Reviewing sessions.
- Negotiating between-session activities.
- Enlisting commitment and checking difficulties in carrying out activities.
- Arranging subsequent contact.

The preparing phase

In Chapter 8, I mentioned that preparation skills were important before starting helping. These skills included trying to ensure that clients' pre-session contact with your helping service was positive. In addition, I stressed arriving early for helping sessions, making sure the room was in order, checking any recording equipment you might use and, if necessary, relaxing yourself. Furthermore, I suggested that you do not allow clients into the interview room before you are ready to devote your full attention to them. Most of the above considerations are just as relevant to preparing for second and subsequent helping sessions as for initial ones.

On introductory counselling skills training courses, students' helping sessions are mainly with peers and, sometimes, with volunteer 'clients'. In many instances, these sessions are recorded for later review by yourself, trainers, supervisors and peers. Students can assign themselves between-session activities. One such activity is to play back any tape of the previous session and review your use of helping skills, how your client responded, what progress s/he made, and the useful-ness of the communication patterns you established with your client. Some introductory counselling skills courses may require students to make such observations in written logs as a prelude to keeping 'professional logs' recording details of each of their supervised placement sessions.

Your trainer and peers can also help you to review the previous session to gain insights into how you might approach the next one. In addition, you can revise helping strategies you intend using to understand their content thoroughly. Furthermore, you can practise delivering the helping strategies. You can also use between-session time to ensure that you have any written material, such as handouts and between-session activity sheets, readily available. However, be careful not to be too rigid in how you plan to approach the next session. Remember that it is vital that you consult with clients as part of establishing a strong working alliance rather than impose your ideas.

The starting phase

The starting phase has three main tasks: re-establishing the relationship and working alliance, reviewing between-session activities and establishing a session agenda. The meeting, greeting and seating skills for subsequent helping sessions are similar to those you require for initial sessions. Possibly you have already obtained permission for recording sessions.

Once clients are comfortably seated, sometimes they will start talking of their own accord. However, on most occasions, you need to make an opening statement. Sample opening statements are provided in Box 14.2. I advocate a 'softly, softly' approach that starts by checking 'where the client is at' rather than by moving directly into helping strategies. Allow clients the psychological safety and space to bring you up to date with information that they select as important to them. By not pushing your agenda, you avoid taking over the session or suppressing significant information that clients may wish to share with you, for instance a death in the family or a car crash. Use your active listening skills to help clients know that you are still interested and concerned in how they see the world and their problem situations.

Once you have allowed clients air time, you may still require further information to help you assess how they have progressed in any between-session activities you negotiated in the previous session. Box 14.2 provides some statements you might make, if you have not already reviewed progress in between-session activities. As appropriate, you can ask additional questions that clarify and expand your own and clients' understanding of progress.

Furthermore, you can encourage clients to acknowledge their agency in bringing about positive changes. For example, Anita, a client prone to angry outbursts, has restrained her anger in a recurring problem situation with her partner Ed and says 'Things are going better in our relationship'. You can help Anita to acknowledge that by changing her behaviour, for instance by replacing negative with calming self-talk, she has helped to bring about the improvement. Anita might now say to herself 'If I use my self-talk skills, then I can restrain my anger and improve my relationship with Ed'.

Near the start of each session in the change stage, consult with clients to establish session agendas. Such agendas may be for all or part of sessions. For example, together you may decide where you will work first and then, later, make another decision regarding where to work next. Alternatively, as part of your initial agenda setting discussion, you may target one area to start and then agree to move on to another area. However, remain flexible once you establish session agendas so that you can respond to developments during sessions.

When establishing session agendas, I favour paying considerable attention to clients' wishes, since I want to encourage their motivation and involvement. If I thought there was some important reason for starting with a particular mind or communication goal, I would share this observation with clients. However, I would still be inclined to allow clients the final say in where we worked. Box 14.2 illustrates the kind of agenda setting statement that a helper might make near the start of a second session. Agendas for later sessions tend to be heavily influenced by work done in and between session activities negotiated in the previous session.

Box 14.2 Some examples of starting phase statements

Opening statements

- 'How's your week been?'
- 'How have you been getting on?'
- 'Where would you like to start today?'

Reviewing between-session activities statements

- 'What progress did you make with your activities?'
- 'What happened when you tried out your changed thoughts/ communications?'
- 'Things didn't just happen, you made them happen by changing [specify what].'

Establishing a session agenda:

- 'In our first session we stated two mind goals for developing your interview skills, using coping rather than negative self-talk and challenging and then replacing your demanding rule about giving perfect answers. We also stated some goals for developing aspects of your verbal, vocal and bodily communication. Where would you like to work first?'

The middle phase

Once session agendas are established, however informally, you can implement helping strategies to assist clients to attain one or more goals. One way of viewing this middle phase is that it is the working phase of the session. However, I have not used the term working phase because it may detract from valuing work performed in the preparing, starting and ending phases.

Already, I have emphasised the importance of client-centred coaching when delivering helping strategies and reviewed some strategies. Be sensitive to the communication patterns or interaction processes you establish with your clients. For example, you may have a tendency to establish communication patterns which are insufficiently client-focused. If so, learn to become aware from your clients' reactions of clues indicating you are doing most of the talking or taking most of the responsibility for session content.

In the middle phase you can involve clients in choices that take place within delivering particular helping strategies, for instance how many rehearsals they require to develop a targeted communication goal. Furthermore, you can involve clients in choices about moving on to different items in your session agenda and refining agendas as appropriate. Together, you may make trade-offs and compromises regarding spending session time: for instance, curtailing time spent in one mind or communication area so that you have time available for another.

Helpers need to keep helping sessions moving at an appropriate pace, neither too fast nor too slow. There are risks in both directions. On the one hand, you may rush through delivering helping strategies in ways that confuse clients and leave them little to take away at the end of the session. Furthermore, you may put too much pressure on clients to reveal themselves and to work at an uncongenial pace.

On the other hand, you may allow 'session drift' – sessions that drift along rather aimlessly with little that is tangible being achieved.

Sometimes session drift occurs because helpers are poor at balancing relationship and task considerations, at the expense of the latter. You may need to develop assertion skills to curtail long and unproductive conversations. Furthermore, you require a repertoire of checking out and moving on statements. Box 14.3 provides examples of such statements.

Though the responsibility should be shared, ultimately it is your responsibility as helper to see that session time is allocated productively. Be careful not to make moving on statements that allow insufficient time to deal with the next agenda items properly. Generally, it is best to avoid getting into new areas towards the end of sessions rather than to start working on them in rushed and hurried ways.

Box 14.3   Examples of statements for the middle and ending phases

Middle phase statements:

- 'Do you want to spend more time now working in this area or are you ready to move on?'
- 'I sense that we've taken working on changing your ___ [specify] as far as we can for now, what do you think?'
- 'Do you want another rehearsal for communicating better in that situation or do you think you can manage all right?'

Ending phase statements:

- 'I notice that we have to end in about 10 minutes . . . and, assuming you want to meet again, perhaps we should spend some of this time looking at what you might do between sessions.'
- 'Before we end it might be a good idea to review what we've done today and see how you can build upon it before we next meet.'
- 'Is there anything you would like to bring up before we end?'

The ending phase

There are various tasks involved in ending sessions skilfully in the changing stage of the RUC model. You need to bring closure to any work on a targeted skill in process during the middle phase. You may want to have either yourself or your client review the session. If clients have not done so already, this may be an opportunity for them to write down their main learnings. In addition, you should leave sufficient time to negotiate and clarify any between-session activities clients will undertake. Furthermore, you and your clients should discuss and be clear about arrangements for your next session.

To allow time to perform the tasks of the ending phase properly, often it is a good idea to make an early structuring statement that allows for a smooth transition from the middle to the ending phase of the session. You might make such a statement about five to 10 minutes before the end of a 40- to 50-minute session. The first two statements in Box 14.3 are examples of some statements you might make in this regard.

Sometimes reviewing a session may help clients clarify and consolidate learnings during a session. However, reviews of sessions are not always necessary, especially if you have been thorough in how you have worked during the session. Furthermore, when you negotiate between-session activities you may cover some of the same ground anyway.

At the ends of Chapter 11 and Chapter 12, I mentioned some ways of increasing clients' compliance in performing between-session activities. At risk of repetition, these ways include: negotiating them rather than imposing them, checking that clients clearly know how to enact the changed thoughts and communications, writing activities instructions and key points down, and discussing with clients any difficulties they anticipate in carrying out the activities.

When ending sessions, you may also check whether clients have any unfinished business, queries or outstanding items that they would like to mention. Some helpers like to check how clients have experienced the session and whether they have any feedback they would like to share with them. Lastly, make sure that you negotiate clear agreements with clients about whether and when you are next going to meet. Maintain boundaries and be careful at the end of sessions not to let working relationships slide into social relationships. Though generally not the case on introductory counselling skills courses, when working as a helper you may want to tell vulnerable 'at risk' clients under what circumstances and how they can contact you between sessions.

Ending helping

Many helping contacts on introductory counselling skills training courses are very brief, say one or two sessions. A discussion of issues restricted to such brief helping might provide an inadequate basis for many readers' current or future work. Consequently, here I discuss some issues connected with ending brief short-term to medium-term helping. However, I stress that beginning helpers need to avoid getting caught up in longer term helping relationships for which they are insufficiently trained.

Length, frequency and number of sessions

Perhaps it is most common for individual helping sessions to be around 45 to 50 minutes long, the so-called '50-minute hour', with the remaining 10 minutes being left for writing up notes, resting and preparing for the next client. However, there are no hard and fast rules. Many considerations determine the length of sessions including: the helper's workload; what is a financially viable length of time to see clients who are fee-paying or paid for by third parties; and the purposes of the session. Some helpers conduct initial sessions of longer than 45 to 50 minutes because they are trying to complete the relating and under-standing stages of the RUC helping process model thoroughly. Some-times subsequent sessions are shorter than 45 to 50 minutes, because helpers are focusing on delivering specific helping strategies.

When you state that a session is going to be of a certain duration, try to adhere to this limit. Reasons for doing so include encouraging clients to speak out within their allotted time, having a break between clients and not keeping subsequent clients waiting. In informal settings, the length of helping contacts varies according to what seems possible and appropriate to both parties at the time.

Frequency of sessions can range from daily to weekly to fortnightly to monthly or to ad hoc arrangements when clients come to see helpers only when in special need. Helpers working in informal sessions may have regular unstructured contact with clients depending on the nature of the service, for example nurses' contacts with hospital patients or prison officers' contacts with juvenile delinquents in residential units.

Most often, helpers conduct interviews with clients on a weekly basis. However, helpers need to keep the time frames of clients' prob-lem situations in mind. For instance, a secondary school student highly anxious about an important exam in two weeks' time or a spouse who has to attend a potentially acrimonious child custody hearing in 10 days' time might require more frequent meetings than once weekly.

In helping that is focused on handling specific problem situations, the number of sessions may range from one to about six. Helping that is focused on helping clients manage broader problems and the underlying problematic skills that sustain them can last from a few to 30 or more sessions. Helping relationships with severely emotionally deprived clients may last longer, sometimes over a year or more. In addition, some clients may return for helping on an ad hoc basic when they have crises, decisions and problems that it is important for them to handle skilfully.

When to end helping

Within the RUC helping model focused on problem situations, when do you end helping? Sometimes clients may terminate of their own accord before you think they are ready. Though this may be either because of a helper–client mismatch or because you did not demonstrate sufficient helping skills to have them return, this is not necessarily the case. Clients may have found their session or sessions with you of value, but think they can continue on their own. Sometimes, external circumstances such as a change of job or illness may prevent them continuing. In addition, some clients just resist the ideas of having to change and of being in helping.

As mentioned in the previous section, many problem situations have their own time frames. On occasions when you are helping clients handle specific upcoming events, clients may only wish to continue in helping up until that event. In informal helping, your contact may end when clients leave settings such as hospitals and residential units for juvenile delinquents. On other occasions, you may end helping when clients have made sufficient progress in either the problem solving or the changing specific communications and thoughts approach to the third stage of the RUC model.

Whether your helping contact is focused on helping clients deal with specific problem situations or involves longer term contact, there are four main sources of information you and clients can use in reviewing when to end helping. First, there is what clients report to you about their feelings and progress. Are they happy with progress and do they feel they can cope better? Second, there are your own observations about clients' progress. Third, there is feedback from significant others in clients' lives, for instance spouses, bosses or peers. This feedback may go direct to clients and then be relayed to you. Alternatively, if you are working in conjunction with a helper's aide, the information may come from them rather than from the client. Lastly, you and your clients may feel more comfortable about ending helping by obtaining evidence of attainment of measurable goals: for example, passing a driving test, saying 'I love you' to a partner at least once a day for a week, or making a given number of sales calls or job applications over a specified time period.

Formats for ending helping

In introductory counselling skills courses, usually you start by doing parts of interviews, then move on to whole interviews, then you may go as far as interviewing the same person for up to two or three sessions. It is rare to go beyond two or three sessions since you are not working with real clients. In most instances, you and your peer or volunteer 'client' will know in advance the duration of your contact.

When working with actual clients, there are a number of different formats for ending. In or around the first interview, you and your client can fix the number of sessions you will spend together. Sometimes, of course, external factors fix the number of sessions. Fixed endings may motivate clients to use helping to best effect. My preferred format is to leave the number of sessions open and then later negotiate with clients when to end. A variation of an open ending is to fade or withdraw helping assistance gradually, say from once a week to once a fortnight and then to once a month.

Sometimes helpers either schedule or leave open the possibility of follow-up or booster sessions. Such sessions may be planned at time of ending – for instance 'We agree to meet again in three months to review progress' – or left to the client's initiative. Helpers can also schedule follow-up phone calls with clients. From follow-up phone calls and booster sessions, helpers can obtain feedback on how successful helping was in assisting clients to manage problem situations better and to maintain targeted changes in specific communication/actions and thoughts.

Assisting maintaining change

Issues surrounding maintaining changes in problem situations should not be left to final sessions. Helpers can assist clients to maintain changes during helping by identifying the key mind and communication skills clients need to develop, training thoroughly, and negotiating relevant between-session activities that help clients transfer what they have learned inside helping to problem situations outside.

The main task in ending helping is to assist clients to consolidate what they have learned so that they may continue to help themselves afterwards. One method of enhancing consolidation is for either helper or client to summarise the main points learned for dealing with problem situations in future. In addition, helpers and clients can spend time anticipating difficulties and setbacks and develop strategies for dealing with them. Some of these strategies may be focused on communication: for instance, how to seek support during attempts to handle a difficult problem situation better.

Other strategies may focus on how clients think. For example, you may help clients develop coping self-talk when they do not succeed in achieving their goals in a particular problem situation. Such self-talk may be written down on reminder cards for use in appropriate circumstances. Furthermore, you can prevent discouragement by distinguishing between a process success and an outcome success: even though clients have used good skills in a problem situation (a process success) they may not get what they want (an outcome success). Not getting what they want does not negate the fact that they still performed competently and can do so again in future.

Stress the importance of clients understanding that often they can retrieve mistakes and always they can learn from them. In addition, where appropriate, challenge clients' demanding rules that 'change must be easy' and 'maintaining change must be effortless'. Encourage clients to replace such rules with more preferential rules stressing that changing and maintaining change can involve effort, practice and overcoming obstacles. Helpers can also emphasise clients' assuming personal responsibility for continuing to cope with their problem situations to the best of their ability.

Sometimes it is appropriate for helpers to explore with clients arrangements for continuing support. Such support may take the form of identifying and using supportive people, referral to another helper, attending a helping group or training course, self-help reading, and self-help audio cassettes or videotapes. In addition, as mentioned previously, helpers can offer review and booster sessions.

Ending final sessions

In brief helping focused on handling problem situations better, issues of dealing with clients' feelings are likely to be of less importance than in longer term helping. Nevertheless, helpers can facilitate discussion of clients' feelings about the future, the helping process and about ending it.

Saying goodbye or the formal leave taking should be a clean cut and respectful finish to what has gone before. Last impressions as well as first impressions are important. Aim to say goodbye in a business-like, yet warm and friendly way. By ending helping sloppily you may undo some of the good work you have done to date and make it more difficult for clients to return if they need to see you in future. Stay in your role as a helper rather than let your own personal agendas intrude.

Summary

You can be most effective with clients if you help them with both your heart and your head. Keep in touch with your humanity and avoid burdening yourself with the need to appear as an expert.

Helping sessions have four phases: preparing, starting, middle and ending. In helper training, preparing skills can include reviewing the previous session with trainer and peers as part of planning how to handle the next one. Also, you can make sure you know how to deliver any helping strategies you intend using.

The starting phase has three main tasks: re-establishing the relationship and working alliance, reviewing between-session activities and establishing a session agenda. Make opening statements that allow clients to share 'where they are at' rather than are solely task oriented. Encourage clients to see their contribution to positive changes. Consult with them and, where feasible, adhere to their wishes regarding session agendas.

The middle phase consists of delivering helping strategies. Remember to keep clients actively involved in the process and to keep sessions moving at an appropriate pace – neither too fast nor too slow. The ending phase may start with a structuring statement that allows sufficient time for ending the session properly. Tasks of the ending phase include negotiating between-session activities and setting up the next appointment.

Helper–client contacts can vary on dimensions of length of sessions and their frequency and overall number. If clients end helping of their own accord, this does not necessarily mean that they did not value their contact with you. There are four main sources of information that you and clients can use about when to end helping: client self-report, helper observations, third-party feedback and progress in attaining measurable goals. Formats for ending helping include stipulating a fixed number of sessions and leaving ending to be negotiated, including withdrawing helping support gradually. In addition, helpers and clients can arrange or leave open the possibility of booster sessions and follow-up phone calls.

Ways of assisting clients to maintain changes include end-of-helping summaries, anticipating difficulties and setbacks and developing strategies to deal with them, and helping clients think in ways that prevent discouragement and encourage persistence. Sometimes helpers need to explore arrangements for continuing support for clients, including referral to another helper. At the end of final sessions, helpers can facilitate discussion of clients' feelings about the future, the helping process, and about ending it. Staying in your role as helper, aim to say goodbye in a businesslike, yet warm and friendly way.

Activities

Activity 14.1   Starting post-initial helping sessions

Part A   *Formulating statements*

Using Box 14.2 as a guide, formulate at least one additional starting phase statement in each of the following categories:

- opening statements;
- reviewing between-session activities statements; and
- establishing a session agenda.

Part B   *Practising the starting phase*

One student acts as helper, another as client, with possibly a third student acting as observer. The client chooses a problem situation of relevance to him/her. Assume that you have conducted an initial session in which helper and client have completed the first two stages of the RUC helping process model. Furthermore, assume that you and your client have identified at least one communication/action and at least one thought to be altered during the changing stage, which may last for at least one more session after this one. If this is not a real second session, you will need to discuss how each participant can best get into their roles. Then conduct the starting phase of a second helping session up to and including the establishment of a session agenda.

Afterwards hold a sharing and feedback discussion. Then, if appropriate, change roles and repeat this activity.

Using audio cassette or videotape recording and playback may add value to the activity.

Activity 14.2   Conducting post-initial helping sessions

Part A   *Formulating statements*

Using Box 14.3 as a guide, formulate at least one additional statement in each of the following categories:

- middle phase statements;
- ending phase statements.

Part B   *Practising conducting second sessions*

One student acts as helper, another as client, with possibly a third student acting as observer. Using the same assumptions, either for the problem situation worked on in Activity 14.1 or for another problem situation conduct a helping session consisting of the following four phases:

- preparing phase (this may include addressing issues connected with your respective roles);
- starting phase;
- middle phase;
- ending phase.

Afterwards hold a sharing and feedback discussion. Then, if appropriate, change roles and repeat this activity.

Using audio cassette or videotape recording and playback may add value to the activity.

Activity 14.3   Ending helping

Part A   *Considerations in ending helping*

1   Critically discuss the importance and validity of each of the following considerations for when helping should end:
    - client self-report;
    - helper observations;
    - third-party feedback;

- attainment of measurable goals; and
- other factors not mentioned above.

2   Critically discuss the merits of each of the following formats for ending helping:
- fixed ending decided in the initial session;
- open ending negotiated between client and helper.

3   Critically discuss the value of each of the following ways of assisting clients to maintain their changes.

Prior to the final session:

- a strong working relationship;
- clear training in changing targeted communications/actions and thoughts;
- relevant between-session activities.

During the final session:

- summarising the main learnings;
- anticipating difficulties and setbacks and developing strategies for dealing with them;
- strategies that focus on how clients can think after helping; and
- exploring arrangements for continuing support.

Part B   Ending a series of helping sessions

One student acts as helper, another as client, with possibly a third student acting as observer. For the problem situation worked on in Activity 14.2 assume that you are now in your third and final helping session. Conduct all or part of this final helping session in which you focus on:

- assisting your client to maintain changes;
- ending helping smoothly;
- saying goodbye.

Afterwards hold a sharing and feedback discussion. Then, if appropriate, change roles and repeat this activity.

Using audio cassette or videotape recording and playback may add value to the activity.

PART 5

PRACTICAL CONSIDERATIONS

15 Introduction to Ethical Issues

Be not too hasty to trust or admire the teachers of morality: they discourse like angels, but they live like men.

Samuel Butler

Chapter outcomes

By studying and doing the activities in this chapter your should be able to:

- *understand the difference between ethics, values and the law;*
- *understand the difference between ethical lapses and ethical dilemmas;*
- *see that the core values of compassion and competence underpin ethical practice;*
- *know about some of the many ethical issues facing helpers;*
- *possess some basic knowledge about codes of ethics and practice;*
- *possess insight into the process of decision making for ethical dilemmas; and*
- *understand some ethical issues and dilemmas for students on introductory counselling skills training courses.*

Ethics are rules of conduct or systems of moral standards for different situations. They address considerations of right and wrong behaviour. All helpers develop implicit and explicit personal systems of ethics about using counselling skills. Furthermore, the different groups to which helpers belong are likely to have developed codes of conduct and guidelines for ethical practice.

Ethics differ from values which are the underlying principles upon which people and groups develop ethical codes and behaviour. Ethics also differ from laws which are rules of behaviour set by the legislature and the courts to establish standards that help society function in an orderly fashion.

Helping ethics is a huge, complex and fascinating topic. Students on introductory counselling skills courses should have an introductory awareness of the area. However, trainers need to refrain from allowing the study of ethical considerations to unbalance courses from their primary aim, which is to develop basic competence in counselling skills. Since helper competence is one of the main ethical issues, attention to developing skills and fostering more ethical helping can go hand in hand.

Counselling skills students cannot avoid many ethical issues both as students and in their subsequent use of counselling skills. This chapter aims to help you either start or continue developing a personal system of ethics for using counselling skills. Your personal system of ethics will be influenced by your underlying humanity, relevant ethical codes and guidelines, and society's moral and legal standards. Furthermore, you can develop a strong commitment to implementing and monitoring and, where necessary, amending your personal system of ethics.

Ethical issues surrounding the use of counselling skills are not always clear-cut. Sometimes, it is obvious when there are ethical lapses on the part of helpers: for instance, engaging in sexual relations with clients. On other occasions, users of counselling skills will be faced with ethical dilemmas involving choices between alternatives regarding how best to act. Confidentiality was the area for ethical dilemmas most frequently reported by British and American psychologists (Lindsey and Colley, 1995; Pope and Vetter, 1992). The same probably holds true for other users of counselling skills. When faced with ethical dilemmas, you require good ethical decision making skills.

This chapter mainly focuses on ethical issues and dilemmas connected with using counselling skills with individuals. Ethical issues attached to using counselling skills with couples, families and groups are both similar and different. Many helpers consider it insufficient to deal with ethical issues only when using counselling skills with individuals and groups. Instead, such helpers use community, organisational and political change agent skills to create environments in which clients and others can develop more of their human potential. For example, helpers who strive for greater racial and multicultural tolerance, understanding and legislative support fall into this category.

Core values: compassion and competence

Whether the ethical issues surround either obvious helper shortcomings or ethical dilemmas of varying degrees of complexity, users of counselling skills need to be guided by a commitment to the core values of compassion and competence.

Commitment to compassion

Compassion involves being kind hearted, benevolent and caring towards others who may be suffering in different ways and in varying degrees. Furthermore, compassion entails possessing a sympathetic identification with all people, regardless of race, culture or other differences, as being made of the same human clay as oneself. In Thailand, where I live, people are extremely sensitive to whether you are 'jai dee', heart good, or 'jai my dee', heart no good, or somewhere in between.

Counselling skills students and helpers can show warmth and concern in ways that do not demean clients by being either possessive or ingratiating. Most of us need to develop our capacity for good-hearted compassion rather than just portray it when it suits us. Compassion entails bringing out the best in ourselves as persons. Being genuinely good hearted to clients requires us to get in touch with and, in disciplined ways, to nurture and reveal our underlying altruistic tendencies.

Helpers tend to hold humanistic values reflecting compassion. In one large-scale study of American counsellors based on 10 value types derived from the Schwartz Universal Values Questionnaire (Schwartz, 1992), two of the three most highly rated value types were benevolence (a concern for the welfare of others with whom one is in frequent personal contact in everyday interactions) and universalism (an appreciative concern for all people and of nature) (Kelly, 1995). Probably, most users of counselling skills share similar compassionate values.

Many ethical shortcomings by helpers can be viewed as failures of compassion. Clients in various ways become viewed as objects rather than prized as separate and unique members of the human race. Any form of discriminatory prejudice by helpers creates suffering and represents insufficient mental, moral and, depending on one's religious stance, spiritual development. Similarly emotional and sexual exploitation that takes place in the power imbalance of the helper–client relationship creates suffering and reflects lack of a strong commitment to the value of compassion. On a more subtle level, failures by counselling skills students and helpers to listen properly can also indicate deficiencies not just in competence, but in compassion as well.

Commitment to competence

Compassion and competence intertwine. If you genuinely care for your clients as separate individuals, you want to help them to ease their psychological pain and develop the knowledge and skills to create more happiness for themselves and others. To achieve these aims you need to be there as competently as possible for them. To do this you require a continuing commitment to acquiring, maintaining and developing competence in using counselling skills.

Where introductory counselling skills are involved, there tends to be a substantial degree of agreement among helpers as to what constitutes competence: for example, how to use active listening skills to under-stand clients' internal perspectives. As you learn more advanced coun-selling skills, the definition of what skills are important and therefore of what constitutes competent performance will vary according to the theoretical orientation of the helping school in which you are being trained; for example, person-centred, cognitive-behavioural, psycho-dynamic or some form of integration of approaches.

Students with a genuine commitment to competence are realistic about their strengths and limitations. On introductory counselling skills courses and in more advanced helper training, they are diligent about learning and practising. This commitment to competence continues in their work as helpers where they maintain and develop existing skills as well as learn new ones. Monitoring their use of counselling skills is taken for granted. Committed users of counselling skills, whether students, counsellors or otherwise, seek assistance in evaluating their work from trainers, supervisors, colleagues and clients who can give honest and constructive feedback.

Developing a genuine commitment to competence can protect counselling skills students from many ethical shortcomings both now and in future. Half-hearted attempts to learn counselling skills are simply not good enough. A small minority of counselling skills students seem more interested in acquiring the qualifications at the end of their courses than the knowledge and skills that these qualifications represent. In later helping practice, a genuine commitment to competence can protect you from sloppy work. Sometimes such a commitment entails helpers in developing better self-care skills, so that their enthusiasm and counselling skills are not adversely affected by emotional fatigue and burnout.

Ethical issues in helping practice

In this section I identify some areas of ethical issues and dilemmas pertinent to using counselling skills in helping practice. Then I review some frameworks for making decisions about ethical issues. Many of these issues are just as relevant for helpers who use counselling skills as part of their jobs as for counsellors and psychotherapists.

Ethical issues and dilemmas

Virtually every aspect of using counselling skills can be performed ethically or unethically. In addition, the use of counselling skills presents many opportunities for ethical dilemmas. Below I briefly present just some of the many areas pertinent to using counselling skills ethically in helping practice.

- *Competence* Issues of competence include how well you listen, deliver helping strategies, work within your limitations, and, in appropriate circumstances, make referrals.
- *Continuing counselling skills development* Monitoring, maintaining and where possible developing competence in using counselling skills.
- *Confidentiality* Confidentiality involves not divulging private information without client permission as well as informing clients of any limits in confidentiality. Helpers also have an ethical responsibility to keep client records and audio cassette and videotape recordings of sessions safe.
- *Permission to record sessions* Obtaining permission to audio record or videotape sessions without undue pressure and with clients fully informed of how the recordings will be used and for how long they will be kept.
- *Warning and protecting third parties* Clients may divulge information about potential harm to third parties; for instance intended physical violence or being HIV positive and having unsafe sex.
- *Readiness to practise* Helpers require appropriate training and practice before they are ready to see clients and to use counselling skills competently with them.
- *Fitness to practise* Issues here concern the helper's ability to use counselling skills competently. Helpers have an ethical responsibility to maintain their own resilience and fitness to help clients. They should do their best to refrain from allowing current personal agendas, for example going through a messy divorce, to adversely influence their helping work.
- *Client autonomy* Helpers need to respect clients as different and separate from themselves and not attempt to impose their own

values and solutions upon them. Clients need to be allowed to retain responsibility for their lives.

- *Informed consent*   Informed consent involves the right of clients to be informed about what the helping process will involve and to consent knowingly and without undue pressure to any helping strategies that are used during it.
- *Dual relationships*   Helpers, in addition to the helping relationship, may either already be in, or consider entering, or enter other kinds of relationships with clients: for instance, friend, lover, colleague, trainer, manager, supervisor, among others. Whether a dual helper–client relationship is unethical, ethical or presents an ethical dilemma depends on the circumstances of the relationship.
- *Prejudice and insensitivity to difference*   Being either prejudiced against or insufficiently sensitive to clients who differ from you on dimensions such as race, culture, social class, gender, sexual and affectionate orientation, age, physical disability and religious beliefs, among others.
- *Using counselling skills with minors*   Many ethical issues surround the boundaries of helper obligations to children and to significant others in their lives, such as parents and teachers.
- *Financial exploitation*   Taking advantage of clients for the purposes of financial gain as contrasted with legitimate fees for service activities.
- *Helper emotional and sexual exploitation of clients*   Using clients to meet helper needs for closeness, intimacy and sex. Sexual harassment can fit into this category.
- *Client emotional and sexual manipulation of helpers*   Dealing ethically with seductive and emotionally manipulative clients.
- *Client and helper safety*   Protecting clients from physically harming either themselves, for instance suicide, or you, for instance threats of physical violence.
- *Basis for suggesting helping strategies*   Being informed about the practical and research literature about the process and outcomes of using different helping strategies for specific problem situations and problems.
- *Ending helping ethically*   Issues include maintaining boundaries, post helping availability, and referral to other helpers or forms of support.
- *Relationships with other helpers*   Dealing ethically with trainers, supervisors, colleagues and helping agencies.
- *Advertising and self-promotion*   Avoiding making false and misleading statements about training, qualifications, experience and the likely outcomes of using counselling skills.

Ethical codes and guidelines

When developing your personal system of helping ethics, monitoring your practice, and dealing with ethical dilemmas, where can you turn? Tim Bond (1999) suggests five sources of 'professional guidance' for helpers: professional codes and guidelines, law, agency policy, ethical analysis based on moral philosophy, and the ethics and values implicit in the helper's theoretical orientation. In addition, helpers can reaffirm their commitments to the core values of compassion and competence.

Students on beginning counselling skills courses should be introduced to the ethical codes and guidelines pertinent to their current and subsequent use of counselling skills. Box 15.1 lists some illustrative ethical codes and guidelines for counselling, psychology and psychotherapy. In addition, different areas such as nursing, social work and human resource management have their own ethical codes and guidelines. Since ethical codes and guidelines tend to get updated, find out about and use the most recent versions.

Box 15.1   Illustrative British and Australian ethical codes and guidelines

Britain
- *British Association for Counselling (BAC)*:
  - BAC Code of ethics and practice guidelines for those using counselling skills in their work
  - BAC Code of ethics and practice for counsellors
- *British Psychological Society (BPS)*:
  - BPS Code of conduct, ethical principles and guidelines
  - BPS Division of Counselling Psychology Guidelines for the professional practice of counselling psychology
- *United Kingdom Council for Psychotherapy (UKCP)*:
  - Ethical guidelines of UKCP

Australia
- *Australian Guidance and Counselling Association (AGCA)*:
  - AGCA Code of ethics
- *Australian Psychological Society (APS)*:
  - APS Code of professional conduct
  - APS Guidelines for therapeutic practice with female clients
  - APS Guidelines for the provision of psychological services for and for the conduct of psychological research with Aboriginal and Torres Strait Islander people of Australia

---

Ethical codes and guidelines are designed to protect both clients and helpers. Such codes and guidelines are statements of what is an acceptable level of conduct and what is not. As such, these codes and guidelines lay down standards of accountability to which helpers can be held responsible. However, many areas of ethical practice are grey rather than black and white. Nevertheless, ethical codes can provide a useful framework that suggests acceptable norms for your area of helping when making ethical decisions in light of the individual circumstances of each unique client.

Ethical codes protect clients by stating guidelines for helpers behaving responsibly towards them. Ethical codes also protect helpers by offering group guidelines rather than leaving a vacuum regarding what constitutes ethical practice. In addition, ethical codes and guidelines have PYRE or 'Protect Your Rear End' value for helpers. Those helpers complying leave themselves less open to complaints and malpractice litigation than those who do not.

Some ethical codes are pertinent to counselling skills training. For instance, the British Association for Counselling publishes a separate Code of Ethics and Practice for Trainers and another for Supervisors of Counsellors. A notable exception is the absence of any student guidelines. A case exists for developing student ethical guidelines, especially since all practitioners, trainers and supervisors start as students. Furthermore, discussion of ethical issues during counselling skills and counsellor training may have more relevance if focused on students' current rather than future helping practice.

Making decisions about ethical issues and dilemmas

American counselling writers Marianne and Gerald Corey (1998) observe that, along with codes of ethics of relevant organisations, possessing a systematic way of approaching difficult ethical dilemmas increases helpers' chances of making sound ethical decisions. Box 15.2 presents two models for ethical decision making: first, that of the Coreys; and second Carol Shillito-Clarke's (1996) development of an earlier six-step model developed by Tim Bond (1993). Models such as those described in Box 15.2 are definitely valuable in listing important considerations and assisting helpers to manage their anxiety when confronted with dilemmas.

Box 15.2   Models of decision making for ethical dilemmas

Corey and Corey's ethical decision making model

1   Identify the problem.
2   Apply the ethical guidelines.
3   Determine the nature and dimensions of the dilemma and seek consultation.
4   Generate possible courses of action.
5   Consider the possible consequences of all options and determine a course of action.
6   Evaluate the selected course of action.
7   Implement the course of action.

Shillito-Clarke's 5 Cs model for working through ethical decisions and dilemmas

1   *Clarify*   Considerations include clarifying the issue at stake, its main elements, and how it might be perceived by those involved.
2   *Consult*   Consult relevant ethical codes and guidelines, legal position (if relevant), and supervisors and colleagues (as appropriate).
3   *Consider*   Generate different courses of action and consider their ethical dimensions and consequences.
4   *Choose*   Choose the best course of action, sleep on it and review it again before implementing it.
5   *Check*   Check the outcomes, whether another solution would have been better, and what you can learn from the experience.

Perhaps rather more than is justified, both the Corey and the Shillito-Clarke models seem to imply that making ethical decisions is a rational process. As the saying goes: 'Who ever said that humans were rational?' Helpers tend to bring different decision making styles to ethical decisions: for example, some avoid making them for as long as possible, others rush into making them, still others worry over every detail. In addition, even when helpers make decisions, they differ in their commitment to them and in their abilities to implement them skilfully.

Furthermore, helpers like clients differ in their mind skills strengths and weaknesses. Here I provide at least one example of how poor skills can interfere with making decisions rationally for each of the mind skills areas of creating self-talk, visual images, rules, perceptions, explanations and expectations. Helpers may use negative self-talk that increases their anxiety about making and implementing decisions on ethical issues: for instance, if they suspect serious misconduct on the part of a colleague or boss. Accompanying their negative self-talk may be unhelpful visual images about the processes and outcomes of acting ethically. Furthermore, helpers may have rules that interfere with ethical action: for instance, a demanding rule like 'I must be approved of all the time' may get in the way of openly discussing an ethically ambiguous situation such as being strongly sexually attracted to a client.

Areas for ethical dilemmas are fertile breeding grounds for creating false perceptions. For instance, controlling helpers may possess little insight into their ethical lapses in the areas of client autonomy, undue pressure and informed consent. Being blind to the existence of their ethical lapses, they are scarcely in the position to embark on an ethical decision making process about the issues and dilemmas associated with their behaviour. Helpers may also create false explanations about why they are spending so much time with certain clients rather than with others. Indeed, a helper may go so far as explaining having sex with a client as a manifestation of depth of love rather than as serious professional misconduct. In addition, helper expectations about the damage to themselves and to clients of any ethical lapses may be far off the mark. For example, helpers who advertise and promote themselves unethically may fail to anticipate the consequences that may be in store for them.

In sum, two rather than three cheers for ethical decision making models. Always, be alert for how you may be turning what is outwardly a rational decision making process into one that is less than completely rational because of your own needs and anxieties. Furthermore, the more you can successfully work on your own mental development both as a person and as a helper, the more likely you are to work your way rationally through ethical dilemmas in helping.

Ethical issues in introductory counselling skills courses

Many of the ethical issues and dilemmas connected with helping practice are present in introductory counselling skills courses. Furthermore, the range of people on counselling skills courses is very similar to the range of people in the helping services. Many counselling skills students are already employed as helpers and others will become so. Consequently, when it comes to ethical issues, students are likely to possess the same strengths and vulnerability to temptation as practising helpers.

I want to avoid this discussion of student ethics from becoming too negative. Just as most helpers and trainers behave very ethically, so do most counselling skills students. Sometimes, where ethical lapses do occur, they are through carelessness rather than from conscious intent. However careless lapses, for instance of confidentiality, can have negative consequences. In addition, counselling skills training can present students with real ethical dilemmas. Some students resolve such ethical dilemmas more successfully than others. I now review three ethical areas relevant to all introductory counselling skills training courses: competence, confidentiality and dual relationships.

Competence

The gaining of basic competence is the main goal of introductory counselling skills courses. Most students work hard at this and some make huge sacrifices to attend counselling skills courses and develop their skills. However, for various reasons, some other students' motivation to gain competence may not be as strong as desirable. Box 15.3 provides some examples of ethical lapses and dilemmas in the area of gaining competence.

Box 15.3   Competence: examples of ethical lapses and dilemmas

Ethical lapses
Student A is admitted to a 12-week two-and-a-half-hour session introductory counselling skills course and then proceeds to go overseas for the first six weeks of class. Student A did not reveal this trip at time of admission to the course.

Student B intentionally does just enough work to achieve the minimum standards for passing an introductory counselling skills course. S/he frequently comes to skills classes very late and misses other classes without contacting the trainer in advance. Student B rarely practises her/his skills.

Ethical dilemmas
Student C has heavy family and work responsibilities and feels stretched and stressed by attending her/his introductory counselling skills course and completing the between-session assignments diligently. As the semester progresses, Student C wonders how s/he is going to manage and what her/his real priorities are.

> Student D is taking an introductory counselling skills course as part of a larger helping services course. The culture of the department in which the course is held values academic work and research more highly than professional competence. Student D feels under considerable pressure to pay more attention to the academic rather than the practical dimensions of her/his course.

If, by any chance, you are a student either tempted or under pressure to reduce your commitment to your introductory counselling skills course, following are some points for you to consider. My assumption is that your course is run by a competent and ethical trainer and its goals were clearly presented before you enrolled. You entered the course either with an explicit or a good faith contract that you would undertake the course diligently. If the course has minimum attendance requirements, for instance attending nine out of 12 sessions, you could be failed for insufficient attendance.

In addition to what you perceive as your interests, any decision by you to short change the course affects the interests of many others. You are making it more difficult for your trainer to achieve her or his goals for your group. You may create a less productive learning environment for your fellow students.

Furthermore, introductory counselling skills courses are not ends in themselves, but the means by which students can offer better services to clients. By paying insufficient attention to your course, you jeopardise the interests of future clients. In addition, if your introductory counselling skills course is a prelude to having a counselling skills placement, you may put yourself and your trainer in an invidious position regarding your readiness to see clients. As a trainer, I resented those few students who expected me to arrange clients for them at the same time as not being diligent about learning counselling skills. Other people with an interest in having students learn properly are the institutions or agencies in which the courses are taught and any accrediting bodies, such as the British Association for Counselling, that are involved. Poor students who then become poor helpers are a credit to neither.

Confidentiality

All people consider it their right to control the flow of personal information that others receive about them. Confidentiality is at the heart of building trust with clients. Some clients find it difficult to trust anyone. Many feel very vulnerable about the nature of the personal information that they reveal to their helpers.

Trainers on introductory counselling skills courses can not only build students' awareness of the importance of confidentiality, but also do their best to see that students translate awareness into action when on their courses. On beginning counselling skills courses, issues of confidentiality can concern disclosures revealed in practice helping sessions, disclosures students share with one another informally, and disclosures made by 'volunteer clients'. Reasons students may breach the ethic of confidentiality include wanting to disclose a good story, enjoying gossiping, careless talk, careless storage of records, and being insufficiently clear about when to keep your mouth shut.

Some students on counselling skills courses do not take the issue of confidentiality sufficiently seriously. Probably most problems of confidentiality on introductory counselling skills courses fall more into the category of ethical lapses than ethical dilemmas. Since students tend to be counselling one another rather than real clients, many situations that make confidentiality a central ethical dilemma for helpers do not occur: for instance, the rights of parents when their children are clients. Box 15.4 provides two examples of ethical lapses in which another student's disclosures have been insufficiently protected: one involving verbal leakage, another involving the potential for pictorial as well as verbal identification.

Box 15.4 Confidentiality: examples of ethical lapses

Student E has been using counselling skills in a practice helping session with Student F as client. Student F discusses a problem in her/his relationship with her/his partner. When Student E gets home s/he talks about contents of the helping session to her/his partner.

Student G makes a videotape in which s/he counsels Student H who discusses a problem situation in her/his life. Student G leaves the videotape lying around in the classroom, with the door unlocked, when the training group goes out for a coffee break.

Some may consider that the example in Box 15.4 of talking to your partner at home about a client's problem is all right as long as you do not identify the client. I disagree. Students need to develop the strict habit of maintaining confidentiality under virtually all circumstances. Furthermore, in Britain many ethical codes request that clients be informed in advance of any limitations of confidentiality, though with differing emphases. Bond (1999) observes: 'BAC requires and BPS recommends that clients be informed in advance, whereas UKCP only requires that any limitations be communicated in response to a direct request from the client' (p. 198).

Within the framework of relevant ethical codes, trainers and students on counselling skills courses can develop rules about confidentiality for their particular groups. Sometimes these rules get formalised into group contractual agreements signed by all concerned. In addition, where students record helping sessions with 'volunteer clients', clients must be informed in advance of any limitations of confidentiality connected with the training process. Furthermore, trainers and students have an ethical obligation to protect confidentiality in how they use, store and dispose of 'volunteer client' recordings.

Dual relationships

When students come on introductory counselling skills training courses, they have a right to assume that they will be treated by their trainers no better or worse than any other students. Furthermore, they have a right to assume that their contact with their trainer will be focused on their counselling skills development rather than meeting the trainer's needs for emotional and sexual intimacy. By virtue of their role, trainers possess a degree of power over students. However, trainers are also vulnerable human beings. Some trainers may have a pattern of exploiting students to meet their own needs. However, other trainers may be vulnerable only in special circumstances, for instance if lonely after a recent separation or divorce.

The majority of students who enrol in introductory counselling skills courses are of mature age. Students also have a responsibility not to engage in trainer–student relationships which may have negative consequences for their fellow students, their trainers and possibly for themselves. Some students may seek special treatment on assessments by becoming friendly with trainers. Others may genuinely possess strong feelings of sexual and emotional attraction to their trainers rather than seek to influence the assessment processes of the course in any way. In some instances it may be appropriate to express these feelings, so long as it is not done seductively or in a way that manipulates the trainer to respond in kind. Box 15.5 provides two examples where students might be perceived as acting unethically in the area of dual relationships. In the first example the trainer then acts unethically too.

Box 15.5 Dual relationships: examples of ethical lapses

Student I persistently asks Trainer X to come out for personal meals and to social events where other students are not invited. Trainer X at first says no, but then gives way and the two develop a close emotional bond that falls short of a sexual relationship. Student I and Trainer X endeavour to keep their relationship secret from the rest of the training group.

Without any encouragement Student J behaves seductively with Trainer Y during a scheduled office hour. Subsequently Student J makes it quite clear to Trainer Y that s/he would like to have sex with her/him.

Counselling skills students may themselves receive messages from their trainers that the training relationship might be accompanied by an emotional or sexual relationship. Mostly students should use assertion skills to nip such advances in the bud. In rare instances, they might suggest to the trainer that the possibility of engaging in a personal relationship be put on hold, pending the end of their course. If sexually harassed, students can go to people like heads of departments, students' rights officers, counselling services, and consider using institutional sexual harassment procedures, assuming they exist.

Not all cases of dual relationships are clear-cut. For example, a student and a trainer may have known one another before the start of the course. Furthermore, some trainers and students may have genuine common interests, for instance tennis or country music, that provides a shared bond between them. Both students and trainers need the freedom to express their humanity at the same time as guarding against the danger of exploiting and being exploited by one another.

Summary

Ethics are rules of conduct or systems of moral standards for different situations. Sometimes ethical issues are not clear-cut, thus presenting ethical dilemmas for helpers. All users of counselling skills develop systems of ethics pertinent to helping. Ethics differ from the law, which are standards laid down by legislatures and courts. Compassion and competence are two core values underlying helping ethics.

Virtually every aspect of using counselling skills can be performed ethically or unethically. Ethical issues pertinent to helping practice include: competence, continuing counselling skills development, confidentiality, permission to record sessions, warning and protecting third parties, readiness to practise, fitness to practise, client autonomy, informed consent, dual relationships, prejudice and insensitivity to difference, using counselling skills with minors, financial exploitation, helper emotional and sexual exploitation of clients, client emotional and sexual manipulation of helpers, client and helper safety, the basis for suggesting helping strategies, ending helping ethically, relationships with other helpers, and advertising and self-promotion.

Ethical codes and guidelines are designed to protect both clients and helpers by suggesting standards for appropriate behaviour. Counselling skills students are encouraged to familiarise themselves with the most recent versions of any ethical codes pertinent to their current or future helping practice. Currently there appear to be no ethical guidelines for counselling skills students.

Ethical decision making models can guide helpers in making decisions about ethical issues and dilemmas rationally and thoroughly. However, helpers have different styles of decision making that may interfere with their effectiveness. In addition, poor mind skills in the areas of creating self-talk, visual images, rules, perceptions, explanations and expectations can each introduce irrational elements into the decision making process. Consequently, when faced with ethical dilemmas, helpers need to protect themselves against their tendencies to irrationality as well as to follow the steps of a rational decision making model.

Many of the ethical issues and dilemmas connected with helping practice are present on introductory counselling skills courses. For example, students differ in their commitment to competence. Ethical lapses include poor attendance, doing the minimum to pass the course, and failing to practise skills sufficiently. Ethical dilemmas related to gaining competence include what priority to give to learning counselling skills when faced with the pressures of work and family life and when influenced by academic cultures that undervalue the learning of applied skills. Students should learn to be strict about confidentiality when first learning counselling skills by protecting one another's disclosures and by safeguarding any recordings made of helping sessions. Students also have a responsibility for avoiding sexual and emotional dual relationships with trainers during counselling skills courses, even when trainers make the first moves.

Activities

Activity 15.1   Ethical issues in helping

Critically discuss how each of the following areas can contain important ethical issues, and possibly dilemmas, for helpers:

- competence;
- continuing counselling skills development;
- confidentiality;
- permission to record sessions;
- warning and protecting third parties;
- readiness to practise;
- fitness to practise;
- client autonomy;
- informed consent;
- dual relationships;
- prejudice and insensitivity to difference;
- using counselling skills with minors;
- financial exploitation;
- helper emotional and sexual exploitation of clients;
- client emotional and sexual manipulation of helpers;
- client and helper safety;
- the basis for suggesting helping strategies;
- ending helping;
- relationships with other helpers; and
- advertising and self-promotion.

1 In what areas do you consider yourself most at risk of unethical helping behaviour?
2 What can you do to protect yourself from engaging in unethical helping behaviour in the areas you have identified?

Activity 15.2   Making decisions about ethical issues and dilemmas

1   Critically discuss the strengths and weaknesses of:
   • Corey and Corey's ethical decision making model
   • Shillito-Clarke's 5 Cs model for working through ethical decisions and dilemmas
2   What factors do you think might interfere with your making decisions about ethical dilemmas rationally:
   2.1   your current style of making decisions (please specify);
   2.2   poor mind skills in one or more of the following areas:
      • creating self-talk;
      • creating visual images;
      • creating rules;
      • creating perceptions;
      • creating explanations;
      • creating expectations;
   2.3   any other factors (please specify).
3   What can you do to improve your ability to make decisions wisely when faced with ethical issues and dilemmas in future?

Activity 15.3   Ethical issues in introductory counselling skills courses

1   Critically discuss the ethical issues and dilemmas for introductory counselling skills students in each of the following areas:
   • gaining competence;
   • confidentiality;
   • dual relationships.
2   What other areas for ethical issues and dilemmas are important and why?
3   If you were to develop a set of Student Guidelines for Ethical Participation in Introductory Counselling Skills Training Courses, what would be its main provisions?

16 Becoming More Skilled and Human

Love begins at home and can spread like a burning fire from house to house.

Mother Teresa

Chapter outcomes

By studying and doing the activities in this chapter your should be able to:

- *monitor your counselling skills for each stage of RUC helping process model;*
- *gain some ideas about self-help methods for maintaining and developing your skills;*
- *gain information about training paths for developing counselling skills;*
- *know some points to check when selecting a training course;*
- *know more about books and journals relevant to counselling skills; and*
- *gain some ideas about how to develop and maintain your humanity.*

This chapter explores how, once you have completed your introductory counselling skills training course, you can both build your skills and develop your humanity. The endings of introductory counselling skills courses are also beginnings. Perhaps your appetite to go further was whetted before your course started. If not, I hope your training experience has been such that you wish to become more skilled. However, becoming more skilled also entails becoming more human. By that I mean developing the better rather than the worse qualities of humankind so that you can become an even more present, humane and compassionate helper.

Monitoring your skills

The term 'reflective practitioner' is used to describe helpers who monitor, evaluate and think deeply about their helping work, often with the aid of others such as supervisors and trusted colleagues. At the end of an introductory counselling course, perhaps a good place to start in reflecting about your future practice is to take stock about where you are at present. By the end of your training course, you will have developed some ideas about how well you are getting on and which counselling skills you need to develop. Your opinion may have been influenced by feedback from your trainer and fellow students as well as by comments made by your 'clients'. In addition, some of you use counselling skills in your outside jobs, so this will be a further source of feedback.

In a sense, the term 'introductory counselling skills' is inaccurate. Possibly, it is better to think of them as fundamental skills that provide the basic tool kit for your helping work, especially if you are planning to become a qualified counsellor. There is no shame in thinking you need to improve your fundamental skills, quite the contrary. High levels of competence can only be attained and maintained by those realistic about how hard it is to become a good practitioner. Students who do not properly monitor their skills, fail to realise their limitations and then rush out to practise well beyond their strengths are dangers on the road who give counselling and helping a bad name.

Activity 16.1 asks you to evaluate your present level of competence at using the counselling skills described in this book for each stage of the relating–understanding–changing (RUC) helping process model. Depending on the length and goals of your course, some of you will have covered more ground than others. Just as with your clients, change involves taking responsibility for developing your skills, being honest about your strengths and limitations, and pinpointing where you need to change. Complete the activity as best you can.

Becoming more skilled

Introductory counselling skills training courses differ in length, format, content and context. In addition, students on introductory counselling skills courses come from a diversity of backgrounds and plan many different futures. Consequently, any suggestions for becoming more skilled need to be taken in the context of your evaluation of your current counselling skills and also of your personal agendas and career aspirations.

Self-help

What are some of the things you can do on your own to maintain and develop your counselling skills? You can observe and listen to demonstrations of skilled counsellors. For instance, cassettes of interviews conducted by leading counsellors and psychotherapists are available for purchase in Britain and Australia. Also, you can purchase or hire videotapes. In Britain, films and videotapes may be hired from the British Association for Counselling. In addition, you may learn from written demonstrations of counselling skills. Transcripts of interviews by leading helpers are available, sometimes accompanying cassettes. Another way you can learn from demonstration is to become the client of a skilled helper, though this should not be your primary motivation for seeking counselling help.

While a whole interview approach to observing, listening to and reading transcripts is valuable, this is not the only way to approach the material. One option is to focus on smaller segments of interviews, say five minutes, and look out for how specific counselling skills are used. In addition to verbal communication, remember to focus on vocal communication and, if observing videos, on bodily communication as well. Furthermore, look out for the communication patterns between helpers and clients as well as how helpers respond to single client statements.

Another option is to turn the audio or video recorder off after each client statement, form your own helper response, and then see how the helper actually responded. When working with transcripts of a session by someone like Carl Rogers, you can go down the page covering up Rogers' responses, form your own, and then check Rogers' responses. Remember that your responses will not necessarily be inferior to those of the more famous helpers.

Co-counselling is a form of peer helping whereby in a given time period, say an hour, each person will have a turn at being both helper and client. You can practise your counselling skills with a colleague, possibly someone who was also on your introductory skills training course, on a co-counselling basis using audio and video feedback where appropriate. In addition, you may be able to form or become part of a learning helping skills peer self-help group in which you work with, comment on and support one another as you develop your counselling skills.

Whether in informal helping contacts or in more formal helping sessions, some of you are already using counselling skills as part of your jobs. In some settings, you may be able to monitor yourself by recording and playing back your sessions, possibly in the presence of supervisors or peers. In addition, you can be sensitive to feedback from clients. Some of this feedback will come in how they respond to your use of counselling skills through their verbal, vocal and bodily communication. In addition, where appropriate, you can ask clients for feedback on how they experienced individual sessions and their overall helping contact with you. You can also develop your own questionnaires to generate client feedback.

Training paths

Where do you go next if you want to gain more training in counselling skills? Given the diversity of introductory counselling skills courses and the different background and goals of students on them, this is a hard question to answer simply. Many of you may be in professions other than counselling, for example social work, where there may be opportunities for further training within your existing undergraduate or postgraduate courses or, if already graduated, on in-service training courses and workshops run by your professional association or by members of it. Others of you may be working in voluntary organisations which may offer their own more advanced counselling skills training courses geared to the populations which they serve.

Readers wishing to become counsellors or counselling psychologists should look out for accredited and/or well-regarded courses. At time of writing there is no accreditation of counselling courses in Australia. However, in Britain the British Association for Counselling accredits courses. You can find further details of training courses in the most recent version of BAC's annually published *The Training in Counselling and Psychotherapy Directory*.

In both Australia and Britain, the main route to becoming a counselling psychologist now is through undergraduate work in psychology followed by a Masters in Counselling Psychology. You can contact the relevant psychological professional association for details of accredited courses.

**Box 16.1   British and Australian counselling and counselling
psychology professional associations**

Britain
Counselling: British Association for Counselling, 1 Regent Place, Rugby,
   Warwickshire CV21 2PJ; Information Tel. 01788 578328; Fax 01788
   562189
Psychology: British Psychological Society, St Andrews House, 48 Princess
   Road East, Leicester LE1 7DR; Tel. 01162 549568; Fax 01162 470787;
   e-mail information requests, enquiry@bps.org.uk

Australia
Counselling: Australian Guidance and Counselling Association,
   Membership Secretary, Clive Budden, 53 Hereford Ave., Trinity
   Gardens, South Australia 5068; Tel. 883668825 (w); fax 883652750
Psychology: Australian Psychological Society, PO Box 126, Carlton South,
   Victoria 3053; Tel. 03 9663 6166 (or toll free 1800 333 497); fax 03
   9663 6177; e-mail, natl-off@aps-nho.mhs.compuserve.com

Graduation from a counselling or counselling psychology course
does not in itself mean you are an accredited practitioner. To obtain
accreditation, you will be required to accumulate a set number of
hours of supervised counselling practice. Afterwards, to maintain your
accreditation, you may be required to have ongoing supervision (as
with the British Association for Counselling) or regularly accumulate
continuing professional development points by attending conferences,
workshops and training courses (as with the Australian Psychological
Society).

A distinction exists between accreditation by a professional association and mandatory registration or licensing by either a national
registration board or, as in Australia, by a state registration board. In
some states in Australia people cannot call themselves counselling
psychologists unless certified as such by the relevant state registration
board. In both Britain and Australia, the trend is towards tightening up
the licensing of counsellors and counselling psychologists. The recent
development of the United Kingdom Register of Counsellors is an
important milestone on the British landscape.

At an appropriate time, check the licensing requirements either in
force or in the pipeline for where you intend to practise. For those
wishing more information about the British scene, Ray Woolfe (1999)
reviews training and accreditation routes for counsellors, counselling
psychologists and psychotherapists. However, when the time comes

for you to seek this information, you may require an even more recent source.

Attending conferences, short courses and workshops can provide an informal training path whereby both counselling skills students and more experienced helpers can improve their knowledge and skills. In Britain details of short courses, workshops and conferences can be found in BAC's quarterly journal *Counselling* and in the BPS's monthly journal *The Psychologist*. In Australia, similar information can be found in the APS's journal *InPsych* and in the Society's state branch newsletters as well as in the AGCA's *Australian Journal of Guidance and Counselling* and its state branch newsletters. In both countries information about short courses, workshops and conferences can be found in the newsletters and journals of other professional associations and of voluntary agencies, such as *Relate News* in Britain.

If interested in developing your skills in a particular approach to helping, enquire whether there is a training centre in your locality. Most major helping approaches have international networks for training and practice. For example, agencies for specialised training in Person-Centred Therapy exist in Britain and for Rational Emotive Behaviour Therapy in both Britain and Australia.

You need to make decisions about further counselling skills training wisely. To help with this process, Box 16.2 provides a checklist for assessing training courses. As appropriate, amend the checklist for workshops, conferences and short courses.

Box 16.2   Checklist for assessing training courses

Following are some factors to bear in mind when choosing a course:

- What are the course's goals?
- How do these goals fit into my helping and personal goals?
- How does the course add to or expand my knowledge and skills?
- What qualification, if any, does successful completion of the course bring?
- What other courses are there that are comparable to this course and how much should I know about them?
- What is the length and format of the course?
- What is the total time commitment, both inside and outside class, expected of students?
- Where is the course located?
- What is the course's accreditation status and by whom?
- What is the course's reputation and how reliable are my sources?
- What are the selection criteria and procedures?

- What are my chances of getting selected and what might I do to improve them?
- What is the course's main theoretical orientation?
- What is the size of the training group?
- What is the breakdown on the course between:
  - theoretical and academic studies;
  - research preparation and projects;
  - applied counselling skills work?
- What is the course content in each area?
- What teaching and learning methods are employed in each area?
- What assessment methods are used in each area?
- What is the staffing situation – for instance, number, qualifications, interests, national or international reputations?
- What and how good is the physical accommodation:
  - for teaching;
  - for skills training?
- How good are the library facilities:
  - books;
  - journals;
  - audiovisual material?
- How good are the computing facilities and what amount of computing support is available?
- What and how satisfactory are the course's placement arrangements?
- What and how satisfactory are the course's supervision of practical work arrangements?
- What requirements, if any, are there for the personal development of students?
- What facilities are there for the personal development of students:
  - on the course;
  - outside the course, for instance a student counselling service?
- Where are recent graduates of the course employed?
- What are the fees and arrangements for paying them?
- Are there any other additional expenses involved?
- Is there any financial assistance available?

Books and journals

Books
There is a large theoretical literature that underpins the use of counselling skills. This can be divided into primary sources, books and articles written by the leading theorists themselves, and secondary sources, books and articles written about the different theoretical approaches by people other than their originators. Ultimately, there is

no substitute for reading primary sources. However, it can be a daunting task for a beginner to know where to start and how to cover the ground. Perhaps it is better to start with a secondary source book that overviews many of the main approaches and lists primary sources that you may follow up. In Britain two leading counselling theory textbooks are Windy Dryden's edited *Handbook of Individual Therapy* (1996), with chapters written by a range of leading British practitioners, and my *Theory and Practice of Counselling* (1995). Even though I wrote all the chapters in my book, I was fortunate enough to be assisted by experts in each approach. These experts included many of the originators of the approaches who provided material and reviewed or arranged for the review of chapters prior to publication. Both these textbooks are readily available in Australia and New Zealand.

The bibliography at the end of this book contains many suggestions for books and articles about counselling skills. Counselling skills textbooks that cover more advanced skills than this introductory book include Gerard Egan's *The Skilled Helper: A Problem Management Approach to Helping* (1998) and my *Practical Counselling and Helping Skills: Text and Exercises for the Lifeskills Counselling Model* (1997).

Elsewhere, I have reviewed some of the main similarities and differences between the Egan 'skilled helper' and the Nelson-Jones 'skilled client' helping process models (Nelson-Jones, 1999b). At risk of overstatement the following are some of the main differences between the models:

- The skilled helper model focuses on problem management whereas the skilled client model also focuses on addressing the problematic skills that position clients for problems both now and in future.
- The skilled helper model has its major emphasis on the problem management process up to and including the stage of planning action strategies. Above all, it appears to be a problem solving or decision making model.
- The skilled client model goes beyond goal setting and planning to emphasise that, if helpers are to be skilled at skilling clients, they require both a repertoire of interventions and the skills to deliver them properly.
- The skilled client model places much greater stress on addressing clients' mental processes than the skilled helper model.

Journals

Journals provide an excellent means of keeping abreast of the counselling skills literature. Some readers of this book are in fields such as nursing, social work and human resource management, whose professional journals may contain some articles about the use of counselling skills .

Box 16.3 provides a list of some of the main counselling and counselling psychology journals. These journals may be of interest not only to counsellors and counselling psychologists, but to those of you using counselling skills either as part of other jobs or on a voluntary basis. These journals offer a mixture of applied practice and research articles, with the exception of the Journal of Counseling Psychology which focuses on research.

Box 16.3   Some leading counselling and counselling psychology journals

Counselling
Australian Journal of Guidance and Counselling
British Journal of Guidance and Counselling
Counselling (British Association for Counselling)
Journal of Counseling and Development (American Counseling Association)
New Zealand Counselling and Guidance Association Journal
International Journal for the Advancement of Counselling

Counselling psychology
The Australian Counselling Psychologist (Australian Psychological Society)
Counselling Psychology Review (British Psychological Society)
Journal of Counseling Psychology (American Psychological Association)
The Counseling Psychologist (American Psychological Association)

Becoming more human

Counselling skills students and helpers face the double challenge of assuming responsibility for becoming and staying not only more skilled, but more human as well. A major theme of this book is that you cannot separate your level of functioning as a human being from how you deliver counselling skills. You are most skilled when you are both a competent helper and a compassionate human being.

Counselling skills students as human beings can ask themselves questions like: 'Where am I now in developing my humanity?', 'What helps me move forward?', 'What is holding me back?' and 'What can I do to become more human?' A useful distinction exists between being weakly and strongly human. In his analysis of what holds course members back most in training to become person-centred counsellors, Dave Mearns (1997) cites the level of fear being too high, self-esteem too low, and difficulty taking responsibility for Self. All of these restraining and retarding factors might be viewed as characteristics of being weakly human.

Being strongly human involves possessing the mind and communication skills to confront, work through and transcend your past. Rather than being fear-governed, you are free to make the choices that affirm and develop your own and your clients' humanity. Your level of mental development is such that you do not need to cling to others, including your clients, for approval. Instead, being strong inside, you have the energy and motivation to transcend yourself in the service of developing your clients' capacity to experience and live their lives more fully.

Helping from a position of inner strength both represents and allows you to have the confidence, serenity and wisdom to be of most benefit to your clients. Nevertheless, helpers who are strongly human still have to struggle to maintain their humanity in face of internal and external factors that might diminish them and, thus, cause them to be less helpful to clients. Being and staying strongly human is a process and life task, not something you can hold on to forever without effort.

Some helpers draw additional strength in their struggle to remain human from their religious faiths or spiritual disciplines. The strong motivation emanating from love of god to be more fully human by serving humanity is well illustrated in the following five lines printed on the late Mother Teresa's 'business card' (Chawla, 1992): 'The fruit of silence is prayer, the fruit of prayer is faith, the fruit of faith is love, the fruit of love is service, the fruit of service is peace.' A simple Buddhist prayer that delivers a similar humble and compassionate message is: 'So long as space remains, so long as suffering remains, I will remain to serve.'

Being your own client

Love begins at home. So does being a humane and compassionate helper. All counselling skills students and helpers need to assume responsibility for being their own most important clients. Successful helpers are continually in the process of using their knowledge and skills to help themselves grow and develop both as persons and service providers.

Following are some suggestions for what you can do to help yourself become a more human and humane helper. Clearly realise that use of counselling skills requires both heart and head. In relating to clients you need to steer a middle course between over and under involvement as a person.

Once committed to developing yourself as a humane helper, you can draw upon your experiences in counselling skills training. For instance, when practising counselling skills you can attempt to come over to clients as a humane and caring person. In addition, you can ask your trainers, supervisors and fellow students to look out for ways in which you either strengthen or weaken the human quality of your interviewing.

Virtually all counselling skills students take time to develop the confidence and skills required for a comfortable interviewing style. If you undergo further counselling skills training in which you gain more experience with clients, you may find yourself letting some fears go and releasing more of your potential for genuine concern and care. However, if you do not practise and are poor at reflecting on what you do, the chances are that you will remain stuck both as a human being and as a helper.

If you identify ways in which you appear wooden or uncaring, use these as signals for exploring what is going on either within you or between you and your client that holds you back from expressing your humanity. Experienced trainers and supervisors can help you to pinpoint roadblocks and work through fears and doubts. In addition, counselling skills students sometimes show excellent skills in offering one another feedback, sharing experiences and giving encouragement.

When reflecting upon the experiences of your daily life, you can also treat yourself as a client. You are still the same person in your everyday roles, for instance partner or parent, as in your helping role. Helper training provides you with tools for improving your own functioning. For example, when faced with problem situations, you can use the RUC helping process model. You can clear a space so that you can relate to yourself calmly and lovingly. Next clarify and expand your understanding of what is going on in the situation and identify unhelpful thoughts and communications. Then, you can set goals, plan and implement your plan for changing unhelpful into helpful behaviours.

As you proceed with helper training, you can apply to yourself the core helping approach adopted on your course. If successful, this process has the double benefit of improving your humanity as well as your skills in applying the approach.

Without becoming dependent, you can use external resources to develop your humanity. Charles Legg (1999) cites three reasons for counselling students undergoing therapy: personal growth; gaining empathic understanding of the client's position; and extending your experience of types of therapy. All three reasons are valid. Personal counselling can be very beneficial in working through blocks to being a happier, more fulfilled and humane person. It is difficult to use any helping approach properly unless you have become skilled at applying it to yourself. Often this is best achieved by first working as a client with a competent practitioner of the approach. You can also consider group counselling and lifeskills training approaches to becoming a stronger and more skilled human being.

Having the experience of being a client should improve your understanding of being in the client role. However, to gain genuine understanding of the helping process from the client's viewpoint, seeking therapy should not simply be a training experience, but grounded in other motivations based on your life experience, hopes and suffering.

The better you understand the client's role, the more humanely you may be able to respond to clients' inevitable ambivalence about being in helping. You may also experience different aspects of your own humanity by working with helpers from different theoretical orientations. However, start with a firm grounding in one approach rather than act like a magpie, hopping from one approach to another.

It is one thing to become more human and another to stay human. There is a vast literature on stress and burnout in the helping professions. Helping can be immensely interesting and rewarding. However, many helpers get emotionally, mentally and physically exhausted. Feeling scarcely human themselves, they are not in a strong position to relate to clients as strong, compassionate and caring human beings. All helpers require skills of self-care and of monitoring their fitness to practise competently and compassionately. Skills for avoiding tiredness and burnout include: managing time well, assertively setting limits, developing support networks, and developing, valuing and using recreational outlets that nourish and re-energise you. If necessary, you can also address issues of burnout in supervision or personal counselling.

Many factors in the modern world make it hard to hold on to your humanity. The rate of technological change is staggering. In addition, Western societies tend to be very materialistic and you may find yourself being measured by the size of your pocket book rather than the size of your heart. Furthermore, the organisations in which some helpers work can be big and impersonal. In addition, academic institutions with their research cultures can compartmentalise knowledge at the expense of a more balanced approach that also values the study of whole persons and the teaching of applied skills. You and your clients require inner strength and the support of like-minded people to hold on to your humanistic values in the face of such pressures. This is a situation that is unlikely to improve in the next decade or so.

Towards more skilled and humane helping

The lotus flower is one of the most powerful images in the Buddhist religion. Starting off in muddy and brackish water, the lotus can grow and unfold into an outstandingly beautiful flower. Along the same lines, as adherents of the Buddhist faith become less anxious and ignorant and move further along the path to enlightenment, the compassion and beauty of their inner Buddha natures unfolds for the world to see.

Counselling students and helpers can also be viewed as being on a path to becoming more humane and enlightened as well as more skilled. In this book I have outlined some introductory counselling skills that are both the first steps and the foundations for later steps on the path to becoming more effective helpers. However, throughout the book, I emphasise that counselling skills students and helpers do not live by skills alone. As a helper you need to develop and use both your heart and your head so that, like lotus flowers, you can unfold and offer your best counselling skills to clients. I wish you strength and happiness along the path to becoming a truly humane helper who offers skills within the context of compassionate and caring relationships. Then, also like lotus flowers, your clients should be able to go some way to unfolding and bringing out what is best and beautiful in themselves.

Summary

Reflective practitioners monitor, evaluate and think deeply about their helping work. You can monitor your present level of competence in using counselling skills.

Self-help approaches to becoming more skilled include observing, listening to and/or reading videotapes, audio cassettes and written transcripts of sessions conducted by skilled helpers. You can interject your own responses before seeing how the helper responds. You can also improve your helping skills by co-counselling, by joining peer self-help groups, and by monitoring your use of counselling skills if you use them as part of your job.

Training paths to becoming more skilled include either continuing on your present course or enrolling in a more advanced course. Professional associations can provide information about counselling and counselling psychology courses. A distinction exists between accreditation of a course from a professional association and obtaining a licence to practise from a national or state registration board. Make decisions about further training wisely and in light of your personal goals and career aspirations. When choosing a course consider many factors including the course's content, teaching and assessment methods as well as its reputation and accreditation status. You can also become more skilled by attending conferences, short courses and workshops.

The counselling skills literature consists of books and journals. Books that may support your skills development include textbooks reviewing different helping approaches as well as textbooks presenting more advanced helping process models and counselling skills. You can also read about counselling skills in counselling and counselling psychology journals as well as, sometimes, in the journals of other helping professions.

Becoming more skilled entails becoming more human. You need to help from a position of inner strength and struggle to maintain your humanity in face of internal and external pressures. Learn to become your own most important client and to use your helping knowledge and skills for your personal growth. Ways of developing your humanity include: taking advantage of opportunities offered during counsellor training and in supervision; reflecting on your everyday experiences and skilfully working through problems and problem situations; and undergoing individual counselling and, possibly, enrolling in group counselling and/or attending lifeskills training courses.

Staying human entails developing your skills of self-care so that you minimise the chances of becoming overtired and burning yourself out. Staying human also involves resisting the dehumanising pressures in modern society.

Counselling skills students and helpers can be viewed as being on a path to becoming more humane and enlightened as well as more skilled. Like lotus flowers, both helpers and clients can unfold to show what is best and beautiful in themselves.

Activities

Activity 16.1   Monitoring my helping skills

Monitor your good and poor skills at using each stage of the RUC helping process model. For each skills area, focus on both your mind and communication skills. In addition, when focusing on your communication skills, remember to assess vocal and bodily as well as verbal communication. For more information about specific skills areas, turn to the relevant chapters.

Stage 1   Relating

Meeting, greeting and seating clients:
- My good skills
- My poor skills

Structuring the start of the helping process:
- My good skills
- My poor skills

Using active listening skills to help clients tell their stories:
- My good skills
- My poor skills

Summarising:
- My good skills
- My poor skills

Stage 2   Understanding

Asking questions:
- My good skills
- My poor skills

Challenging clients' perspectives:
- My good skills
- My poor skills

Providing feedback:
- My good skills
- My poor skills

Identifying unhelpful thinking:
- My good skills
- My poor skills

Using active listening skills when clarifying and expanding understanding:
- My good skills
- My poor skills

Summarising a client's problem situation:
- My good skills
- My poor skills

Stage 3   Changing

Facilitating clients in clarifying goals:
- My good skills
- My poor skills

Generating options to attain goals:
- My good skills
- My poor skills

Translating unhelpful communications and thoughts into goals:
- My good skills
- My poor skills

Client-centred coaching:
- My good skills
- My poor skills

Demonstration skills:
- My good skills
- My poor skills

Rehearsing skills:
- My good skills
- My poor skills

Assisting clients to develop coping self-talk:
- My good skills
- My poor skills

Assisting clients to develop preferential rules:
- My good skills
- My poor skills

Assisting clients to reality test perceptions:
- My good skills
- My poor skills

Negotiating between-session activities:
- My good skills
- My poor skills

Conducting sessions:
- My good skills
- My poor skills

Ending helping:
- My good skills
- My poor skills

1   What are your main counselling skills strengths?
2   What are the main counselling skills areas on which you still need to work?
3   Refer back to the relevant chapters for suggestions on how to improve specific skills and develop and implement a plan to improve your counselling skills.

Activity 16.2   Choosing further counselling skills training

If you are in the position of needing to choose another course to develop your counselling skills, use the checklist provided in Box 16.2 to assess any training course you are considering.

Activity 16.3   Developing my humanity

In the text I suggested that you become your own most important client. Below are listed a number of different ways in which you can develop and maintain your humanity. Assess if and how you might use each of the following in light of your own individual circumstances.

Ways of developing and maintaining humanity

- Clearly realising that use of counselling skills requires both heart and head.
- Drawing upon your experiences in counselling skills training.
- Obtaining more interviewing practice.
- Working with experienced trainers and supervisors.
- Using your helping knowledge and skills to work on personal problems and problem situations.
- Personal counselling.
- Group counselling.
- Lifeskills training.
- Developing self-care skills.
- Working to resist the effects of dehumanising pressures:
  - at the organisational level;
  - at the societal level.

1   What do you consider are the most important ways you can develop and maintain your humanity?
2   State goals and then make and implement a plan for developing and maintaining your humanity.

A Glossary of Helping Terms

Acceptance Unconditional affirmation by helpers of clients as persons.

Action skills Areas of externally observable actions in which people can make good or poor choices, or a mixture of both.

Active listening Accurately understanding clients' communications from their internal perspectives and then communicating back your understanding in a language and manner attuned to their needs. More colloquially, being a good listener and then responding with understanding.

Advising Telling others how they might feel, think, communicate and act rather than letting them come to their own conclusions.

Anxiety Feelings of fear and apprehension which may be either general or associated with specific people and situations. Anxiety may be realistic and proportionate to the threat as well as unrealistic and disproportionate.

Assertive communication The ability to communicate, if necessary backed up by actions, either positive or oppositional thoughts and feelings in appropriate ways that are neither aggressive nor non-assertive and submissive.

Assessment Collecting and analysing information about clients to make decisions about helping strategies, to monitor progress and to evaluate changes.

Avoidance Thinking and acting in ways that avoid dealing directly with the realities of life, for instance by withdrawing.

Awareness Consciousness of and sensitivity to oneself, others and the environment.

Behavioural counselling An approach that views counselling and therapy in learning terms and focuses on reducing anxiety and on altering specific behaviours.

Between-session activities Activities negotiated between helper and client designed to support and consolidate learnings taking place during helping sessions. See **Monitoring**.

Bodily communication Messages that people send with their bodies: for instance, through gaze, eye contact, facial expressions, posture and gestures.

Burnout Depletion of motivation, interest, energy, resilience and, often, of effectiveness on the part of helpers.

Careers counselling Using counselling skills to assist clients with career choice, career development and career transition decisions and issues.

Challenging Expanding clients' awareness by reflections and questions focused on actual and potential inconsistent and illogical ways of thinking and communicating. Clients can also challenge themselves.

Clarifying understanding   Assisting clients to bring out into the open and become clearer about material from their internal perspectives.

Client   An inclusive term to describe all those people with whom helpers use counselling skills either in helping sessions or in informal helping contacts.

Client-centred coaching   An approach to coaching that allows clients to retain ownership of their problems, values their contributions, and draws out and builds upon their abilities to change for the better.

Client-centred counselling   See **Person-centred counselling**.

Cohesive group   A group in which the members are well disposed to one another and stick together to attain common goals.

Cognitive counselling   An approach to counselling and therapy originated by Aaron Beck which focuses on improving clients' abilities to test the accuracy and reality of their perceptions.

Communication   Sending and receiving information by means of verbal, vocal, bodily, touch and/or taking action messages.

Compassion   Being aware of others' suffering and acting with benevolence and care towards them.

Competence   Without seeking perfection, striving for and attaining high standards of performance and of service to clients.

Communication patterns   Ways of communication in which helper's and client's verbal, vocal and bodily communication mutually influence one another to produce a degree of stability: for example, talkative helper–quiet client.

Communication skills   Areas of externally observable communication in which people can make good or poor choices, or a mixture of both.

Confidentiality   Keeping trust with clients and fellow students by not divulging personal information about them unless granted permission. Confidentiality relates to the storage of written records and audio-visual recordings as well as to the spoken word.

Confrontation   See **Challenging**.

Congruence   Genuineness and lack of facade arising from awareness of one's internal processes. Communicating and acting consistently with one's thoughts and feelings.

Conscious thinking   A state of possessing a present awareness of some material in the mind.

Contracting   Making agreements with clients and others which may be either implicit, or verbal, or written and countersigned.

Coping   Dealing with situations by managing them adequately without necessarily mastering them completely.

Coping self-talk   Dimensions of coping self-talk include creating alerting, calming, coaching and affirming statements. See **Self-talk**, **Visualised rehearsal**.

Core conditions   In person-centred approach, in particular, but also in other approaches to helping, the core conditions of the helping relationship are helper-offered empathy, unconditional positive regard, and congruence.

Core values   Competence and compassion are the core values underlying ethical helping practice.

Counselling   A relationship in which helpers assist clients to understand themselves and their problems better. Where appropriate, helpers then use various strategies to enable clients to feel, think, communicate and act more effectively. Approaches to counselling practice differ according to helpers' theoretical orientations.

Counselling skills Helper-offered communication skills, accompanied by appropriate mental processes, for developing relationships with clients, clarifying and expanding their understanding, and, where appropriate, assisting them to develop and implement strategies for changing how they think, act and feel so that they can attain life affirming goals.

Counsellor A suitably trained and qualified person who uses counselling skills in exercising the profession of counselling.

Counter transference Negative and positive feelings, based on unresolved areas in their own lives, which arise in helpers towards clients.

Couples counselling Counselling two relationship partners either jointly or both separately and jointly at different stages.

Crises Situations of excessive stress in which people feel that their coping resources are severely stretched or inadequate to meet the adjustive demands being made upon them.

Cross-cultural helping A helping relationship in which helper and client come from different cultures.

Cross-cultural sensitivity Awareness of actual and potential differences with clients from other cultures and responding carefully and respectfully where these differences either are or might be concerned.

Defensive thinking See **Self-protective thinking**.

Demonstration skills Skills for showing clients what to do and how to think. Demonstrations may be live, recorded, visualised or written.

Denial A self-protective process by which individuals defend themselves from unpleasant, and sometimes pleasing, aspects of themselves and of external reality by avoiding becoming aware of them.

Dependency Clients who are dependent maintain themselves by relying on support from others, for example their helpers, or from drugs rather than by relying on self-support.

Disclosing skills Helper skills of showing involvement and sharing personal experiences. See **Self-disclosure**.

Distortion A self-protective process involving altering unpleasant or discrepant aspects of reality in order to make them less threatening and more consistent with one's existing self-concept.

Dream interpretation Providing interpretations of the manifest and latent content of clients' dreams. Used in helping approaches such as psychoanalysis and Gestalt therapy.

Dual relationships In addition to the helping relationship, helpers may either already be in, or consider entering, or enter other kinds of relationships with clients: for instance, friend, lover, colleague or trainer.

Eclecticism Basing one's helping practice on ideas and helping strategies drawn from more than one theoretical position.

Empathy The capacity to identify yourself mentally and emotionally with and to comprehend accurately your client's internal perspective and to sensitively communicate back this understanding.

Ethical codes Rules of conduct and guidelines for helping practice. In addition to focusing on counsellors, ethical codes can focus on training, supervision and use of counselling skills by people who are not qualified counsellors.

Ethical dilemmas Situations in helping requiring helpers to make their own decisions because the ethical standards for correct conduct either conflict or are otherwise unclear.

Ethical issues   Issues in helping where there are important considerations regarding rules of conduct, moral standards and right and wrong behaviour for different situations.

Empowering mind   Developing mind skills that allow the individual to create life affirming rather than self-defeating thoughts.

Existential counselling   An approach to counselling and therapy emphasising helping clients to take responsibility for affirming and defining their existence within the parameters of death, suffering, freedom and meaninglessness.

Expanding understanding   Using questions and challenges to assist clients to understand problems more fully and to gain new perspectives on them.

Experiments   Helpers can work with clients to design and implement experiments to test the reality of clients' expectations about changing specific communications/ actions and/or thoughts.

Explanations   The reasons people create for what happens in their own and in other people's lives and in their external environments.

Expectations   Anticipations and predictions that people create about their futures.

External perspective   The external viewpoints of other people, such as significant others and helpers, rather than the subjective perceptions and experiences of clients themselves.

Facilitation   Using active listening and other supportive skills to make it easy for clients to talk, explore and experience themselves.

Family counselling   Approaches to counselling and therapy that focus on relationships within families.

Feedback skills   Usually refers to skills of providing feedback or information from the giver's external perspective to another person. However, the term can also refer to the skills of receiving information from another's external perspective about oneself.

Feelings   Emotional processes, accompanied by physical sensations, at varying levels of awareness. People can experience, express and manage feelings.

Feminist counselling   Approaches to counselling and therapy that address women's issues in the context of gender power imbalances in society.

Gay   A colloquial word for people, especially males, who are homosexually oriented. People of varying degrees of bisexuality are much more common than exclusively homosexual people. See **Lesbian and gay counselling**.

Genuineness   Absence of facade and insincerity. Consistency between verbal, vocal, bodily, touch and/or action communications.

Gestalt counselling   An approach to counselling and therapy consisting of the application of a number of techniques focused on making clients aware of how they are blocking making good contact or strong gestalts with their senses and with the environment.

Goals   Implicit or explicit objectives of helping relationships and of specific helping strategies and client plans. Goals can relate to changing specific communications and thoughts as well as to the desired outcomes from solving problems. See **Setting progressive tasks skills**.

Group counselling   The relationships, activities and skills involved in counselling three or more people at the same time.

Guilt Feelings of distress, involving self-devaluation and anxiety, resulting from having transgressed a code of behaviour to which you subscribe.

Habit A learned tendency to respond in a fixed way to a person or situation.

Helper An inclusive term to describe people who use counselling skills, whether as professional or voluntary counsellors, as part of other roles, or informally.

Helper's aides People in clients' home environments who are enlisted to support clients in attaining their goals.

Helping process models Simplified step by step representations of different goals and activities at progressive stages of helping.

Helping relationships The human connections between helpers and clients both face to face and in one another's minds.

Holistic approach Holistic approaches to training and helping emphasise integration, with helpers and clients relating to one another as whole persons rather than focusing on specific behaviours and skills.

Inhibition Inadequately acknowledging, weakening and restraining the demonstration of feelings, thoughts, communications and actions.

'I' statements Owning and directly stating what you feel and think, starting with the words 'I feel . . .' or 'I think . . .'.

Immediacy Helper and, possibly, client comments that focus on the 'here and now' of the helping relationship, perhaps by focusing on what is or has previously been left unsaid. Sometimes expressed as 'you–me' talk.

Information Material relevant to clients' concerns and decisions which they may seek out for themselves or which may be provided by their helpers; for example, careers information.

Inner strength Mental development and toughness involving a high level of competence in the different mind skills and a capacity to deal with reality honestly.

Internal perspective The subjective perceptions and experiences of an individual rather than an external viewpoint of other people.

Interpretation Explanations from helpers' internal perspectives of clients' feelings, thoughts, dreams and communications.

Lesbian and gay counselling Using counselling skills to address problems and issues attached to clients being lesbian or gay.

Lifeskills Sequences of choices that people make in specific skills areas necessary for effective living, for instance the various mind and communication skills required for relating well to others.

Listening Attentively hearing a speaker. Not only receiving sounds but accurately understanding their meaning from vocal and bodily as well as verbal communication.

Medication Medically prescribed drugs used independently or in conjunction with helping.

Men's counselling Counselling focused on developing the human potential of men by freeing them from gender-stereotyped feeling, thinking and communication.

Mental development Entails acquiring, maintaining and developing mind skills for the purposes of inner strength and of communicating and acting effectively.

Microskills approach An approach to helper training in which single communication skills of the helping process are identified and taught as separate units.

Mind The psychological manifestation of the human brain. The seat of awareness, thought, volition and feeling which is capable of thinking about thinking.

Mind skills   Areas for mental processing in which people can make good or poor choices, or a mixture of both.

Modelling   Demonstrating specific communications, thoughts and mental processes so that clients may learn from observation.

Monitoring   Observing and often recording the occurrence of feelings, thoughts and/or communications either inside or outside of formal helping sessions.

Open-ended questions   Questions that allow clients freedom of choice in how to respond rather than curtailing their options.

Opening statements   Helper statements at the start of initial and subsequent sessions. When starting helping, brief opening remarks that give clients permission to talk and tell why they have come.

Paraphrasing   Expressing the meaning of another's statements or series of statements in different words.

Partner skills   The mind skills and communication skills required for creating happiness in close personal relationships.

Perceptions   Thoughts, of varying degrees of accuracy, that the mind creates about oneself, others and the environment.

Person-centred counselling   An approach to counselling and therapy formulated by Carl Rogers that lays great stress on the primacy of clients' subjective experiences and on helping them release their unique actualising tendencies. Rogers considered a warm, respectful, empathic and genuine helping relationship necessary and sufficient for therapeutic change to occur.

Personal responsibility   The process of making the choices that maximise your happiness and fulfilment. Assuming responsibility for the authorship of your life and for dealing with problems and problem situations.

Physical reactions   Bodily changes that accompany feelings.

Plan   A step by step outline, either verbal or written, of the specific actions necessary to attain client goals.

Pre-conscious thinking   Thoughts that can be brought into awareness relatively easily.

Preferential rules   Rules, beliefs or self-standards based on rational and emotional preferences rather than on rigid and childish demands.

Problem ownership   The degree to which clients and/or helpers assume responsibility for resolving clients' problems and problem situations.

Problem situations   Problem situations are specific situations, often within larger problems, where people experience difficulty coping and reaching satisfactory solutions.

Problematic skills   Poor mind and communication skills that create and sustain problems and problem situations.

Progressive muscular relaxation   A helping strategy in which clients are taught to relax by sequentially tensing and relaxing various muscle groupings. Sometimes also combined with mental relaxation involving imagining restful scenes.

Psychiatry   The branch of medicine dealing with understanding, treating and preventing mental disorders.

Psychoanalysis   An approach to counselling and therapy originated by Sigmund Freud that emphasises making conscious and interpreting clients' unconscious thinking. The term also applies to approaches which are later variations of Freud's model.

Psychodrama   A primarily group approach to counselling and therapy involving helpers directing dramatic enactments of scenes relevant to clients' lives and problems.

Psychology   The science and study of human behaviour.

Psychosis   Severe mental disorder involving loss of contact with reality and usually characterised by delusions and/or hallucinations.

Psychotherapy   Often used interchangeably with counselling. May have connotations of moderately to severely disturbed clients seen in medical settings, but not necessarily so. More accurate to speak of the psychotherapies since there are many theoretical and practical approaches to psychotherapy.

Questions   Sentences worded or expressed to seek information: for instance, about specific details of problems or problem situations, personal meanings, and about client strengths.

Rational emotive behaviour counselling   An approach to counselling and therapy originated by Albert Ellis in which helpers assist clients to dispute demanding beliefs and to replace them with preferential beliefs.

Reality counselling   A form of counselling and therapy originated by William Glasser that sees people as control systems who need to acknowledge reality as a basis for responsible behaviour that will enable them to fulfil their needs for love and worth and thus attain a success identity.

Reality-testing perceptions   Testing how closely perceptions based on inference accord to available facts and whether there are more accurate ways of viewing oneself, other people, problems and problem situations.

Records   Helpers may keep records focused on initial assessment, progress during helping and termination details. Records may also take the form of statistical summaries of group information.

Regard   Non-possessive liking or prizing of another, for example the client. Unconditional acceptance of another as a person.

Referral skills   Skills of referring clients to other helpers who may be in a better position to assist them. Referral skills include both knowing when not to refer and when to refer the client's problem for discussion with an appropriate person rather than the client her/himself.

Reflecting feelings   Feeling and accurately understanding the flow of another's emotions and experiencing and sensitively communicating this understanding back to them.

Reflective practitioner   A helper who monitors, evaluates and reflects deeply about her/his helping work, often with the assistance of supervisors and trusted colleagues.

Rehearsing skills   Skills, such as role-playing, for rehearsing clients in changing specific communications and thoughts. Clients can also use rehearsing skills on their own. See **Visualised rehearsal**.

Relaxation   A restful state or one of numerous approaches to gaining that state: for instance imagining restful scenes. See **Progressive muscular relaxation**.

Reluctance   Unwillingness or disinclination on the part of potential or actual clients to enter into the helping process.

Resistance   Any feelings, thoughts and communications on the part of clients that frustrate and prevent them from participating effectively in the helping process. Behaviour that impedes, slows down or stops the helping process.

Role-playing   Engaging in simulated enactments for understanding clients' problems and problem situations better and for rehearsing changed communications and thoughts. See **Rehearsing skills**, **Visualised rehearsal**.

RUC model   A three-stage relating–understanding–changing helping process model for managing problem situations better.

Rules   The standards people have for themselves, others and the environment. Rules vary in how demanding or how preferential they are.

Schizophrenia   A psychosis characterised by the disintegration of personality, emotional withdrawal and disorders of feelings, perception and communication.

Self-acceptance   Accepting oneself as a person while remaining aware of one's strengths and limitations.

Self-awareness   Being aware of one's significant thoughts, feelings and experiences and of the impact that one makes on others.

Self-concept   The ways in which people see themselves and to which they attach terms like 'I' or 'me'.

Self-disclosure   Revealing feelings and sharing personal information, especially by intentional verbal communication.

Self-helping   The ultimate aim of all helping is to help clients to develop thoughts and communications whereby they can help themselves independently of their helpers.

Self-protective thinking   The processes by which people deny and distort information at variance with their conceptions of self when this information threatens their feelings of adequacy and worth.

Self-talk   What people say to themselves before, during or after specific situations.

Self-worth   Sense of adequacy, positive or negative evaluation of oneself as a person.

Session agendas   Agreements between helpers and clients, usually near the beginning of sessions, on what tasks will be addressed during them and in what order. Session agendas can also be developed or amended during sessions.

Setting progressive tasks skills   Skills for assisting clients to break situations down and set themselves progressively more difficult goals and tasks as steps towards attaining their ultimate goal.

Skills   Skills can be defined by area, level or competence, and by the sequences of choices they entail.

Small verbal rewards   Brief expressions of interest designed to encourage another to continue talking.

Social rules   The implicit and explicit rules of conduct which vary according to the social contexts in which communication takes place.

STC framework   A situation–thoughts–consequences framework for analysing the relationships between how people think, feel, physically react and communicate/act. The framework can be used to analyse the effect of mind skills as well as thoughts.

Strengths   Areas of thinking and communication/actions in which clients possess good skills. See **Inner strength**.

Stress   Perceived demands on one's energy and coping abilities.

Stress tolerance   The level of stress or cumulative amount of stressors that an individual can tolerate before experiencing distinct physiological and psychological distress.

Structuring   The verbal, vocal and bodily communications used by helpers at the start of, during and at the end of the overall helping process to explain to clients what is going on and what their respective roles are.

Study skills   Skills for learning efficiently and for getting the most out of studying: for example, reading skills, report writing skills, and test taking skills.

Summarising   Pulling together, clarifying and reflecting back in more succinct form a series of client statements either during a discussion unit, at the end of a discussion unit, or at the beginning or end of helping sessions. Sometimes helpers ask clients to summarise.

Super-conscious thinking   A state of thinking about how you think. Sometimes referred to as meta-conscious thinking.

Support networks   Networks of people available to provide strength and encouragement to one another, especially when in difficulty.

Supportive helping   Offering clients a helping relationship in which they can feel understood and affirmed when they feel that some extra support might assist them through an awkward phase in their lives or help them make a difficult decision better.

Supports   People in clients' home environments who can support their efforts to attain communication, action and thinking goals.

Taking action communication   Messages people send when not face to face with one another through their actions, for instance sending flowers or tidying the house.

Telephone counselling   Counselling and helping clients on the phone, often used in helping clients in crisis, for instance the work of the Samaritans.

Tension   Feeling mentally and physically stretched and under strain.

Termination   The ending of helping sessions and relationships.

Tests   Psychological tests are ways of gathering information about people by taking objective and standardised measures of samples of their behaviour. Tests can also be used to explore subjective reality.

Thinking difficulties   Ways of thinking that cause clients to have negative emotions and to communicate and act less effectively than they might otherwise do.

Threat   Perception of real or imagined danger.

Timing   The 'when' of making helper and client responses and of implementing helping strategies.

Touch communication   Messages that people send by touching one another.

Transactional analysis   An approach to counselling and therapy, originated by Eric Berne, based on the analysis of 'Parent', 'Adult' and 'Child' ego states in interpersonal transactions.

Transference   The process by which clients transfer feelings, perceptions and communications applicable to previous relationships on to their helpers; emphasised in psychoanalysis.

Transition statements   Helper statements which move or suggest moving the content of a session from one topic area to another or from one phase of the session to another.

Transitions   Changes which people undergo during the course of their lives: for example, the birth of a first child or retirement.

Tunnel vision   A narrowing of perception under threat so that the individual focuses only on certain factors in a situation and excludes others which may be important.

Unconditional positive regard   Consists of two dimensions: first, prizing and feeling positively towards clients and, second, non-judgemental acceptance of clients' experiencing and disclosures as their subjective reality.

Unconscious thinking   Thinking that is beneath the level of conscious awareness and frequently inadmissible to consciousness because of the anxiety it generates.

Unfinished business   Unexpressed and, possibly, insufficiently acknowledged and worked through feelings that can negatively affect current functioning.

Unrealistic standards   Standards for behaviour and self-evaluation which are dysfunctional in helping individuals to cope with their lives and meet their physiological and psychological needs. Usually in helping, but not always, such standards are too high rather than too low.

Values   The underlying beliefs or philosophies by which people lead their lives.

Visual images   The pictures that people create in their minds.

Visualised rehearsal   Rehearsing desired communications and actions in imagination prior to enacting them. Can also involve rehearsing accompanying coping self-talk.

Vocal communication   Messages that people send through the voice: for instance, volume, articulation, pitch, emphasis and speech rate.

Voluntary counselling   Use of counselling skills by helpers in an unpaid capacity, frequently under the auspices of a primarily voluntary and non-profit agency, such as Relate or Relationships Australia.

Vulnerability   Being psychologically at risk, especially when faced with negative occurrences and feedback. A tendency to contribute to, if not cause, your own difficulties.

Withdrawal   Mentally, emotionally and/or physically retreating or pulling back from situations and experiences.

Working alliance   Collaboration between helper and client to achieve the goals of helping.

Working through   Facing up to a feeling, problem or decision and mentally working on it until a satisfactory resolution is reached.

Bibliography

Argyle, M. (1992) *The Social Psychology of Everyday Life*. London: Routledge.

Argyle, M. (1994) *The Psychology of Interpersonal Behaviour*, 5th edn. London: Penguin.

Barrett-Lennard, G.T. (1998) *Carl Rogers' Helping System: Journey and Substance*. London: Sage.

Beck, A.T. (1976) *Cognitive Therapy and the Emotional Disorders*. New York: New American Library.

Beck, A.T. (1988) *Love is Never Enough: How Couples Can Overcome Misunderstandings, Resolve Conflicts, and Solve Relationship Problems Through Cognitive Therapy*. New York: Harper and Row.

Beck, A.T. and Weishaar, M.E. (1995) 'Cognitive therapy', in R.J. Corsini and D. Wedding (eds), *Current Psychotherapies*, 5th edn. Itasca, IL: Peacock. pp. 229–61.

Bond, T. (1993) *Standards and Ethics for Counselling in Action*. London: Sage.

Bond, T. (1999) 'Guidelines for professional practice', in R. Bor and M. Watts (eds), *The Trainee Handbook: A Guide for Counselling and Psychotherapy Trainees*. London: Sage. pp. 186–222.

Brammer, L.M. and MacDonald, G. (1996) *The Helping Relationship: Process and Skills*, 6th edn. Boston: Allyn and Bacon.

Chawla, N. (1992) *Mother Teresa*. London: Arrow Books.

Clarkson, P. and Gilbert, M. (1991) 'The training of counsellor trainers and supervisors', in W. Dryden and B. Thorne (eds), *Training and Supervision for Counselling in Action*. London: Sage. pp. 143–69.

Cohen, D. (1997) *Carl Rogers: A Critical Biography*. London: Constable.

Corey, M.S. and Corey, G. (1998) *Becoming a Helper*, 3rd edn. Pacific Grove, CA: Brooks/Cole.

Cormier, W.H. and Cormier, L.S. (1991) *Interviewing Strategies for Helpers: Fundamental Skills and Cognitive Behavioral Interventions*. Pacific Grove, CA: Brooks/Cole.

Dryden, W. (1991) *A Dialogue with Arnold Lazarus: 'It Depends'*. Milton Keynes: Open University Press.

Dryden, W. (ed.) (1996) *Handbook of Individual Therapy*. London: Sage.

Dryden, W., Horton, I. and Mearns, D. (1995) *Issues in Professional Counsellor Training*. London: Cassell.

Duck, S. (1998) *Human Relationships*, 3rd edn. London: Sage.

Edwards, C.E. and Murdoch, N.L. (1994) 'Characteristics of therapist self-disclosure in the counseling process', *Journal of Counseling and Development*, 72 (2): 384–9.

Egan, G. (1998) *The Skilled Helper: A Problem Management Approach to Helping*, 6th edn. Pacific Grove, CA: Brooks/Cole.

Ekman, P., Friesen, W.V. and Ellsworth, P. (1972). *Emotions in the Human Face*. New York: Pergamon Press.

Ellis, A. (1995) 'Rational emotive behaviour therapy', in R.J. Corsini and D. Wedding (eds), *Current Psychotherapies*, 5th edn. Itasca, IL: Peacock. pp. 364–75.

Ellis, A. (1996) *Better, Deeper and More Enduring Brief Therapy: The Rational Emotive Behavior Approach*. New York: Brunner Mazel.

Freud, S. (1976) *The Interpretation of Dreams*. Harmondsworth: Penguin.

Gardner, H. (1993) *Frames of Mind: The Theory of Multiple Intelligences*, 2nd edn. London: Fontana.

Gelso, C.J. and Carter, J.A. (1994) 'Components of the psychotherapy relationship: Their interaction and unfolding during treatment', *Journal of Counseling Psychology*, 41 (3): 296–306.

Gelso, C.J. and Fretz, B. (1992) *Counselling Psychology*. New York: Harcourt Brace Jovanovich.

Goleman, D. (1995) *Emotional Intelligence: Why It Can Matter More than IQ*. London: Routledge.

Gordon, T. (1970) *Parent Effectiveness Training: The Tested New Way to Raise Responsible Children*. New York: Wyden.

Hall, E.T. (1966) *The Hidden Dimension*. New York: Doubleday.

Ho, M.K. (1992) *Minority Children and Adolescents in Therapy*. Newbury Park, CA: Sage.

Holland, J.L. (1973) *Making Vocational Choices: A Theory of Careers*. Englewood Cliffs, NJ: Prentice Hall.

Hutchins, D.E. and Cole, C.G. (1992) *Helping Relationships and Strategies*, 2nd edn. Pacific Grove, CA: Brooks/Cole.

Inskipp, F. (1996) *Skills Training for Counselling*. London: Cassell.

Ivey, A.E. (1994) *Intentional Interviewing and Counseling: Facilitating Client Development in a Multicultural Society*, 3rd edn. Pacific Grove, CA: Brooks/Cole.

Kagan, N. (1975) *Influencing Human Interaction*. Washington: American Personnel and Guidance Association.

Kelly, E.W. (1995) 'Counsellor values: a national survey', *Journal of Counseling & Development*, 73 (4): 648–53.

Kendall, P.C. and Hollon, S.D. (1989) 'Anxious self-talk: development of the anxious self-statements questionnaire (ASSQ)', *Cognitive Therapy and Research*, 13 (1): 81–93.

King, M. (1963) *Strength to Love*. Philadelphia, PA: Fortress Press.

Kitzinger, C., Coyle, A., Wilkinson, S. and Milton, M. (1998) 'Towards lesbian and gay psychology', *The Psychologist*, 11 (11): 529–33.

Knox. S., Hess, S.A., Petersen, D.A. and Hill, C.E. (1997) 'A qualitative analysis of client perceptions of the effects of helpful therapist self-disclosure in long-term therapy', *Journal of Counseling Psychology*, 44 (3): 274–83.

Laungani, P. (1999) 'Client or culture centred counselling', in S. Palmer and P. Laungani (eds), *Counselling in a Multicultural Society*. London: Sage. pp. 134–52.

Lazarus, A.A. (1984) *In the Mind's Eye: The Power of Imagery for Personal Enrichment*. New York: Guilford.

Lazarus, A.A. (1993) 'Tailoring the therapeutic relationship, or being an authentic chameleon', *Psychotherapy*, 30 (3): 404–7.

Legg, C. (1999) 'Getting the most out of personal therapy', in R. Bor and M. Watts (eds), *The Trainee Handbook: A Guide for Counselling and Psychotherapy Trainees*. London: Sage. pp. 131–45.

Lindsay, G. and Colley, A. (1995) 'Ethical dilemmas of members of the Society', *The Psychologist*, 8 (10): 448–52.

Luria, A. (1961) *The Role of Speech in the Regulation of Normal and Abnormal Behaviors*. New York: Liveright.

McKay, M. and Fanning, P. (1992). *Self-esteem: A Proven Program of Cognitive Techniques for Assessing, Improving and Maintaining your Self-esteem*. Oakland, CA: New Harbinger.

McMillan, M. (1997) 'The experiencing of empathy: what is involved in achieving the "as if" condition?', *Counselling*, 8: 205–9.

Mearns, D. (1997) *Person-Centred Counselling Training*. London: Sage.

Mearns, D. and Thorne, B. (1988) *Person-centred Counselling in Action*. London: Sage.

Nelson-Jones, R. (1995) *Theory and Practice of Counselling*, 2nd edn. London: Cassell. Published in Australasia as *Counselling and Personality: Theory and Practice*. Sydney: Allen & Unwin.

Nelson-Jones, R. (1997) *Practical Counselling and Helping Skills: Text and Exercises for the Lifeskills Counselling Model*, 4th edn. London: Cassell. Distributed in Australasia by ASTAM Books: Sydney.

Nelson-Jones, R. (1999a) *Creating Happy Relationships: A Guide to Partner Skills*. London: Cassell.

Nelson-Jones, R. (1999b) 'Process models for counselling psychologists: the skilled helper and the skilled client', *Counselling Psychology Review*, 14 (1): 16–21.

Nelson-Jones, R. (1999c) 'Towards cognitive-humanistic counselling', *Counselling*, 10 (1): 49–54.

Palmer, S. and Laungani, P. (eds) (1999) *Counselling in a Multicultural Society*. London: Sage.

Pope, K.S. and Vetter, V.A. (1992) 'Ethical dilemmas encountered by members of the American Psychological Society', *American Psychologist*, 47: 397–411.

Rennie, D. (1998) *Person-Centred Counselling: An Experiential Approach*. London: Sage.

Roach, F. (1999) 'Culture, counselling and racial issues', in S. Palmer and P. Laungani (eds), *Counselling in a Multicultural Society*. London: Sage. pp. 71–89.

Robinson, W.L. (1974) 'Conscious competency – the mark of a competent instructor', *Personnel Journal*, 53: 538–9.

Rogers, C.R. (1957) 'The necessary and sufficient conditions of therapeutic personality change', *Journal of Consulting Psychology*, 21 (2): 95–104.

Rogers, C.R. (1975) 'Empathy: An unappreciated way of being', *The Counseling Psychologist*, 5 (2): 2–10.

Rogers, C.R. (1980) *A Way of Being*. Boston: Houghton Mifflin.

Schwartz, S.Z. (1992) 'Universals in the content and structure of values: theoretical advances and empirical tests in 20 countries', *Advances in Experimental Psychology*, 25: 1–65

Shillito-Clarke, C. (1996) 'Ethical issues in counselling psychology', in R. Wolfe and W. Dryden (eds), *Handbook of Counselling Psychology*. London: Sage. pp. 555–80.

Sichel, J. and Ellis, A. (1984) *RET Self-help Form*. New York: Institute for Rational-Emotive Therapy.

Sullivan, H.S. (1953) *The Interpersonal Theory of Psychiatry*. New York: W.W. Norton.

Watkins, C.E. (1990) 'The effects of counselor self-disclosure: A research review', *The Counseling Psychologist*, 18 (3): 477–500.

Woolfe, R. (1999) 'Training routes', in R. Bor and M. Watts (eds), *The Trainee Handbook: A Guide for Counselling and Psychotherapy Trainees*. London: Sage. pp. 6–18.

Wolpe, J. (1990) *The Practice of Behavior Therapy*, 4th edn. Oxford: Pergamon.

Name Index

Subject Index

THE HANLEY LIBRARY
AND INFORMATION CENTRE